THE WIRE

THE CULTURAL HISTORY OF TELEVISION

Breaking Bad: *A Cultural History*, by Lara Stache

Cheers: *A Cultural History*, by Joseph J. Darowski and Kate Darowski

Fierce Females on Television: A Cultural History, by Nicole Evelina

Frasier: *A Cultural History*, by Joseph J. Darowski and Kate Darowski

Friends: *A Cultural History*, by Jennifer C. Dunn

Gilmore Girls: *A Cultural History*, by Lara Stache and Rachel Davidson

The Golden Girls: *A Cultural History*, by Bernadette Giacomazzo

In Living Color: *A Cultural History*, by Bernadette Giacomazzo

Mad Men: *A Cultural History*, by M. Keith Booker and Bob Batchelor

Mystery Science Theater 3000: *A Cultural History*, by Matt Foy and Christopher J. Olson

Northern Exposure: *A Cultural History*, by Michael Samuel

Seinfeld: *A Cultural History*, by Paul Arras

Sex and the City: *A Cultural History*, by Nicole Evelina

The Simpsons: *A Cultural History*, by Moritz Fink

Star Trek: *A Cultural History*, by M. Keith Booker

The Wire: *A Cultural History*, by Ben Lamb

THE WIRE

A CULTURAL HISTORY

BEN LAMB

ROWMAN & LITTLEFIELD

Lanham • Boulder • New York • London

Published by Rowman & Littlefield
An imprint of The Rowman & Littlefield Publishing Group, Inc.
4501 Forbes Boulevard, Suite 200, Lanham, Maryland 20706
www.rowman.com

86-90 Paul Street, London EC2A 4NE

British Library Cataloguing in Publication Information Available

Library of Congress Cataloging-in-Publication Data

Names: Lamb, Ben, (Lecturer in media studies), author.
Title: The Wire: a cultural history / Ben Lamb.
Description: Lanham : Rowman & Littlefield, [2025] | Series: The cultural history of
    television | Includes bibliographical references and index.
Identifiers: LCCN 2024037996 | ISBN 9781538181201 (cloth) | ISBN 9781538181218
    (ebook)
Subjects: LCSH: Wire (Television program) | Television cop shows—United States—
    History and criticism. | Drug traffic on television. | Baltimore (Md.)—On television.
Classification: LCC PN1992.77.W53 L36 2025 | DDC 791.45/72—dc23/eng/20241021
LC record available at https://lccn.loc.gov/2024037996

♾™ The paper used in this publication meets the minimum requirements of American
National Standard for Information Sciences—Permanence of Paper for Printed Library
Materials, ANSI/NISO Z39.48-1992.

To Joanna Lamb, an exceptional mother, for buying me *The Wire* DVD box set and encouraging me to study the show for my Film and Television MA at The University of Warwick, 2009–2010

CONTENTS

Introduction   ix

1   Producing a Television Classic: How *The Wire* Came to Be   1

2   Casting the Characters   17

3   Season 1: A Classic Cop Show   37

4   Season 2: The Port of Baltimore   71

5   Season 3: The War on Drugs   95

6   Season 4: Education   119

7   Season 5: Populism   145

Conclusion: The Lasting Impact of *The Wire*   169

The Episodes: An Opinionated Compendium   183

Notes   189

Bibliography   201

Index   215

About the Author   221

INTRODUCTION

THE BEST TELEVISION SHOW OF ALL TIME?

The Wire (2002–2008) should not exist. Against all economic logic, HBO repeatedly took chances on a show unable to attract subscribers to their cable channel. Ratings peaked at a mere 4.3 million viewers at the start of the second season before declining into a death spiral. Season 3 managed to average a sobering 1.9 million viewers per episode. The fifth and final season received its lowest-ever viewing figures. High-profile awards equally snubbed the program. In a tokenistic gesture, the coveted Primetime Emmy Awards nominated season 3, episode 11, "Middle Ground," and the last-ever episode "30," for Best Writing awards. Needless to say, *The Wire* emerged from both ceremonies empty-handed. On June 2, 2002, the show debuted to a mixed critical reception. The *Chicago Tribune* found *The Wire*'s ability to "spin the conventions of cop drama . . . surprising."[1] Meanwhile, the *New York Post* felt that "*The Wire* looks and feels like an ordinary show from some other network."[2] Fast-forward 20 years, and a BBC critics' poll has crowned *The Wire* the greatest TV series of the twenty-first century.[3] Half the 206 critics polled across 43 countries put the show in their top 10 with a quarter of all critics ranking it in first place. Similarly, streaming service Max prominently features *The Wire* in marketing campaigns as flagship content to continuously generate new subscribers. This is a complete turnaround for showrunners David Simon and Ed Burns. Simon, crime reporter for *The Baltimore Sun* turned novelist, teamed up with Burns, a Baltimore homicide detective turned public school teacher, to provide a damning indictment of America's War on Drugs. Over five seasons, Simon and Burns expand the reach of the series to explore the decline of working-class opportunity among the police force, the criminal justice system, dockland workers, local government, school infrastructure, and the newspaper industry.

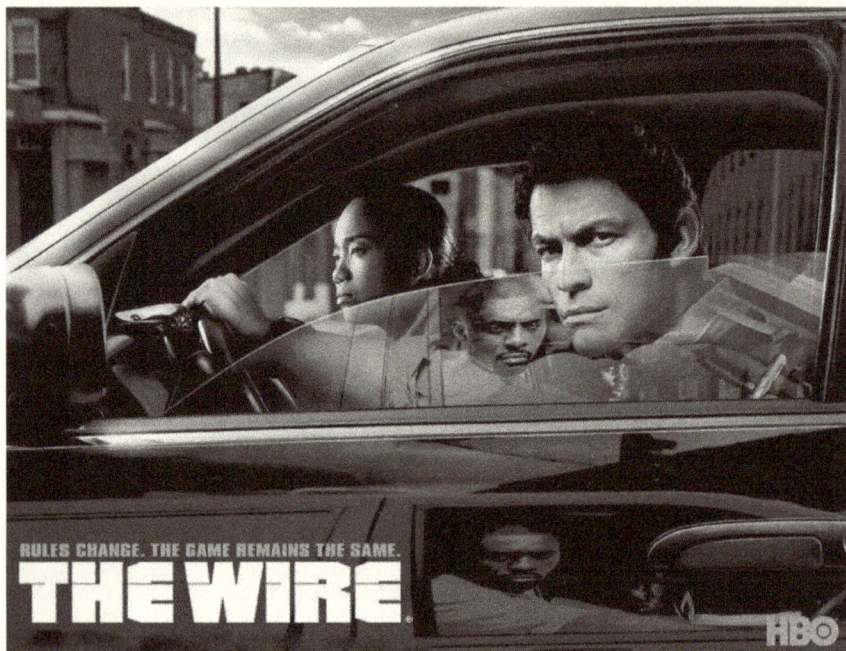

Figure 0.1. A promotional poster still used to generate new Max subscribers. HBO/Photofest © HBO.

The term *"The Wire"* refers not only to the police's wiretapping of drug dealers but also to the thin boundary that exists between an American dream, promising that hard work leads to wealth, and the "game" of drug dealing that propagates social exclusion. With 58 hour-long episodes in total, Maryland's Baltimore City is exposed as a depressingly neglected Wild West environment. Violence reigns supreme in an area undergoing perpetual decline.

So, why is *The Wire* now considered by many to be the best television show ever made?

Spearheaded a New Era of Quality TV

The Wire revolutionized the television industry's relationship with its audience. Up until 2002, "quality television" was used as a critical term to distinguish prime-time hour-long dramas from generic programming. *Hill Street Blues* (1981–1987), *St. Elsewhere* (1982–1988), *Miami Vice* (1984–1989), *Twin Peaks* (1990–1991), *NYPD Blue* (1993–2005), *ER* (1994–2009), *The*

West Wing (1999–2006), *The Sopranos* (1999–2007), and *24* (2001–2010) have all been identified as quality TV. From the late 1970s to the late 1990s, television networks would put considerable resources into these select number of high-profile dramas that boasted cinematic production values, large ensemble casts, highly paid star performers, conviction in a showrunner's writing genius, a subversion of audience genre expectations, and controversial subject matter. Throughout this 30-year period, quality TV's purpose was to utilize this prescribed mixture of techniques to attract the largest audience share at peak hours.

The Wire is the first show to contain all the ingredients of traditional quality television yet continuously lose viewers over five seasons. Given the increased capabilities of cable networks, flat-screen high-definition televisions, digital surround sound, Blu-ray DVDs, TiVO boxes, and broadband internet connections, HBO gambled on *The Wire*, gradually building a constituency of viewers outside of its scheduled broadcasting hours. As part of the "It's not TV. It's HBO" campaign, *The Wire* sought to attract the younger, educated, metropolitan, and wealthy bracket of the television audience market prepared to invest time, attention, technology, and money into the consumption of television programs increasingly subject to connoisseur appreciation. *The Wire* was the first show to prove that viewing figures no longer mattered and that a television audience is composed of microcultures and niche markets rather than a mass homogeneous whole. Subsequent companies AMC and Netflix have since deliberately utilized the HBO model to build their brands around programs like *Mad Men* (2007–2015), *Breaking Bad* (2008–2013), *House of Cards* (2013–2018), and *Better Call Saul* (2015–2022). Cultivating an intense appeal to the young and affluent share of television consumers is now standard practice, as companies can survive off the intense commitment of their cult following. Overseeing a reduced yet loyal viewership would have been impossible in previous years when an audience share of 30 percent was the base threshold for a show's continuation. Nevertheless, HBO's gamble paid off and paved the way for Netflix. Retaining small yet enthusiastic audiences across quality outputs is the dominant economic strategy across the broadcasting and streaming industries.

Following *The Wire*, American television now produces edgier, riskier, and more complex programming en masse. Quality TV drama before *The Wire*, broadcast on one of three major American television networks or a select few cable channels, would promote a conservative ideology whereby colleagues could unearth the supposedly lost familial intimacy of previous generations at their workplace in the face of longer shifts, less pay, and increasingly demanding conditions. *Hill Street Blues* and *The West Wing* endorse the collegiate workplace as a viable alternative to idealized notions of the nuclear family as characters would work through issues of commitment, belonging, and companionship on a weekly basis. But with cable channels able to bypass Federal Communications Commission regulations, Simon grabbed at the opportunity to break the ideological mold of American quality TV. In response to programs like *M*A*S*H* (1972–1983) and *ER*, where unstable, inhumane working conditions can be overcome through a familial intimacy between colleagues, *The Wire* calls for complete top-down infrastructural change. It makes the case for drug law reform and substantial state reinvestment in industry and civic services to improve the working-class quality of life. *The Wire* spearheaded a new era of quality TV both economically and ideologically. Its reconceptualizing of broadcasting economics has become adopted by streaming service giants ranging from Amazon Prime to Disney+. Yet Simon believes that *The Wire*'s greatest "legacy" lies in its arguing for revolutionary change in the face of quality TV's previously inherent conservatism.[4]

Enhanced Televisual Storytelling

It took audiences the world over four seasons to find *The Wire*. Its deliberately slow pace and distinct lack of episodic closure was unintentionally more suited to the DVD format. Simon claims that the DVD evolution "caught up with the show and so our ratings became more and more meaningless with every season."[5] Here viewers now had the autonomy to structure their television viewing habits around their own commitments and domestic rhythms. This better fit with the program's narrative that requires viewers to actively memorize the intricacies of one complex case pursued over 13 hours of content per season. Viewers could now choose to binge-watch episodes when they were best suited to actively engage with the nuances of the multifarious plotlines. Audience numbers of the original HBO broadcasts trailed off into nothingness because the traditional broadcasting model of consuming one episode per week was frustrating. Viewers found themselves more liable to forget precise details and so felt unfulfilled with the lack of episodic closure provided.

Up until this point, American quality TV from the 1970s to late 1990s across both terrestrial networks and cable television had adopted flexi-narratives. This narrative device balances overriding season-long story arcs with shorter episodically concluded story lines to maximize pleasure for both regular and occasional viewers. *The Wire* was not designed to appeal to infrequent viewers as David Simon's talk at the 2009 Edinburgh International Television Festival titled "Fuck the Casual Viewer" attests. At this time, before broadband capabilities were strong enough to accommodate streaming services, the rise in the popularity of DVD apexed at the perfect moment to become the natural home of *The Wire*. Ten million DVDs were sold within ten months of the first three seasons being simultaneously released worldwide. Therefore, television's home video practices were brought more into line with those of film, as the relationship between advertiser, broadcaster, and viewer could be overridden. Thus, quality television dramas were converted from being primarily ephemeral moments in a schedule to symbolically bounded objects more akin to artworks or novels maximizing audience immersion and closeness to narrative worlds and characters. While film had prospered on home video in this manner for two decades, television had not due to the space required to store tapes. Every single episode of *The X-Files* (1993–2002) on a complete videotape collection, for example, would have occupied 10 square feet of shelf space compared to DVDs, whereby an entire season occupies the same space as one single videocassette. Simon found that HBO's subscription funding model alongside their investment in DVD releases came together in a perfect storm to liberate him from "the economic construct of advertising."[6]

With the conditions for this "emancipation of story" in place, *The Wire*'s aim was to be "a novel for television."[7] Although Simon had worked on network TV's police procedural *Homicide: Life on the Street* (1993–1999), based on his novel *Homicide: A Year on the Killing Streets*, he had no interest in the familiar structure of episodic television. An episode of *The Wire* does not function on its own, nor does it provide any degree of satisfying closure because they are written by published novelists. These prose writers were unfamiliar with the beats of traditional television that take weeklong gaps between episodes and commercial breaks into account. Novelists George Pelecanos, Richard Price, and Dennis Lehane worked under experienced nonfiction writers Simon and Burns to invest the show with the same slow-burning propulsive energy and thematic density of Price's *Clockers* and Lehane's *Gone, Baby Gone*. Each installment of *The Wire* builds on itself like chapters in a book to make viewers pay closer attention to the thematic connections that are rarely italicized or foregrounded. Lester Freamon's motto underpinning his wiretapping operation, "all the pieces matter," actually applies to the show itself. You will rarely see "Top 10 Episodes of *The Wire*" articles because it is difficult to delineate episodes from one another within each 12- to 13-hour-long story. If an episode reaches a resolution, it does so to create a host of new problems to be dealt with farther down the line.

As well as harnessing the narrative complexity and detail of the novel-istic form, *The Wire* also shares an ideological purpose with the traditional novel. In the same way the novel first emerged as a new genre of writing to document the industrializing of society, *The Wire* arrived as a new form of televisual storytelling to document the social impact of Baltimore's contin-ued deindustrialization and outdated drug policies. Like the Brontës, Dick-ens, Austen, and Hardy, both Simon and Burns are motivated by a deep conviction that they, like their novelist progenitors, can provide a vivid and immediate depiction of the "totality of society" and reveal its pattern of development within a particular social structure and historical period.[8] Focusing on the inner workings of a different institution in each season, *The Wire* also inhabits a profoundly moral role akin to the traditional literary novel, as it also produces a sustained and powerful criticism of the con-straints and limitations imposed on human behavior by social institutions.

Portrays Baltimore City as a Character

Operating free from the constraints of advertising and traditional appoint-ment viewing figures, Simon, Burns, and their writing team were able to expand the micro- and macroscale of television storytelling to a size not experienced on television before or since. *The Wire*'s first season has 11 cast regulars, with at least two dozen other significant recurring players. Here viewers witness the Baltimore Police Department establish a new detail, ini-tiated by renegade detective Jimmy McNulty (Dominic West), and pursue elusive drug kingpin Avon Barksdale (Wood Harris) and his crew of West Baltimore drug dealers. Season 2 then expands the show's scope to intro-duce a litany of characters who work in the Port of Baltimore. In exposing how drugs get to dealers, viewers witness how blue-collar cargo handlers and checkers like Frank Sobotka (Chris Bauer) are being left behind with no choice but to turn to crime to make ends meet. Season 3 then casts its eye over City Hall to illustrate how difficult attempts to reform the War on Drugs are. Season 4 orients itself around a quartet of middle school friends to dem-onstrate how the failings of the public school system turn youths to drug dealing. The final season enters *The Baltimore Sun* newsroom to explore how depleted local media resources are failing to convey the truth and scale of the problem to its public.

Using each series to focus on a host of new characters located within a different institution, alongside the usual cast of homicide detectives and drug dealers, means that every element of the drug chain is richly drawn. From kingpins to low-level lookouts to drug users, *The Wire* provides an entire ecosystem. From the start, Simon's goal was to build an entire city and perform a systemic analysis of it that would dramatize the dire need for policy reform. Casting the city of Baltimore as a character distinguishes *The Wire* from other quality TV programs that were traditionally structured around the family or familial-like relationships. Even Simon and Burns's previous critically revered HBO miniseries *The Corner* (2000), adapted from their novel, focuses on the family unit as a microcosm of wider society. From the courts to the longshoremen's union, from the mayor's office to the homeless community, *The Wire* provides a sociological analysis at all levels of society, revealing how power dynamics, interpersonal relationships, and even snap decisions can impact Baltimore and entire swathes of its people. The closing montage in the final episode of each season is an integral device for portraying the city as an entity. Each "conclusion" delivers some narrative closure but overwhelmingly maintains that the real Baltimore and its systemic problems will continue to worsen beyond the confines of the television drama. Here selfish careerists—councilman turned governor Tommy Carcetti (Aidan Gillen), homicide commanding officer turned superintendent of the Maryland State Police William Rawls (John Doman), Pulitzer Prize–winning journalist Scott Templeton (Tom McCarthy), and others—are continuously rewarded for their dishonesty with promotions. In contrast, those with integrity who tried to improve the system—McNulty, Cedric Daniels (Lance Reddick), Lester Freamon (Clarke Peters), and more—are largely shut out of the hierarchy of their institutions, where their commitment could have made a difference. Through these distinctive montages, key buildings are isolated in close-up, changes to the urban landscape are highlighted, and shots of Baltimore's cityscape bookend the fates of characters to maintain a strong parity between both city and citizen.[9] The systematic analysis of the city resonates, however, because it is emotionally anchored by a rich ensemble of characters.

Provides Ample In-Depth Characters

Despite the deep pessimism of *The Wire*'s systemic analysis of Baltimore, it is important not to lose sight of the undercurrent of hope that runs through all five seasons. Promising and intelligent characters with the capacity to change the city do keep appearing, regardless of race, class, gender, sexual persuasion, or generation, on both sides of the law. The emotional power of the series depends on this dynamic tension between, on the one hand, having so many vibrant characters with enormous potential and, on the other, seeing how the culture is wired to destroy them. Every character, no matter how minor, is imbued with enough depth that nobody is ever allowed to operate as a plot functionary, as entire plotlines can emanate from every person. *The Wire*'s treatment of character is different from HBO's previous series because the navigation of community is no longer driven by focus of a charismatic antihero's commanding perspective. Compared to *Sex and the City* (1998–2004) and *The Sopranos*, plot now emerges from the tensions that arise between institutions and a wide range of autonomous characters.

The casting process was integral to creating characters who are believable yet can draw viewers in. Casting directors Alexa Fogel and Pat Moran were given free rein to discover actors who were then not in high-profile projects, so viewers had no preconceptions of how characters' fates would play out. Thus, another of *The Wire*'s greatest legacies is how it provided A-list household names across both sides of the Atlantic with their first big break. Before the days of *Game of Thrones* (2011–2019), *The Wire* had an unusually large number of British actors for an American television show. Fogel put her entire reputation on the line to cast Dominic West as McNulty to break free of American cop stereotypes. Following this big break, Dominic West has had success from historical action epic *300* (2006) to the BBC's *Les Misérables* (2019) and Netflix's *The Crown* (2016–). Idris Elba, who turned up to his Stringer Bell audition with a thick Hackney accent, has since built a career ranging from Marvel and DC blockbuster movies to BBC's *Luther* (2010–2019). In terms of American talent, providing Michael B. Jordan with his first-ever acting role has led him to playing criminal antihero Erik Killmonger in *Black Panther* (2018) and the lead role in the *Rocky* spinoff franchise *Creed* (2015). Then there's the late Michael K. Williams, who was nominated for an Emmy in his stint on *Lovecraft Country* (2020).

Another legacy of Fogel and Moran's casting process is its inclusion of African American actors. Three years before *The Wire* was first broadcast, the National Association for the Advancement of Colored People reported that U.S. television's fall broadcast schedule did not have a single lead actor of color.[10] African American actors were then among the most underutilized actors in Hollywood. As Baltimore is a city that is 65 percent black, *The Wire*'s emphasis on a varied ensemble of black characters marks an important departure from successful quality TV precursors. Even *The Sopranos*' Italian American characters outwardly occupy middle America's racism toward their African American rivals. In contrast to all previous quality TV, *The Wire* covers almost every major aspect of urban black life. Cutting across age, class, and sexuality, the show captures in each case authentic street vernacular. By casting black Baltimore residents who were untrained actors, like real-life drug kingpin Melvin Williams playing a deacon and real-life drug dealer–robbing bandit Donnie Andrews playing Omar Little's (Michael K. Williams) hired bodyguard, a heightened sense of how West Baltimore residents would realistically talk, act, maneuver, think, and express themselves is achieved.

Brought British Social Realism to American TV

The Wire's approach to casting and character is a practice widely regarded as social realism. This is a form of drama that reveals the effects of "environmental factors on the development of character" to present "gritty character studies of the underbelly of urban life."[11] Another reason *The Wire* is considered to be one of the best programs ever conceived is because it also brings the traditions and techniques of British social realism into an American context to a scale never before conceived, hence why actors from the British Isles—Elba, West, Peters, and Gillen—were able to thrive on a project that spoke to their native acting traditions. While the creators may have never referenced the term "social realism," the central tenets of the form are ever present for all to see. Simon's and Burns's intention was to move away from American TV's usual preoccupation with redemption and affirmation to make a show that provides "political dissent," arguing how "our systems are not functioning" and "policies are incorrect."[12]

This approach to writing, casting, and storytelling is identical to the British traditions of social realism as defined by Raymond Williams. In reference to British television dramas of the 1960s, Williams first defines social realism as a form of television that puts redemption and affirmation to one side to provide a secular drama drawn to logic and reason rather than superstition. Second, according to Williams, social realist television occupies a contemporary setting and addresses current social issues. *The Wire* achieves this by filming all its scenes in real Baltimore locations—row houses, projects, and neighborhoods—capturing native residents who are not trained in acting occupying roles ranging from extras to full-blown characters. The third tenet of social realism according to Williams is "social extension," whereby viewers are exposed to downtrodden communities of people who have hitherto received little exposure.[13] One of *The Wire*'s greatest legacies is familiarizing people the world over with the impact that America's War on Drugs has had on Baltimore's impoverished black community. Finally, Williams claims that drama can be classified as social realism when it is socially engaged enough to provide its audiences with a political hypothesis. Social realism is a form of drama that not only reflects the world but also seeks to interpret it and offer a politically imagined possibility. In exposing the cracks within every major element of Baltimore's social structure, Simon's and Burns's interpretation and solution to the tragic inequalities of Baltimore and black America are simple: legalize drugs and invest heavily in industry, civic society, and community initiatives to create a society that is more in keeping with the principles of the American dream that is no longer marred by inequality.

Compared to other American quality TV of the same era, especially those emulating futuristic sci-fi visuals like *Battlestar Galactica* (2004–2009) and *Lost* (2004–2010), *The Wire* utilizes a mise-en-scène that is functionalist, non-expressionistic, and unobtrusive. Polish cinematographer Uta Briesewitz, well versed in her native European social realist traditions, developed *The Wire*'s distinctive look. She would deliberately occupy vacant row houses and use only natural lighting, much to the annoyance of her directors and production designer. Technically, *The Wire* breaks with conventional police drama and quality TV in how it shoots on location, intermixes professional and nonprofessional actors, has no music soundtrack, and relies wholly on the street vernacular of Baltimore's working class. Even the sound mixers recorded dialogue that was deliberately unpolished so as to capture the natural sounds of Baltimorean neighborhoods. Viewers are therefore required to listen closely to decipher dialogue as if they themselves are detectives eavesdropping on wiretapped conversations.

Educates Viewers in Greek Mythology and the Classics

The Wire meets all the essentials of social realism partly because Simon deliberately sought to emulate the logic of ancient Greek mythology. Underpinning the show's social realist outlook and accompanying political hypothesis are government institutions occupying the same roles as Greek gods. The system a citizen is born into and serves has complete control over a person's fate as the gods were once believed to. As such, McNulty's story mirrors that of Bellerophon. The Greek hero wins the god Athena's favor to slay the fire-breathing Chimea but has his hubris punished by Zeus and so suffers the rest of his life in solitude. This character's trajectory parallels McNulty, who charms Judge Phelan (Peter Gerety) into getting the approval required to defeat monstrous drug-dealing kingpin Avon Barksdale. Nevertheless, these heroic efforts are also punished, as McNulty gets ideas above his station and so is consistently demoted. The fate of McNulty's contemporary on the other side of the law, Avon Barksdale's cousin D'Angelo (Lawrence Gilliard Jr.), is a modern reimagining of the 12 Labors of Heracles. D'Angelo, like Heracles, must atone for an unsanctioned and instinctual killing that dishonors his family. D'Angelo, as witnessed in the tale of Heracles, must partake in menial tasks beneath his station as determined by his extended family. D'Angelo is demoted from running a tower to the low-rises and then does prison time to protect the Barksdale family name akin to the way in which Heracles has to clean the Augean Stables and then navigate the underworld. Despite D'Angelo's errors in judgment, the punishment that D'Angelo has undertaken permits him to receive a hero's funeral in the same way that Heracles subsequently ascends to Mount Olympus.

Key characters bear a lot of similarities to a whole host of Greek myths. Omar and his crew share a strong affinity with Jason and the Argonauts for regularly facing certain death in robbing monstrous entities of their most prized possessions. Correspondingly, both Jason and Omar endure mundane deaths following their heartbreak for a dead lover. Furthermore, Avon Barksdale himself operates as if he is Hades, ruler of the underworld. Both are rich for possessing precious metals of the earth (drugs in Avon's case), both are rarely seen outside of their territory (no photograph of Avon exists in police records), and both equally pride themselves on claiming "subjects" for their kingdom who are unable to leave with their mortality intact.

Following his deliberate emulation of Greek mythology, Simon also considers *The Wire* to be a contemporary Dickens novel. Central to Dickensian realism are industrial settings and the objects that populate them, dehumanizing human subjects. Human qualities are transposed to descriptions of inanimate objects to suggest that human beings are losing their humanity to repressive industrial environments and the commerce they represent. The Sobotka family of *The Wire*'s season 2, the latest in a long lineage of longshoremen, have their emotional agency constricted by the materialistic objects surrounding them. The commanding sight of the dilapidated grain pier and prosperous economic memories associated with it haunt Frank into undertaking criminal acts to keep the docks financially viable. Abiding by Dickensian logic means that those who treat humans as objects are destined to become objects themselves. The Sobotkas' decision to comply in human trafficking alongside their smuggling of drugs and goods kick-starts their desensitization. Compared to Dickens, though, *The Wire* occupies a decidedly more fatalistic outlook, as there is no capacity for the Sobotka characters to reverse their fate. Attempting to cease their human trafficking operations results in Frank's murder, Ziggy's incarceration, and Nick's confinement to witness protection, unable to work. Dickens endorses rekindling family connections to lessen the excesses of rampant capitalism and transcend one's class with social responsibility. In *The Wire*'s deindustrialized Baltimore, however, its overriding classism ensures that the Sobotkas can never escape their sealed fate.

Shifted the War on Drugs Debate

The Wire's defeatist disposition has largely enabled the series to intervene in the War on Drugs debate over time. Its social realist argument underpinned by classicism is that society has become much more determinist and far less meritocratic and that a person's fate is prescribed to them at birth. Until there is real meaningful top-down policy development and institutional change, the actions of heroic individuals at the bottom will be forever meaningless. Until then, these dysfunctional structures—in law enforcement, politics, education, labor unions, the media, and drug gangs—will continue to chug along, serving the interests of the powerful and chewing up average people unlucky enough to get caught in their wake. *The Wire*'s greatest legacy, then, is the key role it has had in making the world increasingly skeptical of America's War on Drugs. Reframing U.S. drug policies as a humanitarian crisis is why season 4 received the strongest critical reception yet. Its portrayal of schoolchildren being forced into a life of drug abuse against their will was commended for the extent to which drug addiction should be treated as a health problem rather than a law-and-order issue.

In a testament to just how much the show has since changed opinion, during his first presidential campaign, Barack Obama said, "Omar's a great guy."[14] While Obama was keen to point out that he was not endorsing the character's lawbreaking, *The Wire* nonetheless helped instigate a global debate as to whether America's War on Drugs is worth its escalating cost in terms of human lives and taxpayer money. At the president's request, Simon met Obama at the White House, where the pair discussed the toll of the War on Drugs on communities, incarceration rates, and law enforcement. Simon has since vowed that he will write a sixth season if drugs are legalized nationally in the United States. Nevertheless, it is hard to envision a world where legislation now treating drug addiction as a health problem, (across Holland, Portugal, Uruguay, Switzerland, the United Kingdom, and others) continues to receive widespread favorable media exposure, political endorsement, and public goodwill had *The Wire* never existed.

In a classic case of life imitating art, March 2021 saw Baltimore state attorney Marilyn Mosby announce that Baltimore would no longer prosecute drug possession for personal consumption. Her office's one-year experiment in not prosecuting minor offenses to decrease the spread of COVID-19 behind bars proved successful. Mosby announced, "America's war on drug users is over in the city of Baltimore." She explained to reporters that "we leave behind the era of tough-on-crime prosecution and zero-tolerance policing and no longer default to the status quo to criminalize mostly people of color for addiction." These COVID criminal justice policies, developed with public health authorities, surprisingly resulted in a reduction in crime akin to *The Wire*'s third season, where drug-tolerant "Hamsterdam" zones are established. Instead of prosecuting people arrested for minor crimes, including drug and drug paraphernalia possession, Mosby's policy has led to a decrease in violent crimes by 20 percent, and property crimes by 36 percent. *The Wire* provides the vision of a community so hamstrung by issues that it is unable to fully recognize its problems much less address them. Twenty years later, Baltimore has begun to take action, as the show has been a key tool in enabling the community to acknowledge its problems and begin pushing back against 50 years of a zero-tolerance federal approach to drug use.[15]

Predicted the Future Political Landscape

As time passes, even season 5—ridiculed for allowing "daftness" to creep in—grows ever more relevant.[16] In this final season, McNulty manages to spark public interest in human bodies littered throughout empty row houses by faking strangulation and bite marks to give the impression that all the cadavers have been victims of a serial killer. As a result of his actions and the arrest of a subsequent copycat murderer, McNulty receives FBI resources, Mayor Carcetti launches his campaign for governor, and *The Baltimore Sun* reporter Templeton receives a Pulitzer Prize for publishing fake news stories. Characters begin to exploit the lack of a credible vision for shared prosperity to promote themselves. Put simply, viewers of season 5 witness the beginnings of populism, a strategic approach to politics that America has since experienced under Donald Trump's election campaigning and presidential tenure. "Populism" is a term that refers to politicians who deliberately characterize society as being divided between hardworking, virtuous, and honorable people (whom they portray themselves as belonging to) who must homogenize to overthrow a "corrupt elite" who have harbored power for too long. A populist leader is somebody who offers straightforward "commonsense" solutions to society's complex problems and in so doing adopts a forceful yet colloquial mode of communication to galvanize those who have lost faith in traditional politics and its representatives.[17] A public appetite for a blasé dismissal of the truth in the face of more compelling narratives was what *The Wire*'s final season envisions and what the entire globe has since experienced under the Philippines' Rodrigo Duterte, Turkey's Recep Tayyip Erdoğan, Brazil's Jair Bolsonaro, U.S. president Donald Trump, and British prime minister Boris Johnson. All harnessed this populist strategy to secure power and capitalize on the electorate's increasing feelings of marginalization following economic and cultural globalization, increasing levels of immigration, and the decline of ideological class politics. Simon may have since claimed that he did not quite anticipate the complete collapse of "truth" and "the idea of you can just boldly lie your way to the top," but it is undeniable that in criticizing "the media culture that could allow the events witnessed in the previous four seasons to go on," he stumbled on the beginnings of populism.[18]

It Laid the Foundations for Streaming TV

Superficially, *The Wire*'s legacy can be felt among all streaming service dramas that dispense with the traditional flexi-narratives of broadcast television and follow the "every season is a 12-hour-long film" strategy. Programs like *Killing Eve* (2018–2022), *Stranger Things* (2016–), and even *Making a Murderer* (2015–2018) were found by the majority of their fans through the ability of streaming services to attract attentive viewers who are required to sift through the nuanced detail of an ever-meandering 12-hour-long storyline. But let's not get carried away; *The Wire* has very little in common with this kind of algorithm bait that drags itself out to boost a platform's minutes-per-subscriber metric. There may be no contemporary television that has reproduced the look, slow narrative pace, or social ambition of *The Wire*, but this does not make it a failure. It is proof of concept. There have been occasional attempts, like *American Crime* (2015–2017), to re-create *The Wire*'s ability to build an entire city through a network of social institutions across five seasons. However, the broadcasting industry's continued disinterest to do so illustrates what a rare feat Simon and Burns pulled off—sometimes imitated, rarely duplicated, never enhanced. As Burns recently admitted, *The Wire* would "definitely not" have been green-lit if pitched today. Now "it's got to be *Game of Thrones*. . . . It's got to be big. It's got to be disconnected from stepping on anybody's toes." Simon and Burns happened to catch HBO at a unique time when networks were beginning to think, "Oh, we need a show for this group of people." It is nearly impossible to pull off a perspective-shifting dense Balzacian drama without losing an audience. It is an even rarer feat to extrapolate a television drama from a series of institutional critiques guided by Greek philosophy without sounding like a textbook or lecturing its audience. We probably won't see a show like *The Wire* produced ever again because the job is massive, and the commercial payoffs, historically, are not. Even Simon and Burns's most recent Baltimore Police Department–based HBO drama *We Own This City* (2022) is a mere five-episode-long miniseries. But that's okay; the void we continue to feel 20 years later is an ever-present reminder of *The Wire*'s masterpiece status.[19]

Its Social Impact Lives On

A lot has happened since HBO first broadcast *The Wire*'s final episode on March 7, 2008. The United States feels completely unrecognizable in relation to the message of hope that Obama's then presidential campaign promised. The 2020s has grown into the country's most socially fractious decade since the Civil War. The country has witnessed Baltimore's 2015 riots, the 2020 murder of George Floyd and subsequent protests, a 2021 attempted Capitol Hill insurrection, and the rise of the Black Lives Matter (BLM) movement and "defund the police" campaigns in what has been the biggest spate of civil rights campaigning since the 1960s. As other cities keep a close eye on how Baltimore pushes back against 50 years of America's War on Drugs, now is the perfect time to look into how the program predicated this shift in consciousness. While *The Wire* actor Wendell Pierce (Bunk) publicly endorsed BLM in how it "speaks truth to power," little connection has since been drawn between the BLM movement and how the show helped lay the foundations for this community awareness.[20] Meanwhile, America has seen domestic terrorism increase, race relations become ever tenser, political populism become increasingly sectarian, health inequalities worsen, incarnation rates of black people skyrocket, and grassroots racial activism grow. Following the COVID-19 pandemic, the United States is rebuilding itself through the biggest state spending plan in its history, by continuing to consider scaling back on international military interventionism for the first time since World War II, and by decriminalizing personal drug use in particular states. While the country faces its biggest socioeconomic crossroads for generations, *The Wire: A Cultural History* reflects, through the benefit of hindsight, how the show has navigated, and continues to navigate, old and new fans through this epoch.

Chapter 1 walks through David Simon's life story and how he came to devise *The Wire*. It illustrates how the showrunner's life experiences came to inform the show's unique writing process, production practices, and outlook. Chapter 2 relives how *The Wire*'s leading roles were cast and uncovers the stories behind the real-life counterparts of each principal character to demonstrate how racial stereotypes are challenged. Chapter 3 journeys through a complete history of the American cop show to deduce which key programs *The Wire*'s first season emulates and challenges. Chapter 4 traces the entire economic, social, and racial history of the Port of Baltimore. In so doing, the chapter discerns how the longshoremen of season 2, descended from Polish immigrants, interact with the landscape differently than their Barksdale counterparts and their continued combating of historically prominent racial stereotypes. Chapter 5 explores how America's War on Drugs was established and upscaled and thus impacted Baltimore from 1971 to today. Leading criminological fieldwork into drug dealing and drug addiction then helps the chapter uncover why the fictional depiction of decriminalized drug–taking "Hamsterdam" zones of season 3 work to a point. Chapter 6 paints an evocative history of the racial inequities that have befallen Baltimore's school system before adopting critical race theory to determine how the depiction of certain classes across season 4 provide breakthroughs for inner-city pupils. Then the chapter explores how four principal schoolboy characters—Randy, Dukie, Michael, and Namond—each come of age compared to the well-trodden paths laid by their protagonist forebearers in African American literature. Finally, chapter 7 outlines how *The Baltimore Sun* newspaper's USP was established and evolved before considering how the final series predicted the rise of populism across world politics and the increasing significance of popular criminology in local crime reporting. Finally, all chapter findings considered, a conclusion explains how 20 years on *The Wire* continues to inform university courses, change Baltimore City itself following the 2015 Freddie Gray riots, impact the 2020 rise of the BLM movement, and influence worldwide drug-taking laws. The book draws to a close by considering the role that Simon's and Burns's latest Baltimore-set HBO drama, *We Own This City*, has in this continuing set of cultural conversations.

But before we get into all that, how did David Simon come to create *The Wire*?

CHAPTER 1

PRODUCING A TELEVISION CLASSIC

How *The Wire* Came to Be

David Simon was destined for a life of journalism. It "was just in the ether of my house."[1] His father, Bernie, was the public relations director of B'nai B'rith. Overseeing the comms of a nongovernmental organization committed to combating anti-Semitism worldwide required reporters to constantly gather at the Simon family home. Subscriptions to the *Washington Times*, the *Washington Post*, and the *Washington Star* meant that the Simons not only discussed current events daily but also critiqued the writing style of reporters. Here Simon quietly absorbed intense political discussion untypical for a six-year-old. One of Simon's first memories, at age eight, is witnessing blazing rows of fury erupt between his family of Democrats across the dinner table. Amidst the 1968 presidential primary, Simon's sister Linda was a fervent supporter of a youthful Robert F. Kennedy Sr., his brother, Gary, was a fan of the anti–Vietnam War Eugene McCarthy, and his father was committed to establishment candidate Hubert Humphrey. The very nature of these heated intellectual discussions led Gary's future wife to ask, "Why do you guys hate each other?" But Simon's upbringing had just left him intrinsically poised to argue through his ideas as a creative process—so much so that he felt befuddled in later life when people interpreted his spirited war of words as personal feuds. Before long, Simon majored in journalism at the University of Maryland, editing the student newspaper *The Diamondback*. Fellow reporter and *The Corner* (2000) screenplay cowriter David Mills recalls Simon producing biting yet humorous put-downs. Simon had "a full-blown writing personality as an undergraduate. He was always getting parking tickets, so he did these rambling, profane, angry pieces about the student ticketers, his nemeses."[2] Growing up alongside the Watergate scandal and Vietnam War, Simon was accustomed to the government lying to its citizens, compared to his father, who, before the outbreak of World War II, wrote life-affirming "America can do" pieces for the *Hudson Dispatch*. Simon found his voice by rebelling against his father's generation of war-torn New Deal Democrats who trusted and believed in presidential administrations. Simon's acerbic questioning of authority emboldened him to work as a stringer for *The Baltimore Sun* in his senior year. Here Simon unearthed a university scandal involving a Terrapin basketball player suspended for sexual misconduct. With the head coach allegedly harassing the female accuser to refute her accusation, Simon's story was published in the *Washington Post*. After a year of covering the College Park campus, in 1980, Simon was offered a six-month *Sun* contract. His dream had come true. At only age 22, he was working at a prestigious paper.

Being assigned to the police beat immediately ignited Simon's lifelong fascination with Maryland's city of Baltimore. Riding along on night patrols from 4:00 p.m. to 12:00 a.m. every weekend, in addition to a full work-week of reporting, meant that Simon came to understand his city's crime culture and racial politics firsthand. Simon obsessively pulled double shifts, drank into the small hours with his cop buddies, and spent what little free time he had left poring over piles of notebooks in his unfurnished bachelor pad. Compulsively charting a wider view of the goings-on of the Baltimore Police Department (BPD) may have contributed to his marital breakdown. But being so immersed in the police force's inner workings enabled the reporter to recall who was assigned to what shift faster than most detectives. Having grown up in the Silver Spring suburbs of Maryland, Simon threw himself headfirst into a city that had an unremitting rate of poverty, high rates of drug abuse, and a capacity for violence. Alongside scribing standard newspaper fare, Simon honed a unique ability for crafting multipart stories on how the interplay of cocaine and semiautomatic weapons jacked up the city's murder rate. His five-part chronicling of Little Melvin Williams's rise and fall from kingpin status remains a gripping yet informative read. Years of reporting in Baltimore's inner-city neighborhoods in this way left Simon at ease as the only white person in a room. "To be a decent city reporter, I had to listen to people who were different from me. . . . I had to not be uncomfortable asking stupid questions or being on the outside."[3] Both in the newsroom and in the police force, Simon found kinship in the jocularity, camaraderie, and sense of purpose instilled across both vocations. Here he perfected an ability to authentically dramatize the experiences, vernacular, and needs of Baltimore's black community alongside condemning the city and police culture that solely blamed drug addicts for their afflictions.

By 1986, working conditions were already worsening. The *Sun* was bought by the Times Mirror Company, which curtailed staff medical coverage despite the paper being at its most profitable. Simon was incensed yet reluctant to sacrifice a job he loved so dearly. So his employers agreed to a year's leave of absence in the event their crime correspondent secured a book deal. Simon wrote to Baltimore police commissioner Edward J. Tilghman asking, with feigned innocence, whether he could observe Tilghman's detectives for a year. To his surprise, Tilghman agreed. To this day, Simon has not received an explanation for Tilghman's decision despite the deputy commissioner of operations being thoroughly against the idea. It mattered little to the aspiring novelist, who in 1988, began what would become *Homicide: A Year on the Killing Streets*. From January to December of that year, Simon documents the inner workings of a department of 36 detectives tasked with investigating 240 murders per year on average. The idea came when Detective Donald Kincaid offhandedly suggested to the young idealistic crime reporter that "if someone just wrote down what happens in this place for one year, they'd have a goddamn book." So that's exactly what Simon did. Gradually, he earned the detectives' trust by strictly abiding by their three rules: he would not communicate what he witnessed to his newspaper employers, he would obey orders of the supervisors and investigators, and, above all, he could not quote anyone by name unless they agreed. Simon stuck to these conditions so stringently that when the manuscript was complete, the Legal Affairs Division requested no changes. The process of writing a novel had been a creative awakening, as Simon could now tell a much longer story in more detailed yet sophisticated prose.

Reading *Homicide* is like reading elements of *The Wire* in novel form. As in the show, the real poetry of police work emerges not from large set pieces or moments of redemption but from the way a couple of detectives recline in the back room looking over ballistics. Here Simon developed his ability to capture the authenticity of detectives' voices amid the unrelenting character of the institutions that envelop them. The book is a stark, unromantic, and claustrophobic exposé of the repetitive nature of detective work within an under-resourced homicide department. The book begins by informing its readers,

This is the job:

You sit behind a government-issue metal desk on the sixth of ten floors in a gleaming, steel-frame death trap with poor ventilation, dysfunctional air conditioning, and enough free-floating asbestos to pad the devil's own jumpsuit. You eat $2.50 pizza specials and Italian cold cuts with extra hots from Marco's on Exeter Street while watching reruns of *Hawaii Five-O* on the communal nineteen-inch set with insubordinate horizontal hold. You answer the phone on the second or third beat because Baltimore abandoned its AT&T equipment as a cost-saving measure and the new phone system doesn't ring so much as it emits metallic, sheeplike sounds. If a police dispatcher is on the other end of the call, you write down an address, the time, and the dispatcher's unit number on a piece of scratch paper or the back of a used three-by-five pawn shop submission card.[4]

Simon grounds this matter-of-fact realism directly in response to popular film and literary representations of the detective. His debut novel dispels the myth that "coroners are capable of telling *Kojak* that his victim stopped breathing between 10:30 and 10:45." In truth, medical experts can often provide "no more than a rough guess for a victim's time of death." While Simon agrees that the enjoyment of reading Dashiell Hammett and Agatha Christie comes from their view that "to track a murderer, the motive must first be established," here motive "matters little." Shootings, stabbings, bludgeonings, overdoses, seizures, suicides, accidental falls, drownings, crib deaths, and autoerotic strangulation "all receive the same attention from the same detective who has, at any given moment, case files for three open homicides on his desk." Up against the clock, the most successful homicide detectives are guided by their instincts. Philosophically, as in *The Wire*, the detectives are the playthings of forces outside of their control with little to no agency over their own fate. While attempting to solve unspeakably violent murders, they all must endure an even more unrelenting chain of command, frothing at the prospect of disciplining its workers for the increasing rate of unsolved homicides. When the superiors are "asking for a piece of meat to hang on the wall," Simon noticed that a detective "learns how to make himself invisible." A detective's efforts, no matter how honorable or heroic, stand for very little. There is no satisfying closure to be found in this 646-page chronicling of a year in the life of Baltimore's Homicide Department. The investigation that occupies the most pages, the sexually assaulted, stabbed, and strangled 11-year-old Latonya Kim Wallace, produces no charged suspects regardless of the detectives' repeated efforts. Just like the signature montages that conclude each season of *The Wire*, despite the small victories that characters may achieve, the murders of West Baltimore never deescalate in frequency or in bloody intensity. The life of the maligned underclasses wearily trudges on because "in a city with 240 murders a year there will always be another body."[5]

Despite some positive critical reception, including a 1992 Edgar Award and Hollywood director William Friedkin phoning Simon personally to congratulate the debut novelist on his achievement, *Homicide* was no bestseller. Soon, hardback copies were consigned from displays to the true crime section. Squad Supervisor Roger Nolan confiscated Simon's police ID so that the journalist could continue to ply his trade at the *Sun* as the detectives' world returned to being unexamined. Simon resumed encountering detectives from the other side of the crime scene tape as if the book had never happened. Working on the rewrite desk and doing night shifts, Simon experienced a prize culture taking over. New editor John Carroll, veteran of the *Philadelphia Inquirer*, sought not to comprehensively address what Baltimore's problems were and instead steered his journalists toward hunting Pulitzer Prize–winning stories that could be picked up by bigger newspapers within their corporate chain. Simon occasionally penned the kind of stories he wanted, such as his four-part "Crisis in Blue" (1994), arguing that the BPD's increasing dysfunctionality was due to institutional failure rather than the fault of individuals. But such writing opportunities were minimal.

With the *Sun* ceasing to produce what Simon regarded as valuable journalism and his agent unable to broker a *Homicide* film deal, Simon reached out to Baltimore television producer Barry Levinson directly. Levinson's company agreed to option Simon's book at the author's request, as they needed to make something for the NBC network. Simon was happy to receive a check, hoped the show would lead to more book sales, but didn't expect it would change his life all that much. It was only when Levinson's associate producer Gale Mutrix asked Simon to write an episode that he entered the television business. Once a template for *Homicide: Life on the Street* (1993–1999) was established, loosely based on Simon's novel, the crime reporter turned novelist learned the basics of television writing. He called up his old *Diamondback* colleague David Mills, now reporting for the *Washington Post*, to collaborate on a script. With no television industry experience between them, both men wrote an episode called "Bop Gun." A defenseless tourist is needlessly murdered in the cold, hard light of day in front of her young children. Network executives considered the episode too dark and flatly refused to produce it. Simon's fortunes would turn only after producer Mark Johnson convinced Robin Williams to play the grieving husband. "Bop Gun" was filmed for season 2 and won a Writers Guild award. While Mills went on to write for *NYPD Blue*, Simon's pride was wounded. The wannabe TV writer could not get over the fact that producers Tom Fontanta and Jim Yoshirura cut 50 percent of his and his friend's screenplay. Despite this being the industry standard for first-time writers, Simon resented the edits as a personal failure. Instead, the self-proclaimed "failed" TV writer took another year from the *Sun* to begin a second novel, *The Corner*, a humanistic exploration into how drug addiction impacts the lives of people living at the intersection of Fayette and Monroe, West Baltimore's open-air drug market.

Compared to *Homicide*'s forensic exploration of BPD office culture, guided by the jaded outlook of its detectives, *The Corner* is far more empathetically invested in the lives of a poverty-stricken family caught up in Baltimore's illicit drug trade. Through 1993, Simon adopted a slightly different reporting methodology for this new book, one he calls "stand around and watch journalism." Both he and his cowriter Ed Burns would stand on the Fayette and Monroe corner each day with a notepad and pen. As they gradually earned people's trust, both men would follow the residents around, observing them through the course of their lives. Compared to Simon's debut novel, there is now a concerted attempt to understand the plight of those who fall afoul of the law. In *Homicide*, the detectives' perspective of

Figure 1.1. Robin Williams guest stars in the "Bop Gun" episode of *Homicide* written by David Simon. NBC/Photofest © NBC.

civilians living in poverty, while not uncaring, is detached from the conditions of those they stumble across. In places, *Homicide* reads like a wildlife documentary narration observing creatures in their habitat. For example, in a Newington Avenue row house, Simon observes that "two dozen human beings have learned to leave food where it falls, to pile soiled clothes and diapers in a corner of the room, to lie strangely still when parasites crawl across the sheets, to empty a bottle of Mad Dog or T-Bird and then piss its contents into a plastic bucket at the edge of the bed, to regard a bathroom cleaning product and a plastic bag as an evening's entertainment." In order to protect their own well-being, *Homicide* detectives are compelled to reduce the most appalling of tragedies down to a clinical level. On that basis, even the sight of "a young child sprawled across the pavement—her torso gutted, her neck contorted—becomes, after an initial moment of shock, a matter of evidence."[6]

In comparison, *The Corner* emulates the structure of a classic tragedy, as it is concerned with the way people born into Baltimore's open-air drug markets descend into drug taking and crime because of community peer pressure and lack of legal job opportunities. All residents are doomed to deteriorate materialistically, cognitively, and physically no matter how much promise they occupy in earlier life. Like *Homicide*, the protagonists are trapped in an existential crisis through an oppressive day-to-day routine that informs their behaviors and habits. Only this time, single mother Fran Boyd cannot escape her predicament at the end of a working shift or even in her sleep. She fights "for a thin sliver of the single mattress" shared with her two sons in their 8-by-10-foot second-floor room, while "myriad forms of human dysfunction take place just outside the bedroom door." Fran is imbued with more depth than a piece of evidence as *Homicide* would have been inclined to portray her. She is a human being whose home pressures and drug addiction have impacted how she appears to people living outside her neighborhood. Fran "has a face for the corner, armored by hard-boiled eyes that float in sienna tea—a cold glare to deny even the suggestion of complex feelings. But behind that front is a woman with battered, but still usable conscience—a caring soul that time and again proves itself a burdensome source of pain."[7]

This injection of humanism, empathy, and tragedy comes in part from Simon's cowriter Ed Burns. Simon first met Burns in 1984. Researching his four-part Melvin Williams story, Simon brashly confronted the homicide detective in the Baltimore County Library. Simon spotted Burns being issued a pile of books at the checkout desk comprising *The Magus* by John Fowles, *Veil* by Bob Woodward, and collected essays by Hannah Arendt.

Attempting to schmooze the detective for intel on Williams, Simon broke the ice, exclaiming, "You're not really a cop, are you!?" given the lawman's penchant for intellectual literature.[8] Simon clearly left no impression, as Burns recalls first encountering his future cowriter later in Baltimore's Drug Enforcement Administration (DEA) office. A plucky young journalist had managed to evade security, declaring that he had permission from the police department to listen to the wiretaps that Burns had issued on Williams. The thinking man's detective retorted, "I'm going to show it to you and you can listen. But then I'm going to lock you up and you'll get charged with intervening in an investigation and the penalty I think is like 10 years. So, you wanna do that?"[9]

"No," an uncharacteristically feeble Simon replied. He had met his scholarly match. Nevertheless, both men soon bonded, as they were brazen, fiercely intelligent, and morally outraged by societal inequality. Before long, Burns became Simon's most trusted informant when reporting on crime for the *Sun*. Whereas Simon had sought to capture the attitude of traditional detectives in his first book, *The Corner* formulated a different perspective because of his new cowriter, who thought differently from most police.

The future cocreator of *The Wire* was 14 years Simon's senior and had experienced conflict as an infantryman during the Vietnam War. Stationed to the central coast near My Lai, Burns walked point for a platoon constantly besieged with casualties. It was Burns's job to spot land mines and sniper traps alongside his 19-year-old Vietnamese scout named Ba. Such an exposed and practically suicidal undertaking educated Burns in institutional idiocy and the futility of an occupying army facing an entrenched insurgency. Burns likened joining Baltimore Police in 1969 to his experience of combat, stating, "I did the same thing I did walking point in Vietnam" albeit this time with the drug and vice squads.[10] Here in the Western District (or "wild west" as it is known), Burns found the poverty that rippled through the district of more than 33,000 people astonishing. Unlike other cops, he always found himself drawn to the courage of the people he met. It inspired him to learn more about their world. Burns would meet people on the street and help alleviate residents of their small charges. In so doing, Burns could better understand the whole economic structure underpinning the drug trade. Through this unorthodox method of gathering intelligence, Burns convinced his superiors to wiretap Warren Boardley's drug gang, which directly led to convictions right through to the head of the organization. Burns wasted no time in following this success by writing an extensive proposal for a specialized unit that could conduct long-term investigations into violent drug crews, what would become *The Wire*'s fictional Major Crimes Unit. When that proposal disappeared on the eighth floor without so much as a response, Burns was exasperated. He retired from the force early in 1992 to begin a teaching career. Burns "decided it would be fun to teach in an inner-city school. And that's pretty much the amount of thought I gave it until I walked into the room."[11] In his first cohort of 120 seventh graders, 13 had been shot. This subsequent vocation, which would eventually inform *The Wire*'s depiction of education in season 4, was soon put on hold for two years as Simon convinced Burns to cowrite *The Corner* with him instead.

Following *The Corner*'s publication, Simon returned to his *Sun* desk, where, after a further series of buyouts, talented veteran reporters were being driven out to other newspapers. Simon felt that his newspaper was increasingly the playground of "tone deaf out of town hacks."[12] Simon had written *The Metal Men*, a series of articles that follow the socioeconomic repercussions of two men's scavenging metal from an empty Fulton Avenue row house in West Baltimore. Through the course of the story, readers learn how Kenny's and Tyrone's actions detrimentally impact the directors of a nonprofit corporation and a housing commission, both seeking to restore row houses. Consequently, Baltimore police colonel Roland Daniel lacks the officers he needs to contain the widespread theft. But *Metal Men* proved to be Simon's journalistic swan song. *Sun* editor John Carrol attempted to kill Simon's story because of the complex connections drawn between the characters and the obvious sympathy that Simon held for the thieves. Although the story eventually ran as a singular nine-page piece in the *Sun* magazine, by this time, Simon had had enough. With a series of articles on race rejected, the well-versed crime reporter took up a standing offer to write for the *Homicide* TV show permanently.

Simon moved across town to *Homicide*'s writing staff under the wing of producers Barry Levinson and Tom Fontana in 1995. As Simon's second *Homicide* script had been accepted with few alterations, this was the only persuasion the reporter needed to leave the journalism game altogether and immerse himself in screenwriting. During the production of *Homicide*'s fourth season, Simon worked as a producer and wrote the teleplay for the episodes "Justice: Part 2" and "Scene of the Crime." Here Fontana, who was starting to make *Oz* (1997–2003) for HBO, acted as Simon's mentor. Fontana was committed to growing his writers and producers. Script by script, Fontana shaved Simon's prose until "the pacing and dialogue began to show muscle."[13] Every line had to justify itself. Digress from the plot, and a writer has to know what they're doing to serve the story. As Simon became more comfortable writing in this way, Fontana slowly began giving Simon more responsibilities, including sending him to set calls, casting sessions, and the editing suite. Here producer Jim Finnerty also taught writers the practicalities of crew management. But it was by no means a frictionless transition. Actor Clark Johnson (Detective Meldrick Lewis), who would go on to direct *The Wire* and play journalist Gus Haynes, resisted Simon's wholesale aversion to ad-libbing. Yet many years later, the actor/director admitted that Simon's scripts did not require changes. The "white Jewish guy from the suburbs of Baltimore would be getting us black guys current with our own street lingo!"[14] Eventually winning over his new peers, Simon was now confident enough to adapt *The Corner* for television.

Fontana and Levinson didn't see *The Corner* as material for a continuing drama, but Fontana was generous enough to call Anne Thomopoulos at HBO. At a resulting meeting, it became clear that the cable channel was willing to take a shot provided that Simon could pair himself with a black writer. Thinking on his feet, Simon asked the executives, "How about David Mills?" His former coeditor of their student newspaper and cowriter of *Homicide*'s "Bop Gun" was now a revered scriptwriter on *NYPD Blue* and *ER*. Taken-aback HBO executive Kary Antholis quizzically scoffed, "You *know* David Mills?" "Yeah we're friends," Simon nonchalantly riposted. "I worked on my college newspaper with him. We wrote our first script together." Antholis had known about Mills for a long time and left Simon with an ultimatum. If Simon could secure Mills's involvement, then he would have a show. Having unofficially volunteered his friend as *The Corner*'s executive producer, Simon reached for his cell phone while exiting HBO's lobby. "Hey David," Simon told his startled friend settling at home for the evening, "I know what you're doing for the next year."[15]

Soon, the crew that Simon would work with consistently throughout *The Wire* began to assemble. On the production side, Jim Finnerty volunteered his protégé. Nina Noble had been first assistant director on the premier season of *Homicide* and had worked her way up in Fontana's crew. Simon immediately agreed to the partnership, as a recommendation from Finnerty was good enough for him. Noble would go on to produce 52 episodes of *The Wire*. Having recruited Mills and Noble, Simon had all the producing talent he needed for a six-hour miniseries—or so he thought. HBO had doubts aplenty, and their executives demanded that they add their own visual producer into the mix. Antholis arranged interviews in New York with several candidates. Enter Bob Colesberry. His two-decade-long résumé of producing high-end features initially made Simon wary. There was little trust in Antholis's tense office that day. You could cut the tension with a knife, particularly when Simon, Mills, and Noble walked in and saw a copy of *The*

Corner splayed open in front of Colesberry, its pages already forensically marked up in two different colors of ink. Knowing what he now knows, Simon might have taken this as a good sign: "here was a producer a veteran of an industry—where studio suits reduce all stories to single sentence concepts—endeavouring to read the 550 page novel and then begin carrying scenes and shots in his head." Instead, Simon didn't trust Colesberry and promised to consider the man's script notes before coolly reminding him, the veteran producer, that the decision was Simon's alone. Months later with *The Corner* cast and crewed and with Charles S. Dutton turning in magnificent footage as the director, Simon thought back to that first meeting with Colesberry. The debut showrunner now realized, "I did not want to put anything to film ever again without" his experienced producer.[16] Conversely, black director Dutton, who had grown up among drug addiction on Baltimore's impoverished corners, found Simon's attempts to steer his vision on set, as a middle-class suburban white man, condescending. So using Colesberry as a go-between proved to be a diplomatic masterstroke going forward. The crew had assembled like a shotgun wedding but had blossomed into a faithful marriage. The scripts had probed the human dimension of the drug war. The failure of policy, however, could only be implied within an intimate six-episode portrayal of a family. A sustained investigation into a wider society's failings would require a longer series to unpick the issues in far more detail.

Successfully delivering an HBO miniseries guaranteed the 40-year-old Simon an audience with CEO Chris Albrecht and Entertainment Division president Carolyn Strauss. Here Simon pitched *The Wire* as "the anti-cop show, a rebellion of sorts against all the horseshit police procedurals afflicting American television."[17] A pilot script was commissioned and strategically delivered a few months after HBO had collected a trio of Emmy awards for *The Corner*, including Outstanding Limited Series, Writing, and Directing. For Simon, the timing felt right. Why not "just write some checks and send us back to Baltimore where we belong," the critically accomplished showrunner now impatiently thought to himself. But HBO would continue to harbor doubts and concerns. The cable provider had developed a reputation with their fan base for breaking away from traditional television genres. Producing a cop show that they had worked hard to distance themselves from left the executives feeling uneasy.

Simon would have to iron out *The Wire*'s format carefully to reassure the bigwigs at HBO. To do so, Ed Burns was brought back into the fray as they set out to create a police drama loosely based on Burns's experiences working on protracted investigations of violent drug dealers using surveillance technology. Together, both writers began developing a template for the series. *The Wire* began as a story wedged between two American myths. The first is the myth that "if you are smarter than the next man . . . if you get there first with the best idea, you will succeed beyond your wildest imaginations." While this is true of most American millionaires, for Simon and Burns, a further supporting myth has come to "validate the amassed wealth of the wise and fortunate." Those "who are neither slick nor cunning, yet willing to get up every day and work their asses off and come home and stay committed to their families . . . will have a place."[18] The term "The Wire" not only denotes the police wiretapping but also refers to a boundary between a functional, postindustrial economy that is "minting new millionaires every day" and the other America "amputated surgically from the rest of the economic culture," concealing a permanent underclass for whom both American myths, each propagating the view that hard work leads to reward, are unobtainable.[19]

When Simon and Burns were developing this basis for their new show, certain narratives were playing out within American culture: the shocking frauds at the heart of Enron and WorldCom, not to mention the institutional cover-up of child sexual abuse in the Catholic Church. To the writers back in 2002, there was something "hollow and ugly at our institutional core." From what Ed Burns understood of the BPD and the school system and from what Simon had witnessed at the heart of the city's newspaper, "the institutional and systemic corruption of our national life seemed near universal." America was fast becoming the land of "the juked statistic—the false quarterly profit statement, the hyped school test score, the non-existent decline in crime, the impossible campaign promise, the hyped Pulitzer prize." For Simon and Burns, the American dream had become parasitic, promoting profit at all costs at the expense of a Social Security infrastructure that was rapidly being dismantled. Throughout American society, there was a "growing inability to recognize our problems, much less deal honestly with them." *The Wire* is a line in the sand, an attempt to at least recognize America's flaws. "We had a good argument as far as we knew," says Simon, but "in the beginning we didn't know how good" given the lies and self-delusions that would later lead to the invasion of Iraq in 2003; the federal government's lackluster response to Hurricane Katrina in 2005; the 2008 financial crash; Flint, Michigan's, contaminated water supply and subsequent public health crisis in 2014; and the murder and controversial police cover-up of Baltimore's Freddie Gray in 2015.[20] Even the 2016 election of Donald Trump feels like a nod to the culture of false truths at play within *The Wire*.

Despite Simon's and Burn's best efforts at channeling all their frustrations with contemporary American politics into a pilot script, HBO was still reluctant to commission the show in full. The cable channel wanted three more scripts so that they could make an informed decision. To help develop their show out from its ideological foundations, Simon approached established crime novelist George Pelecanos. Both had grown up in Silver Spring, Maryland, and been to the University of Maryland without crossing paths. In fact, Simon had been reluctant to read Pelecanos's work when it was first recommended to him as a *Sun* journalist. It felt as if their shared interest in the fate of the American city and its black urban residents encroached on Simon's territory as a writer. However, on finally reading *The Sweet Forever* at his wife Laura Lippman's request, Simon changed his mind. The two met at the funeral of a mutual friend shortly after Simon delivered the pilot episode. After the funeral, Pelecanos gave Simon a ride home. Here Simon told him that *The Wire* would be a novel for television. Each episode would be like a chapter in a book, and "you could digress, in the way a novel does . . . about the social aspects of crime." For Pelecanos, "that struck home, because if it's not about something more than the mystery, the thriller part, I'm not going to do it. Life's too short."[21] Pelecanos was in.

Pelecanos was offered a core role in the writers' room with a front-row seat to Simon and Burns's full-blown arguments. The professional relationship between the creator and cocreator had always been tense, thriving as they did on conflict and confrontation in a markedly different manner from the NBC programs where Simon cut his teeth. Their collaboration emulated Simon's family upbringing and dinnertime debating more so than a traditional TV writers' room. Pelecanos was stunned. Sometimes, people would be "standing up putting their fingers in another guy's chest or screaming at the other guy," but "it got to be just business as usual." Burns was forever the aggressor, quick to anger, but the final decision rested with the forthright Simon, who would often say, "I'd agree with you but then we'd both be wrong." The more quietly spoken Pelecanos would regularly find himself working as peacemaker. After spending a full week fixating over how regularly sim cards would be discarded from the Barksdale organization's phones, it was Pelecanos who urged them to move on. From Simon's perspective, Burns was the "ideas guy." He would have 20 good ideas thematically, and Simon would narrow them down to six or seven to avoid "too much fat on the skeleton" as he had heeded from his days of working under Fontana. For Simon, a thoughtful individual would think "they're doing 4 to 6 of my main themes," but Burns "looks at the 13 you left on the floor and says I am betrayed." Burns rationalizes his passions differently. He "wanted to write the best script every season and that sense of competition kind of lifted all of us . . . everybody was trying to do the best work that they could, out of pride." Noble credits Simon with fine-tuning her skills in persuasion: "you really have to prepare your argument know all your facts and have to not be shy about presenting them if you really feel strongly about something."[22] The final decision was always Simon's, but he encouraged debate and was open to being persuaded by watertight arguments.

Over the next five years, Simon and Burns would refine their team's distinctive approach to television writing down to a fine art. The final season's writers' meetings were "equal parts urban-studies seminar, reporters' bull session, and Hollywood story conference." Simon's ruthless focus on never detracting from the story without purpose (drilled into him from his *Homicide* days) was coupled with Burns's ability to think about larger societal structures and the empathetic characters who populate them. This dogged focus on story and ideology within a heated cauldron of argument (not dissimilar from Simon's upbringing) was underpinned by Colesberry's forensic ability to boil complex imagery down into pragmatic visual planning through a system of color coding, something that Colesberry bestowed to his team of producers before his untimely passing in 2004. All approaches manifested into a long sheet of butcher paper displayed prominently on the wall of the writers' room. Divided into a grid, the paper would feature the name of each member of the show's ensemble written in marker on the side. Then the episodes, identified by number, were noted along the top. Above the butcher paper were headshots of all the major actors on the show. As the writers decided what would happen to each character, they would write a brief description of that plot point, or "beat," on a colored index card and pushpin it to the appropriate box on the grid. Much like their fictional detective counterparts, Simon's team was building a complex case where "all the pieces matter." Nevertheless, a lot of the discussion had to do with the larger political themes of the show,[23] a focus that always guided Simon's and Burns's approach from the pilot that continued to make the show so unique.

Ultimately, having gone on a painstaking process of argumentative debate to produce three scripts, without any promise of a commission, it was largely Simon's tenacious determination and silver tongue that finally convinced HBO to commission his show. It was not just the pilot script, the accompanying three scripts, or the length to which the writers had gone to devise a program with real ideological heft and rigorous attention to detail. Burns had even taken it on himself to write a 79-page story bible that would guide all the writers who worked on *The Wire*. No, it was the following memo that Simon wrote to Chris Albrecht and Carolyn Strauss on June 27, 2001, that finally assuaged their fears. The memo asserts,

The argument is this: It is a significant victory for HBO to counterprogram alternative, inaccessible worlds against standard network fare. But it would, I will argue, be a more profound victory for HBO to take the essence of network fare and smartly turn it on its head, so that no one who sees HBO's take on the culture of crime and crime fighting can watch anything like *CSI*, or *NYPD Blue*, or *Law & Order* again without knowing that every punch was pulled on those shows. For HBO to step toe-to-toe with NBC or ABC and create a cop show that seizes the highest qualitative ground through realism, good writing, and a more honest and more brutal assessment of police, police work, and the drug culture—this may not be the beginning of the end for network dramas as industry standard, but it is certainly the end of the beginning for HBO . . . because that world of cops and robbers is so central to the American TV experience, *The Wire* would stand as even more of a threat to the established order than a show that was marginalized because it offered a world (prison, gangsters, sex) where some viewers are reluctant to tread on any terms.

Simon concludes,

This is a smart series. It is good storytelling. And it could be the best work on television that I've done so far. Pull the trigger, guys. As with *The Corner*, you will only be proud.[24]

Needless to say, the trigger was indeed pulled. HBO was finally convinced that Simon, over the course of his life, had amassed enough experiences and developed his talents to the point where he was now ready to take the reins of a large project that would beat network television at its own game. Strauss and Albrecht placed their loyalty in Simon to enhance the cop show format and take it to the darker areas of American life to which the mainstream networks would dare not venture. This would coalesce with the HBO brand and satisfy their avid subscribers, who craved unconventional intelligent programming. David Simon finally got his own show, but he would now need a cast.

CASTING THE CHARACTERS

The casting had to be faultless. Actors picked for *The Wire* required a certain degree of charisma to emotionally draw viewers into a slower pace of televisual storytelling. They would also need to be as true to real life as possible. A star too well known with immaculate good looks and a finely polished delivery of their lines would be unconvincing. After all, the scripts focused on working-class Baltimoreans relentlessly browbeaten by their city's under-resourced institutions. This was the impossible challenge placed squarely on the shoulders of *The Wire*'s casting director, Alexa Fogel. With some experience working on *NYPD Blue* (1994–2005) and *Oz* (1997–2003), Fogel understood Simon and Burns's vision and so opted to break with industry norms by assembling a richly textured cast of stage actors, Britons, musicians, underused veterans, promising newcomers, and complete novices. Even former cops, gangsters, and politicians came to play parts, although the biggest challenge of all came in finding a leading man.

DOMINIC WEST AS JIMMY MCNULTY

Several weeks of fruitless searching for a lead actor was beginning to "weigh on all the souls" of Simon's production team. Every American auditionee had read McNulty's part the way they expected a heroic cop to sound on a traditional police procedural. Think *CSI: Crime Scene Investigation* (2000–2015), where established Hollywood leads dispense impeccably timed one-liners straight to camera with a grin. Instead, Simon and

Burns had always conceived of their McNulty as more jaded, over the hill, and given up on life. Initially, HBO was keen on securing British actor Ray Winstone. But after 9/11 and a subsequent grounding of flights, Winstone dropped out of consideration when he managed to return home. Then Simon had his heart set on John C. Reilly, who was open to the idea. But Simon's hopes were dashed when Reilly called Simon's mobile phone during a family day out. Reilly informed the writer that "there's no way" his wife was moving to Baltimore. Close to giving up, Simon and his team were all knocked off guard when a bizarre videotape landed in their offices shipped from a London address. On-screen, a young actor was racing through the scene where McNulty and Bunk find D'Angelo Barksdale's pager when apprehending the young dealer in the second episode, "The Detail." Curiously, this British actor was reading McNulty's lines with a questionable American accent. The Brit regularly paused to react to silences where the responding lines should have been delivered by supporting performances. Although Fogel had encouraged Dominic West to send a tape in, the amateur footage sideswiped Simon. He and executive producer Bob Colesberry watched the "weird half scene" before falling from their chairs laughing. Overhearing a commotion, director Clark Johnson rushed in to see what all the raucousness was about. In a matter of seconds, the director fell to the floor in hysterics alongside both men. "What the hell is this goofy motherfucker doing?" Clark howled.[1] The audition tape was amateur, but the performance was not. When the three men finally composed themselves to concentrate on what the actor had going for him, all were impressed. West was providing a more jack-the-lad character than the downtrodden protagonist Simon and Burns had envisaged, but it worked.

Nonetheless, HBO executives were not impressed by West's amateurism. Fogel stuck her professional reputation on the line by continuously fighting hard for her preferred leading man. The most important quality to McNulty's character was that "he was lost," and the British thespian understood this. By now, Simon's team had settled on their lead actor a few days before they were due to start filming on the streets of Baltimore. In fact, West was the only person to read McNulty's lines in-person to HBO executives. After West delivered his lines to Chris Albrecht in his plush HBO corner office, Fogel turned to the HBO CEO and explained "the essence of his character" in a way nobody else could. Personally unconvinced with her unorthodox choice and irritated by the lack of competition being considered for the role, Albrecht waited for Fogel to finish. When her pleading ceased, Albrecht menacingly extended his index finger out toward the casting director. "You'd better be right," he threatened.[2] From that moment on, Fogel would not sleep for three weeks straight.

Even West himself needed convincing. Within 10 days of his makeshift audition tape, he was in Baltimore shadowing a homicide cop. Cowering in the corner of a hospital trauma unit alongside the family of a guy who had just been shot in the head three times, West prayed that nobody would speak to him. He had not yet learned the Baltimore accent. Things were moving too fast, and West categorically did not want the job. To placate the confounded actor, West's agent reassured him, "Don't worry you won't get it, you're totally wrong." Despite his aversion to living in Baltimore for six months away from his daughter, the process soon snowballed beyond West's control. By the time West found himself in Los Angeles reading lines for the HBO executives, he "didn't give a shit." At this point, he thought to himself, "I don't want this part. I want to go home. I've made a terrible mistake. I don't know what these people are thinking," to the point where he had "no nerves at all." Usually in such scenarios, West would have "dissolved in nervous exhaustion but here he was able to just play it straight; I think that's why I got the job; they liked that." West reflects, "I did everything possible not to get the part but thank God it got the better of me."[3]

To a point, McNulty is a fictionalization of Burns's detective career. Much like his dramatic creation, Burns also circumnavigated the BPD's chain of command to instigate a protracted investigation into a drug kingpin. For Burns, "wars were being fought within the BPD as much as they were on the street." Endlessly insisting to his superiors that "this guy over here is dangerous . . . just let me have the time to get him" was akin to banging his head against the wall. After failing to convince his captain, Burns went directly to the state attorney, who relieved Burns from his role in the Homicide Department. Eighteen months later, Burns and his team brought down a major drug organization. West's cockier self-assured approach to the McNulty role stresses how Burns was not committed to tearing down drug gangs solely for honorable intentions. Sending down drug lord Melvin Williams and later Warren Boardley was about "the challenge of the pursuit," the ability for Burns to showcase his intelligence and gain some comeuppance over his institutionalized superiors. Throughout the investigation, as with McNulty, Burns found himself stuck between a rock and a hard place. Homicide was resentful that Burns was no longer working for their understaffed department, which was endlessly up against the country's highest per-capita murder rate. Conversely, the Narcotics Department was irked by a homicide detective muscling in on their territory. This division was central to Simon and Burns's depiction of the BPD. Drama emanates from the police department's office politics, where McNulty manages to provoke his superiors into keeping the Barksdale Detail operational without maddening them far enough into shutting it down. The key to getting this balance right, for Burns, is "good communication . . . with a second person."[4] Enter McNulty's best friend, Homicide working partner and confidant Bunk Moreland.

WENDELL PIERCE AS BUNK MORELAND

Although Fogel needed an actor who could share great on-screen chemistry with West's McNulty, Bunk Moreland had been cast before their leading man. It was clear to the production team that Wendell Pierce could hold his own, offering a lot more than the periodic silences that West had been working with on his audition tape. Pierce secured the part not necessarily for his acting talents. On his way to the audition, Pierce got into a dispute with a taxi driver for opting to pick up a white passenger over himself. The altercation soon escalated to the point where the taxi driver threw a punch at Pierce, and he swung back. Pierce came in harried, like a bear who had pawed a hornet's nest. Struggling to focus on the scene and repeatedly apologizing for his frazzled demeanor, Simon saw in Pierce the essence of a "put-upon

Figure 2.1. David Simon and Wendell Pierce exchange a joke on set. HBO/Photofest © HBO.

work-a-day Baltimore homicide detective."[5] Pierce's complaining about that taxi ride secured him the gig. They had found their actor, a man who, like his real-life BPD counterpart Detective Oscar "Rick" Requer, could plausibly puff away at fat cigars, befit pinstriped clothing, and express himself through lawyerly affectations.

On securing the role, Pierce was contracted to ride along with the BPD to conceptualize what being a Baltimore cop felt like. As soon as he fastened himself into a squad car, Pierce was troubled by the dysfunction he witnessed. A couple of cops felt compelled to provoke suspects to impress their Hollywood guest. After days of haranguing people through the streets and interrogation suites, the tipping point came when all were in a woman's house responding to a theft. The detectives turned to Pierce, asking, "Detective, do you have any questions?"[6] From that moment on, the actor refused to ride along with the police. Being perturbed by the lack of due care and attention to legal procedure, which could compromise a civilian's civil rights, hardened Pierce's commitment to his role. *The Wire* was to be different, drawing a light on the institutional power structures that lead to the heavy-handed policing that Pierce experienced. Sending West to New York to read with Pierce, shortly before dispatching the Briton to read for Albrecht in Los Angeles, confirmed in the creators' minds that they had chosen the right leading man. Ideally, a leading actor is chosen first, and the supporting role is cast following how well they interact with the star. Luckily, both men hit it off pretty well, and *"that's* what kicked the show into start."[7]

IDRIS ELBA AS STRINGER BELL

For McNulty and Bunk to meet their match, the heads of the Barksdale drug-dealing outfit would need to be believable adversaries, men who are fiercely intelligent enough to run a watertight organization that does not implicate them directly in wrongdoing. Simultaneously, they must be intimidating enough to exude authority and instill loyalty in those who break the law for them. Originally, Idris Elba wanted to be head honcho Avon Barksdale. But it was the actor's elegance that meant that the unknown Elba would land the role of Stringer Bell instead, a suave character capable of breaking bread with wealthy businessmen, property developers, and politicians. The actor's fate at this time, however, could not have been any farther from his character. For four years, the Hackney-born actor had been living in New York but had hardly secured any acting work save for the occasional gig back in the United Kingdom. "That was a very,

very tough time," reveals Elba. "I was in a competitive market of actors that were born and raised there." Close to giving up, Elba vowed that if he had not made it as an actor in America once his daughter was born, he would return home to the United Kingdom. Islan Elba was due in January. Elba had been auditioning tirelessly all through November and December knowing that if he didn't get a job, he "would have to pack up sticks and move back to the UK where there was more of a support system and maybe more work."[8] The day before his daughter was born, Elba secured the part of Bell.

Living undercover worked in Elba's favor. Since moving to the United States, he never dropped his American accent for anyone. Through his readings for the part, David Simon had a bet going with his producer as to whether Elba was American. At the last audition, Elba was asked, "Where are you *really* from?" "East London," came the actor's reply in his native cockney accent. The whole room erupted in astonishment. Simon had lost the bet, so he promised the actor there and then that "I'm going to give you the job because you had me fooled." This ability to hide in plain sight and mislead inquisitive minds is vital to the Bell role. The character is based largely on Lamont "Chin" Farmer, the favored lieutenant of Melvin Williams (a chief inspiration for Bell's boss Avon Barksdale). The second in command was the brains behind Williams's complex communications system utilizing beepers, pay phones, and coded conversations to evade telephone wiretaps. Farmer was so cautious that he would drive miles, changing direction repeatedly to avoid police surveillance. He was right to. On one occasion, the encroaching blades of a police helicopter began piercing the sky. The lieutenant wasted no time in dropping the pay phone handset and speeding off in his car, all within the blink of an eye. While the chopper was responding to an unrelated emergency, Farmer was also being tailed by detectives expecting to catch him red-handed ordering his next large drug shipment. On this occasion, an act of happenstance, twinned with his continual paranoia, had saved him from police capture. But working his way up from street dealer, Farmer was still something of a scholar. He excelled in local college business courses, funneled drug money into legitimate businesses (a printshop and towing firm), and lectured family members on economics. He also subscribed to legal journals to keep abreast of changes in criminal law. Likewise, Bell attends business classes, runs a printshop, and uses his funeral parlor to discuss economic theories with his mid-level dealers. Spotting a copy of *The Wealth of Nations* by Adam Smith while searching Bell's opulent apartment leads a dumbfounded McNulty to reflect "who the fuck was I chasing?" Cast on his ability to be just as charming, intelligent, yet inconspicuous, for Elba, "it was exciting to watch the evolution" of a secondary role, especially as Bell comes to oversee the drug empire during Barksdale's imprisonment from season 2 onward. Whatever initial misgivings Elba may have had about the character he was given, *The Wire* changed the trajectory of his life beyond anyone's comprehension.[9]

WOOD HARRIS AS AVON BARKSDALE

As for Avon Barksdale, the role went to a slightly more experienced American screen actor who had managed to hold his own against Tupac Shakur in *Above the Rim* (1994) and Denzel Washington in *Remember the Titans* (2000), and had the lead role in Showtime's *Hendrix* (2000). Wood Harris's character is a composite of real-life drug kingpins that Ed Burns investigated and David Simon reported on. The first is a man named "Little" Melvin Williams, who revolutionized Baltimore's drug culture in the 1960s. Son to a cabdriver and nurse, Williams was a skilled pool player hustling through Pennsylvania Avenue tables, earning thousands of dollars most evenings. Here the teenage math prodigy caught the eye of Julius "The Lord" Salsbury, a lieutenant of organized crime boss Meyer Lansky. As heroin overtook gambling as the dominant criminal enterprise, Williams transitioned to drug distribution. Soon, he was sent to New York as Lansky's representative with suitcases stuffed full of money to negotiate product for Baltimore territories with the country's singular most successful drug trafficker, Frank "Pee Wee" Matthews. Following a 1968 prison sentence for his efforts, Williams was released into a drug-dealing vacuum in 1973, as Lansky had fled the country to avoid federal tax evasion charges. Williams wasted no time utilizing his connections with high-profile suppliers and low-level dealers to build a larger yet more close-knit drug ring that controlled the entire drug supply chain from East to West Baltimore. A four-year prison stretch was all prosecutors could pin on Williams in 1975 through evidence secured via informants. It was Ed Burns's more comprehensive 1984 wiretap that would incarcerate Williams until 2004. According to conservative estimates, Williams had led an organization worth millions.

Like Barksdale's character, Williams maintained great levels of personal discipline. Following his 1968 release, the reformed 31-year-old no longer drove Cadillacs, wore fur coats, or adorned custom-made diamond rings. His younger days of openly threatening to execute everyone in a Mount Street bar with a submachine gun over minor disagreements were long gone. Investigators would see pigs fly before they would find the teetotal vegetarian flashing cash, openly communicating with other suspects, or appearing in a room with his product. Similarly, in *The Wire*, Avon Barksdale is sentenced only for "attempted possession" in season 1's final episode, "Sentencing," following coded instructions obtained from a hidden-camera recording. Williams's personal discipline percolated through his intricately devised system of lieutenants, mid-level dealers, street-level dealers, and street-level enforcers, a judiciousness mirrored by Barksdale, who sits above an intricate system of drug dealers (hoppers), "touts" attracting customers, "runners" handing drugs to customers, and "lookouts" warning of police or stickup gangs. Underlying such restraint at every level of Williams's and Barksdale's organizations is a commitment to their community. Williams gifted rent money, groceries, and Thanksgiving turkeys to the poorest of West Baltimore, not to mention fitting dilapidated community playgrounds with fresh basketball nets. Just before his 1968 arrest, Williams even managed to quell race riots earlier that year. In the wake of Martin Luther King Jr.'s murder, Williams stood alongside the National Guard. His instructing bloodthirsty crowds to "go home" was met with rapturous applause and instant dispersal. Williams's consistent commitment to restraint and community, maintained through the majority of his adult life, is something the former drug lord attributes to being a student of martial arts from the age of 15. Barksdale is similarly grounded by the boxing successes of his adolescence. His poster still hangs on the wall of local gyms, and his Golden Gloves accolade is fondly remembered by the boxing community. In season 3's penultimate episode, "Middle Ground," retired enforcer Dennis "Cutty" Wise (Chad Coleman) references both achievements when appealing for help. He asks Barksdale for $10,000 to renovate a run-down gym with fresh equipment to teach children boxing. Barksdale gives Cutty $15,000 in cash without hesitation. In return, Barksdale does not want his name on the wall, only Cutty's promise that the boxing trainer will "take care of them young'uns." To a large degree, his strict discipline is community oriented, a predilection affirmed by Barksdale's earlier donations to a high school's pupil, teacher, and basketball program when recruiting players for season 1's "Game Day"—an annual tournament hosted between East and West Baltimore.

The fictional Avon Barksdale's commitment to discipline and loyalty toward younger members of West Baltimore is underscored and eventually undermined by a proclivity for violence, inspired by the brutal existence led by real-life Nathan "Bodie" Barksdale, who worked as a mid-level dealer for Williams. Bodie rose to notoriety in the 1980s for running a heroin-dealing operation from public housing complexes. Compared to Williams, Nathan Barksdale was directly exposed to violence. Growing up, he was shot more than 20 times and had his right leg amputated below the knee following a dispute with a car owner. The would-be kingpin's leg was deliberately crushed between the reversing vehicle and a brick wall. The teenager's crime? Eating the driver's lunch. Barksdale learned how to maintain control through fear, having been locked in a basement and set on by a German shepherd for allegedly stealing money from gang leader Frank Hopper. As an adult, Barksdale had Hopper assassinated and with that seized control of the dead man's assets. Barksdale would now run a drug ring out of the (since demolished) Lexington Terrace Apartments and George B. Murphy Homes. Both were public housing complexes consisting of high-rise apartment buildings on which *The Wire*'s fictional Franklin Terrace towers are modeled. These towers were Baltimore's 24-hour supermarket for heroin and cocaine. Here Barksdale meted out irregular methods of rough justice, as people he suspected of robbing him were violated with hot curling irons, lit cigarettes, knives, and guns within his own custom-built torture chamber on the Murphy building's eleventh floor, the same punishment that the fictional Avon Barksdale has inflicted on Brandon Wright (Michael Kevin Darnall) for robbing the drug lord's stash houses alongside Omar Little. In season 1's episode 6, "The Wire," Wright's bloody carcass is openly strewn across the hood of a car to ensure that all dealers obey Avon's orders. Likewise, at the peak of a three-year reign of terror, violence attributable to Nathan Barksdale became a daily occurrence. Residents would bolt their doors shut, and security guards would look the other way while stairwells, hallways, and courtyards boiled over into war zones. Even Williams's high-ranking lieutenant Chin Farmer would keep one hand on his gun whenever supplying Nathan Barksdale with drugs to sell.

As with Avon Barksdale, Nathan Barksdale's penchant for maintaining authority through violence was the source of his downfall. Nathan would receive 15 years in prison when he and his street dealer Roland Bell were involved in the prolonged torture and attempted murder of three people. Even the most hardened homicide veterans were left feeling queasy. The mid-level dealer misidentified Myra Tyson alongside two male associates looking to buy cocaine as acquaintances of enemy Michael Stewart. One by one, Tyson and her escorts were forced at gunpoint to Barksdale's eleventh-floor Mengele-esque dungeon. Incorrectly perceiving them as seeking revenge for Stewart's recent murder, Nathan Barksdale went further with his usual methods of vengeance. At one point, he attempted to saw second victim Timothy Franklin's ear off using a serrated steak knife. By the time third victim Michael Stokes was dragged into the apartment, all three were herded into the bathroom and force-fed speedballs, a potent mixture of cocaine and heroin. Several hours later, Barksdale and his men debated how to dispose of the bodies. Stokes wasted no time in seizing his opportunity. Grabbing a gun from distracted street enforcer Victor Smith, Stokes shot his way to freedom. Smith was hit with four bullets, and Barksdale had one pierce his arm as Stokes kept running until he found a police officer. When emergency responders entered the room, they found the victims still breathing among a slurry of weapons, blood, and narcotics, as if they had entered a scene lifted directly from *Scarface* (1983).

David Simon has always maintained that there are only anecdotal connections between these real-life Baltimoreans and his characters. But it is clear that the Avon Barksdale character played by Wood Harris is a balance between "Little" Melvin Williams's indefatigable intelligence and self-discipline and the real Nathan "Bodie" Barksdale's ruthlessness. This appetite for mercilessness is also what consumes Harris's Barksdale. Despite Bell's diplomatic efforts to negotiate with Proposition Joe's (Robert F. Chew) cooperative of drug dealers, Barksdale keeps opting to execute members of Marlo Stanfield's (Jamie Hector) rival gang and take his territories back by force using any means necessary. Being outnumbered and outgunned by Stanfield and acting against the co-op's wishes diminishes Avon Barksdale's supply of drugs and soldiers. Frustrated by his deteriorating influence, the fictional Barksdale relapses into heroin use, as would happen to the real Barksdale. Nathan died in a North Carolina federal medical prison in 2016 at age 54, riddled with sickness from his addictions.

ANDRE ROYO AS BUBBLES

While critics are interested largely in *The Wire*'s representation of institutional failings for many viewers, it is the plight of characters who separate themselves from Baltimore's institutions that make for compelling viewing. Prominent cultural theorist, anthropologist, and ethnographer bell hooks argues that within segregated black communities, the "traveling black man" is an age-old archetype that has been concurrently admired yet indicted for failing to achieve material success and influence within societal infrastructure.[10] In the twentieth century, she elaborates, contemporary equivalents that society continues to remain fascinated by are those who are unemployed or in prison given their adventuresome lifestyles. One such character adhering to the former is heroin addict Reginald "Bubbles" Cousins.

Bubbles, nicknamed as such for blowing spit bubbles during heroin-induced stupors, survives day to day on the streets thieving stolen goods and then selling them to afford his next fix. Bubbles is the emotional core of the show given his ability to repeatedly battle addiction. He is a rare example of a character on *The Wire* achieving redemption when he maintains a degree of control over his addiction and reconnects with his family by the show's end. Nonetheless, stage actor Andre Royo was not convinced. Making a name for himself in the world of theater, the Bronx-born actor was called out of the blue by his manager, urging him to audition for HBO. "The Wire? What the fuck is that?" he rebuked. Royo was insulted by a part with such a trivial name. "Bubbles?!?" he lambasted, felt like a step backward for his stage career. But Royo's manager convinced the New Yorker to use the audition as an opportunity to introduce himself to the film and television world. Pitching the audition to Royo as a challenge lit a fire in the actor's belly. By the third callback, Royo was thriving off the more competitive nature of the television casting process, using his auditions to challenge Fogel into finding "somebody better than me I dare you." But when Royo finally secured the part, he knew very little about drug addiction, so much so that his mother took umbrage at the show's creators for seeing her son exuding the "essence of a junkie." To prepare, Royo studied Al Pacino's performance from *The Panic in Needle Park* (1971). Royo then made a list of things that he did every day without thinking and cut them all out. Removing sugar, television, and sex from his life completely left a jittering Royo climbing the walls of his apartment. This was his technique for "finding that itch. To want something that is right in front of you, but you can't have." His efforts and the work of Debi Young's makeup department soon paid off. While filming, Royo was approached by a man who handed him a small package of heroin. "Man, you need a fix more than I do," said the benevolent stranger. Royo calls this his "street Oscar."[11]

Royo had worked hard to encapsulate the authenticity of Bubbles, a character based largely on police informant "Possum." With his real name protected at his family's behest, the real heroin addict had a drug sentence dropped in exchange for turning over criminals at $50 to $100 per head. Using hats to mark potential criminal targets for police surveillance "gave us at least 500 escapees," remembers Leo Smith of the BPD's escape-and-apprehension squad. "His information was always dead-on," confirms homicide detective Willie Collie. "If he told me right now to go kick in a door, I'd kick in that door." Possum first became addicted to heroin at age 15 when an older friend paid him a debt with leftovers from a $6 bag. Two years later, he was firing drugs almost every day and earning his keep as a street vendor by day and sneak thief by night. Caught in the act of thieving, he was given an ultimatum. Either Possum would give up names, or he'd go to the Southern District lockup. And that began it. Before long, Possum was churning out information on burglaries, robberies, and fugitives. The man had a photographic memory for faces, clothing, and locations. After a time, he could simply memorize photographs and against the odds find those faces on the street. Possum moved through the city unnoticed by everyone, as he always had a reason to be wandering through any neighborhood at any time, be it buying dope, selling goods, or stealing copper piping or metal gutters and finding junkmen to sell the metals to. Over time, Possum's capacity for survival would take a dark turn. After being mugged three or four times, Possum replaced the heroin in his shirt pocket with battery acid. After a couple of days, Possum's tormentor eventually fired it and fell dead. Another person would die simply because they fired acid-contaminated heroin alongside Possum. "I felt bad for that person, but hey, it's all in [the game]," he would say.[12] David Simon's dramatization of these events are rather more tear fueled, as Bubbles's character does not get his comeuppance against his tormentor in season 4. In the season's final episode, "That's Got His Own," Bubbles's young apprentice Sherrod (Rashad Orange) accidentally shoots up the battery acid the night before Bubbles plots to poison his terrorizer. Far less callous than his real-life counterpart, Bubbles's immovable grief comes to underlie his determination to eventually kick his habit.

MICHAEL K. WILLIAMS AS OMAR LITTLE

The extreme plight endured by the "traveling black man" archetype and the decisions they are forced to make to survive the fringes of Baltimore's institutions are a key draw for fans. At the other side of the spectrum is far and away the show's most popular character, Omar Little. A 2009 IMDb poll revealed that Omar was most people's favorite character, President Barack Obama has publicly cited the character as his own personal favorite, and in 2021, the Baltimore Ravens of the National Football League even walked out to the sound of Omar's whistling during their home opener at M&T Bank Stadium.[13] The larger-than-life gun-toting outlaw robs from drug-dealing crews armed with his signature trench coat, sawed-off shotgun, scarred face, and smile, all the while merrily whistling "The Farmer in the Dell." His brazen ability to take what he wants, underscored by a strict moral code that prevents him from hurting innocent bystanders, sees Omar redistribute his stolen money to those in need. Refraining from so much as swearing makes him a character unlike any other. Omar is David to the Goliath Barksdale organization, as he robs their stash houses and then starts targeting, maiming, and murdering their enforcers one by one as a personal vendetta for his lover Brandon Wright being tortured to death. Despite HBO asking Simon to cut Omar out of early scripts for being a character too far, Omar's Robin Hood–esque and spaghetti western outlaw–style catharsis is an important draw for many people.

From the start, casting director Fogel only had one actor in mind for Omar, but she couldn't remember his name. Fogel spent hours going back through files on characters she had cast for *Oz*, searching for the man with that scar. For Fogel, not only did Williams look the part, but she "knew he'd been a dancer and that he had a kind of beautiful calm about him that would serve the character." A skilled choreographer who had appeared in Madonna's music video for "Secret," Tupac cast Williams from his Polaroid alone for *Bullet* (1996). Williams had since secured bit parts in Martin Scorsese's *Bringing Out the Dead* (1999) and *The Sopranos*. His facial scar, which has always helped Williams get noticed and had drawn Fogel back to him, was the result of being on the wrong side of a razor blade during a twenty-fifth-birthday barroom brawl. That said, a gangster he is not. In the first scene he shot, where Omar cocks a shotgun, Williams nervously approached Burns, asking, "Hey excuse me sir, sir, how do you open this?" Burns thought to himself, "Well this character's not going to last." But Burns needed to show the dancer turned actor only once. When the cameras started rolling, "you would have thought when Michael was a baby his mom put a shotgun in the crib with him."[14] The contrast between Williams's scarred face, graceful movements, and inherently polite nature brought to life the habits and traits of a variety of real-life stickup artists whom the character was based on, including Shorty Boyd, Donnie Andrews, Ferdinand Harvin, Billy Outlaw, and Anthony Hollie.

Donnie Andrews, Omar's chief influence, was born Larry Donnell Andrews in 1954. One of Andrew's earliest memories was seeing a man bludgeoned to death in a launderette for 15 cents in the West Baltimore projects. Aged 10, "I made up my mind that I would never be a victim, I would never be the prey, I'd be the hunter." In a neighborhood plagued by gang warfare, Andrews felt that a "lone wolf" mentality would leave him less likely to be caught for criminal acts. After his first arrest at age 16 robbing stores for $200 to $300 each time, he soon found it more lucrative to rob hustlers. Before long, he exuded so much terror that he shouted up to a window, "Hey yo if I gotta come up there it's gonna be bad," and the dealers dropped their heroin down onto the pavement, a scene replicated by Omar in season 1's "Game Day." But by the 1980s, heroin use began clouding Andrews's judgment. At this point, he'd graduated from robbery to murder for hire at the request of drug kingpin Warren Boardley. Boardley hired Andrews and Reggie Gross, a former heavyweight boxer who once fought Mike Tyson, as assassins. By that time, with Melvin Williams and Nathan Barksdale banged up in prison, the Boardley gang violently ruled the Lexington Terrace and Poe Homes projects. They saw rival drug dealers Zachary Roach and Rodney "Touche" Young as enemies. For $5,000 and two ounces of heroin, Andrews and Gross used MAC-11 machine pistols to kill Roach and Young in what became known as the Gold Street murders. As Gross's Uzi unloaded into Young, Roach tried fleeing up the street. Andrews fired into Roach's back, forcing him to fall. Andrews homed in on his prey to finish the job with a final bullet to the head. The dying man looked up at Andrews, stared him straight in the eye, and asked, "Why?" For Andrews, "it was like I was frozen in time. It stuck with me, and I couldn't get it out of my head."[15] Wracked with guilt, Andrews handed himself in to Burns.

Burns knew that Andrews was capable of violence, but beneath his tough exterior, he was not cut out for cold-blooded execution. So Burns offered Andrews a second chance at life. The gun for hire agreed to confess to the double murder and wear a wire to unlock crucial information about the Baltimore drug trade. In exchange, Andrews believed that he would receive a 10-year prison sentence instead of two consecutive life terms. Despite Andrews's cooperation, the district attorney reneged on the agreement, and Andrews was sentenced to life in prison anyway. Simon and Burns turned to Andrews through his incarceration to shed light on various aspects of Baltimore crime so that each could do their respective jobs as detective and reporter even more effectively. Simon and Burns lobbied for Andrews's release. Even Scheeler, the lead federal prosecutor who secured Andrews's conviction, eventually championed a release after watching the former hitman's transformation in prison. After 17 years, Andrews was released in 2005. His first job was becoming an official consultant on *The Wire*. Two years later, he married Fran Boyd (whose life is documented as chief protagonist in *The Corner*) with Simon serving as Andrews's best man. As an actor, Andrews made his debut appearance in season 4's episode 6, "Margin of Error," as Omar's hired muscle who tapes magazines to the stickup man's chest to repel prison stabbings. Meanwhile, Andrews continued his gang outreach program and founded a nonprofit organization called Why Murder?—inspired by the last words of his final victim. In 2012, Donnie Andrews passed away after complications stemming from a heart procedure. On his passing, Simon reflects, "On paper, he's a murderer. We've constructed a criminal justice system that doesn't allow for the idea of redemption." Donnie's life (and, by extension, Omar's character) "puts a lie to that."[16]

Omar is fondly remembered not only for his cathartic ability to live out-side oppressive state institutions such as bell hooks's "traveling black man" but also for challenging black gay stereotypes. While Andrews was straight, Billy Outlaw was a stickup artist who was softly spoken and never cursed, so Burns felt it would be interesting to make Omar an outwardly gay character. When discussing the timeless allure of the traveling man in black subculture, bell hooks argues that while the lone traveler challenges traditional models of patriarchal manhood, "black nationalist circles still demand compulsory heterosexuality" alongside the "persecution and hatred of homosexuals."[17] Collins's cultural analysis of black masculinity develops this point further, arguing that popular representations of gay black men before Omar's char-acter were reduced to simply being a "punk," "sissy," or "faggot," shorthand for an "effeminate and derogated black masculinity." Thus, representations of gay African Americans were "peripheral characters," often in comedic roles that "border on ridicule." The purpose of such stereotypes is to con-struct homosexual black men as less manly for exhibiting a sexual identity that symbolizes a "chosen emasculation."[18]

It was precisely due to these "stubborn stereotypes" that Michael K. Williams was scared to play a gay character. The actor was worried about how playing a gay role would preclude him from future work given how "the stubborn stereotypes of gay characters" outlined by bell hooks and Collins had been prevalent throughout his upbringing and the "community that raised me." So Williams made a conscious choice: "I made Omar my own. He wasn't written as a type, and I wouldn't play him as one." This changed how masculinity was perceived and discussed at that time. Simon and Burns kept writing, "Omar rubs the boy's lips. Omar rubs the boy's hair. Omar holds the boy's hand," to which Williams protested, "Don't gay people fuck? You know what I mean? Don't they kiss? Don't they grab each other?" Williams overruled both creators, imploring, "Listen, we've got to step it up."[19] It is hard to imagine characters like Captain Raymond Holt (Andre Braugher) of *Brooklyn Nine-Nine* (2013–2021), Chrion (Ashton Sanders) of the Oscar-winning *Moonlight* (2016), and Kelly (Gugu Mbatha-Raw) of *Black Mirror*'s "San Junipero" (2016) existing as such powerful three-dimensional characters had Williams not first played Omar as a homosexual authentically freed from stereotype.

Omar challenged the dominant stereotypes identified by Collins, still prevalent in the Bronx communities where Royo's family resided, because "Omar was so open and expressive and fearless about his emotions he wore it on his sleeve. We didn't really see much of that in our culture on screen." Omar embodied a "certain inner strength. For us black people strength was big muscle tough not teary eyed not crying not being sensitive."[20] Omar's scenes, much like the previously mentioned characters whom he has subsequently inspired, often reveal that sensitivity and machismo are not mutually exclusive. Once Omar and Brandon have first robbed the Barksdale crew in season 1's episode 5, "The Pager," they vacate their base to evade Barksdale's enforcers. The scene begins with both Omar and Wright dressed in bulletproof vests. Wright stuffs their gym bags with the stolen money as Omar cocks his handgun and holsters it. The third member of their gang, Bailey, has not turned up at the agreed time, but they are instead opting to leave. Complaining about Bailey's tardiness, Wright is galled by what he sees as a "fucking dope fiend who can't be fucking relied on." Omar pulls up Wright for his cuss words, explaining that "nobody wants to hear those words" as Omar lifts his hand up to stroke Wright's face, elaborating "especially from such a beautiful mouth." After both men lean into one another to tenderly kiss, the camera cuts to Omar's shotgun lying on the bed in close-up and tracks along with it as Omar lifts it up off the bed and cocks it as they leave the room. This is certainly a character who is no "less manly" or who has "chosen emasculation" as Collins describes, as the hands that tenderly and sexually penetrate Brandon's face are the very same hands that confidently operate the shotgun that will maim and execute Barksdale's most ruthless and trusted enforcers. Omar asserts himself as the most physically dominant and smartest male in the whole season, as his love for Wright is what drives him to vengeful murder and helps bring the Barksdale organization to its knees in later seasons. The prior division in black culture between mental and physical toughness (previously coded as heterosexual) and emotional sensitivity (previously coded as homosexual) has been thoroughly breached and presented as two sides of the same coin. Omar is a man who in season 4's episode 3, "Home Rooms," can proudly walk through the impoverished crime-ridden streets of West Baltimore in a bright purple silk dressing gown to buy his boyfriend cereal from the corner shop without fear. Here Omar casually robs a stash house while returning home simply by pausing to smoke a cigarette outside the building in his traditionally feminine undergarments. Gay black characters are no longer ridiculed or sidelined but respected.

SONJA SOHN AS SHAKIMA GREGGS

Before *The Wire*, American cop shows were largely "co-opted by the ideology of sexism," as they would endorse the most brutal aspects of patriarchal authority as necessary to protect society from dissenting criminals.[21] White heteronormative masculinity's imperfections and contradictions are precisely what maintain order. *The Wire* partly challenges this notion given the sheer number of first-time African American actors it cast. Sonja Sohn's character, Detective Kima Greggs, was the first mixed-race black lesbian on American television. For her, *The Wire* ushered in a new interest in African American stories. First spotted at a poetry reading contest by producer Marc Levin, who promptly cast her in his film *Slam* (1998), Sohn was no stranger to underserved communities. Raised in Virginia's Newport News, Sohn's Korean mother—brought home by an American soldier after the Korean War—had a hard time keeping her daughter on the straight and narrow. Sohn's childhood was besieged by drug addiction from age 11, an abusive father, and the murder of her drug-dealing brother. Initially, Sohn struggled to remember her lines on set and came close to quitting *The Wire* on several occassions. Over time, Sohn came to realize that "I was working in neighborhoods that were very reminiscent of the neighborhoods that I grew up in. I was seeing people that reminded me of the people I grew up with. I was essentially, on some level, experiencing a retraumatization. And my brain was just short-circuiting all over the place."[22] Luckily, Sohn persevered, and her character was able to challenge lesbian stereotypes.

Greggs's character develops the precedent pioneered by *Cagney and Lacey* (1981–1988), the first police drama to challenge prevailing stereotypes of women on television that had yet to be matched. Greggs continues the show's legacy by destabilizing and problematizing "commonsense" notions about sexual difference through acerbic, witty put-downs of her surrounding male colleagues as her progenitors frequently did. In the very first episode during a sting operation, her fellow DEA detectives' adrenaline-fueled machismo is undercut by her cold, calm assuredness. Herc (Domenick Lombardozzi) and Carver (Seth Gilliam) struggle to maintain control as the handheld insecure camera replicates their boyhood giddiness. A suspect escapes, and both detectives keep barking increasingly panicked and conflicting orders at the remaining unsuspecting couple in the car, on whom they draw their police guns. Once both suspects surrender on the ground, both detectives seek approval from Greggs by attempting to boast about their superiority over others as she arrives on the scene. Carver proclaims, "You should see the way the bitch was looking at me Kima," and Herc beams with pride that the other "ugly little fucker almost shit his pants he was so scared." Compared to the unstable handheld camerawork that captured the arrest and quick cross cutting between all four characters, in one unbroken shot, Greggs assuredly walks over to the car, calmly searches the back seat in her own time, and produces a smaller gun that they missed. The camera then cuts to a close-up of Carver, whose cocky smile falters into a frown, and both men stop laughing, embarrassed not only that they missed a second gun but also that there is little incriminating evidence to charge the suspects in the car. Similarly, when McNulty tries to seductively charm Greggs in season 1's episode 4, "Old Cases," she again deciphers this bravado as solipsistic. Turning up on a doorstep unannounced and smiling is enough to seduce Assistant State Attorney Rhonda Pearlman (Deirdre Lovejoy) into repeatedly pumping her for information. Conversely, after McNulty thanks Greggs for her help at work, she accepts by saying, "No problem good night" and slams the door in his face. In both of Greggs's scenes, the behavior of her male colleagues is revealed to be short sighted, unprofessional, and unproductive, as it is propelled by immediate gratification. Attempting to assert needless dominance over others is of little help to the investigations and achieves only personal satisfaction.

Greggs furthers *Cagney and Lacey*'s precedent. Unlike her straight white foremothers, Greggs is a homicide detective working in an unrelenting Homicide Department. She does not function as a de facto probation officer or social worker maligned simply to care for victims of the system as was the responsibility of the 1980s duo. Furthermore, while *Cagney and Lacey*

Figure 2.2. Herc's and Carver's gung-ho masculinity is initially exposed as being shortsighted and a hindrance to investigations. HBO/Photofest © HBO.

was the first cop drama to expose gender discrimination and would often privilege the point of view of oppressed ethnic and homosexual minorities, it never portrayed gay women. This is rectified by *The Wire* as Greggs and Cheryl (Melanie Nicholls-King) share tender and intimate moments where they provide their perspective on events, uncover the continued problems with their artificially inseminated pregnancy, and consider the discrimination they experience at the hands of the police force. Lying in a critical condition in season 1's episode 11, "The Hunt," nobody thinks to contact Greggs's partner, as according to the BPD, she is not technically family. Having waited at the hospital for some time, Carver asks his superiors, Lieutenant Daniels and Deputy Ops Burrell, whether somebody could talk to Kima's "girl." Initially, Burrell mistakes Cheryl for Greggs's daughter, as to him, this is the only conceivable way that both women could be family despite their clearly belonging to the same age bracket. Lieutenant Daniels sheepishly corrects Burrell by referring to Cheryl as Greggs's "roommate" rather than explicitly disclosing the true nature of the two women's relationship. Given what "roommate" infers, Commissioner Frazier refuses to console Cheryl and instead sends over his deputy Burrell to provide Cheryl with emotional support. Greggs's girlfriend sits alone in the hospital corridor isolated from the gaggle of uniformed BPD personnel at the reception desk. She is rejected by the larger BPD family to the point where she is not permitted to share the camera's frame with them because of their institutionalized prejudice.

Given how Greggs and Omar subvert traditional notions of masculinity, race, and heterosexuality from traditional television drama, it is now time for the next chapter to tell the story of the American cop show, specifically, how the genre came into being in the 1950s and how landmark shows were commissioned and developed up until 2002 so as to discern what elements from popular programs *The Wire* borrows from and challenges in more detail.

SEASON 1

A Classic Cop Show

Critics are quick to distance *The Wire* from "horseshit police procedurals."[1] McMillan claims that the HBO drama subverts cop show heroism to "rebel against" the genre's "traditional legitimizing" of the American criminal justice system.[2] Williams concurs that it "ceases to be an ordinary police procedural" from the very first court scene.[3] Nichols-Pethick believes that *The Wire* is concerned more with "locating truth" over engaging with the central tenets of the traditional detective drama.[4] Turnbull stresses that each episode conveys an appearance of "no-style" to break from the visual and thematic traditions of the American police genre.[5] Vint acknowledges that *The Wire* owes a significant debt to earlier dramas that take interest in the minutiae of police work. Although to her, the show is more concerned with "contingent, contextual, and social explanations of crime" neglected by previous cop dramas.[6] Barrett even argues that *The Wire* is an all-out "subversion of television codes and conventions."[7] Nevertheless, its depiction of the BPD assembling a special unit to pursue drug lord Avon Barksdale (Wood Harris) shares a closer relationship to the American cop show than previous studies would have you believe. The first season is saturated with references from the morally righteous American cop shows of the 1950s to the liberal series of the 1960s. No show is left unturned, from the rogue cop traditions of the 1970s to the gritty antiheroic cops of the 1980s as well as the empathetic, in-control cops of the 1990s. This chapter explores the history and development of the American cop show. It investigates how previous shows came to be and what their purpose was to uncover where *The Wire* adopts elements of classic franchises and to what end. Simon convincing HBO to commission his work as "a more honest and more brutal assessment of police, police work, and the drug culture" is a tale as old as the American cop show itself. A showrunner has always refreshed the format to imbue their work with greater authenticity than their predecessors. Both Dennis Lehane and George Pelecanos have consistently tempered their boss's attacks on the genre. Both men understood *The Wire* to be a "cop show in its DNA" when writing its scripts.[8] For TV academic Jenner, it is precisely this being "safely situated" within the police procedural genre that an "in-depth analysis of 'the system' emerges."[9] Mittel concurs that "the procedural elements of cop shows. . . are quite vital to *The Wire*."[10] How exactly *The Wire* is stationed within the police genre, and the ideological effect this has had, has not been fully considered—until now.

Season 1's analysis of America's law-and-order system begins when Detective James "Jimmy" McNulty (Dominic West) of the BPD Homicide Unit catches the eye of Judge Daniel Phelan (Peter Gerety) in court. Drug dealer D'Angelo Barksdale (Larry Gilliard Jr.) has been acquitted of committing murder. In private, McNulty explains to Judge Phelan that witness Nakeesha Lyles (Ingrid Cornell) was intimidated by D'Angelo Barksdale's uncle's enforcers to retract her initial eyewitness statement. McNulty vents that nobody is investigating Avon Barksdale and his right-hand man Stringer Bell (Idris Elba), whose crew is responsible for overseeing West Baltimore's drug trade and several unsolved homicides. Phelan swiftly calls Deputy Ops Ervin Burrell (Frankie Faison) demanding that a detail be assembled specifically dedicated to investigating Barksdale. From the outset, Homicide commander William Rawls (John Doman) and Burrell are embarrassed that the chain of command has been breached and repeatedly try to thwart the investigation at every opportunity. Lieutenant Cedric Daniels (Lance Reddick) heads the new Barksdale Detail. The lieutenant supervises three detectives he has worked alongside in the Narcotics Division: Ellis Carver (Seth Gilliam), Kima Greggs (Sonja Sohn), and Thomas "Herc" Hauk (Domenick Lombardozzi). Roland "Prez" Pryzbylewski (Jim True-Frost) is assigned from the Casualty Division, Lester Freamon (Clarke Peters) from the Pawnshop Unit, and McNulty from Homicide. Additional help is also provided from McNulty's Homicide partner Bunk Moreland (Wendell Pierce), heroin addict informant Bubbles (Andre Royo), and Assistant State Attorney Rhonda Pearlman (Deirdre Lovejoy). Over time, the investigation monitors the Barksdale organization through wiretapping, cloned pagers, a hidden camera, and a car tracker. Eventually, key players within the drug-dealing network are convicted. But amassing the all-important evidence needed to secure charges and convictions is what drives the convoluted investigation. So to decipher which cop shows *The Wire* emulates and subverts, our journey begins with *Dragnet*.

Figure 3.1. From left to right: Roland "Prez" Pryzbylewski, Shakima Greggs, Lester Freamon, and Jimmy McNulty all grow to develop essential roles in the Barksdale Detail and then the Major Crimes Unit. HBO/Photofest © HBO.

DRAGNET (1952–1959)

Actor Jack Webb was a man of many talents. He devised, produced, starred in, and directed America's first popular cop show. Attracting 30 million viewers per evening (20 percent of the population) over its 263-episode run made *Dragnet* NBC's highest-rated show from 1952 to 1956.[11] The idea came in 1948, when Webb was cast as a crime lab technician on *He Walked by Night* (1948), a part noir, part documentary film that depicts Erwin "Machine-Gun" Walker's crime spree of burglaries, robberies, and shoot-outs across Los Angeles from 1945 to 1946. Webb struck up a friendship with police officer Martin Wynn, who took Webb for ride-alongs in his police car responding to calls while translating police jargon. With access to police files, Webb strove to devise a police drama with a new level of authenticity. Unable to secure permission to film in the headquarters of the Los Angeles Police Department (LAPD), Webb made do with reconstructions in Disney's Burbank studios. Guided by photographs of City Hall interiors, office sets were replicated right down to the design of the doorknobs. Police consultants also checked scripts for accuracy. *Star Trek* creator Gene Roddenberry got his first big break by gathering stories from police officers, writing them up for submission, and then cutting his $100 fee in half with his LAPD contact. Webb purposefully avoided film noir's fascination with the perverse nature of criminals. He also sidestepped the postwar detective novel's obsessions with gimmicky hard-boiled Chandleresque private investigators. The American TV police procedural was born.

Network executives initially disliked the show's "slow pace," documentary-style "attention to detail," and "lack of gunplay and violence."[12] But Webb's prioritizing of procedure over sensationalism established the police procedural's conventions, which are still prevalent today. First, the show's focus is on the processing of evidence guided by a pragmatic obsession with "what's enough to go to court?" Joe Friday (Jack Webb) and his partner strictly follow police protocols as they conduct interrogations and gather results from the crime lab to charge their suspect. Second, there is an unnatural focus on official terminology to the point where Friday can casually recall, "We filed for violation of the state penal code chapter 339 statutes of 1923 as amended 1947 subsection 2." Third, in stylistic terms, Webb's budget limitations confined his drama to interior sets, long takes, and lengthy scenes to avoid set changes. As a result, each scene has a distinct editing rhythm whereby a series of "tight close-ups" between characters working through evidence are "bookended by long shots without the medium shots that conventionally mediate between these extremes within Hollywood film." Fourth, narration anchors each stage of the investigation. Friday narrates key scene changes stipulating the date, time, location, and/or personnel he works with. Often, this unemotive narration underscores montages of Los Angeles landscapes and talks through scenes of mundane police work to evidence the show's authenticity and expedite narrative. Finally, in not seeing anything beyond Friday's perspective, *Dragnet* is ideologically conservative given its "unswerving belief in the system to continually discipline offenders and protect the innocent by reacting to ever-present threats and manifestations of crime."[13] *The Wire* shares an affinity with *Dragnet* narratively and stylistically. Despite the HBO show outrightly rejecting an unwavering belief in U.S. law-and-order infrastructure, McNulty operates as a Friday figure. Through the first season, he spearheads a legally and technologically advanced investigation, with the added pressure of navigating BPD politics, to diligently gather enough evidence to sentence Avon Barksdale. While many characters come and go, the audience is directly allotted with McNulty's vision of what he deems to be "real police [work]."

Scenes of the BPD's divisional headquarters follow the same visual grammar as *Dragnet*, not to mention other 1950s series that carbon copied its template, including *Highway Patrol* (1955–1959), *The Man behind the*

Badge (1953–1954), and *The Lineup* (1954–1960). All these 1950s series combine narration alongside a focus on procedure, an adherence to official terminology, and distinctive editing rhythm between long shots and close-ups to produce a reverence for police iconography. At the beginning of every *Dragnet* episode, commanding brass music plays loudly as Friday's police badge fades into view in close-up. His rank (sergeant), institution (LAPD), and number (714) are prominently displayed. An authoritative voiceover announces, "The story you are about to see is true. Only the names have been changed to protect the innocent." Intertitles displaying the word "Drag-net" then overlay the badge as the music crescendos. Every week, this close-up shot of Friday's polished badge transitions into a long shot of the skyline of Los Angeles with Friday's narration dispensing facts about the city before introducing the episode's case. For example, in the debut episode, "The Big Jump" (1952), Friday informs viewers of City Hall's longitudinal coordi-nates and its height and details the worldwide materials sourced to construct the building he works in. "They put it up to stay," affirms Friday as the cam-era pans across a long shot of the skyline. Another shot then tracks slowly upward to the tower's tip in awe of its visual grandeur.

Collectively, these 1950s series and the montages used at the beginning and end of each episode utilize on-screen intertitles displaying official legal terminology, an oscillation between close-ups and long shots, a commanding narrator, and triumphant brass music to ensure that police insignias (namely, badges used by real-life squads) are revered. Despite *The Wire*'s attempts to subvert the police series genre, this grammar is replicated. Repeatedly throughout the first season, Baltimore's Homicide Unit and Narcotics Divi-sion are introduced via shots that draw attention to the size and scale of each office block and their operations. In the first episode, after bringing Judge Phelan's attention to Avon Barksdale in the privacy of his courtroom office, the close-up exchanges between McNulty and Phelan are ceased by a montage of three separate long shots of office buildings. The first is mid-way up the side of a glass skyscraper, the second displays the building's entranceway at ground level, and the last is a low-angle shot of the office skyscraper's roof piercing the sky. Combined, all mimic the allure of City Hall in *Dragnet*'s debut episode. The final low-angle shot of the skyscraper then cuts to a low-angle shot of the Narcotics Division's front glass door on the inside. Inscribed on the glass door is the BPD's badge logo with "Nar-cotics Division" written above it in block capitals and "Baltimore Police" engraved along its base. The camera observes this logo in silence before a detective walks through the door. Viewers then wait as the door slowly closes to prominently display the badge engraving again. Like *Dragnet*'s first episode, transitions between long shots of the police headquarters' opulent exterior and close-ups of a police badge emblem function to leave a striking yet imposing impression on the viewer.

As in *Dragnet*, these long establishing shots then transition into an exchange of close-ups between detectives (Herc, Carver, and Greggs) processing the arrest of two suspects they made earlier in the episode. The visuals of the sequence mirror a typical *Dragnet* scene where long establishing shots of the location cut to close-ups of the detectives cross-checking mug shots, memos, and crime lab reports to track down their suspect. In *The Wire*, however, the close-ups now undercut the previous long shots' reverence for police insignia. Close-ups frame Greggs's fingers applying Tipp-Ex to correct a mistake on her arrest report while she curses, Herc's and Carver's facial reactions as they childishly throw a tennis ball at one another, Greggs asserting that Herc needs three separate Violent Crime Unit numbers for the contraband seized at the earlier arrest, Carver grammatically correcting Herc that "shit rolls" and "piss trickles" following Herc's evocative metaphor for how their "chain of command" works, and Herc protesting that if Greggs wants paperwork "done properly," she should "do it your own self." Instead of close-ups underlining detectives' adherence to and faith in procedural technicalities, they now demonstrate the degree to which detectives make errors, cuss, criticize superiors, and avoid administrative responsibilities.

In a following sequence, a *Dragnet*-style deference is upheld toward the police badge once more. After the interchange between Greggs, Herc, and Carver, McNulty enters the Homicide Department. Again, exterior long shots of the BPD's office complex are accompanied by the sounds of traffic. The camera then cuts to a low-angle shot of the BPD badge logo on an interior glass entrance door with "Homicide" written above the logo in block capitals. The camera pulls focus from people inside the offices and tilts backward to capture the emblem and accompanying lettering on the front of the door. This deference is then subsequently undercut by an exchange that McNulty has with Major Rawls through close-ups. McNulty's superior presents both middle fingers, declaring one is going up his "ass" and the other his eye as he goes on a tirade declaring that McNulty is a "backstabbing piece of shit for talking to a shitbag judge about some project n——r I never even heard of." Rawls then furiously flicks through his collection of "H card files" unable to find the details of an unsolved homicide associated with Barksdale. Again, facial close-ups draw attention to the curse words used alongside official terminology, a disregard for actively maintaining accurate recordkeeping, and the act of disciplining subordinates. Proceeding this scene, later on in the pilot episode, another camera shot takes a moment to admire the BPD badge displayed on the front of Burrell's glass office door with the accompanying lettering "Deputy Commissioner of Operations Ervin H. Burrell." Having admired the logo and rank, a series of close-ups promptly unfold as Burrell instructs Daniels to deny the Barksdale Detail surveillance, KEL recorders, and DNRs because he wants to "get in and out as quick as possible." In three separate moments, *Dragnet*'s distinctive editing rhythm is embodied as long deferential shots of the police office building make way for the close-up of a police badge logo filmed in silence at a low angle. Like *Dragnet*, the sound mixing helps these badge shots stand out. Here an unusual lack of sound isolates the badge from the rest of the drama compared to *Dragnet*'s commanding narrator and stirring brass score highlighting the two close-ups of Friday's badge that envelop each episode. However, this *Dragnet*-style admiration for police symbols is undercut by subsequent close-ups of negligent detectives exchanging profanities in the same breath as procedural acronyms to scold those increasing their workload. While *The Wire*'s office scenes continue to abide by *Dragnet*'s sequence of shot scales, a reverence for police insignia has become severely diminished by a management culture prioritizing case clearance rates over traditional detective work.

To leave a comparison between *Dragnet* and *The Wire* here would be to misunderstand the full extent of its ideological affinity with the 1950s show. The Barksdale Detail is eventually successful when their operatives are given the time and space to forensically obtain and examine records. A breakthrough comes when Lester Freamon assumes a Joe Friday role in episode 9, "Game Day," and narrates a series of events through a montage laced with technical speak while mentoring Prez and Leander Sydnor (Corey Parker Robinson). Here Freamon instructs both detectives to research all Barksdale's front companies, limited partnerships, and limited liability corporations. As Freamon begins instructing Prez to visit the corporate charter office, his dialogue transitions into narration as the scene jumps forward in time. Prez is uncovering information in the immediate future, while Freamon's instructions anchor the scene in the present. Freamon instructs Prez to research the records of B&B Enterprises (Barksdale and Bell's business) on a reel of microfilm in the corporate charter office. Once the word "microfilm" is uttered, the camera cuts to Prez holding and looking through a piece of microfilm. Then as Freamon instructs Prez to "write every name you see," the camera cuts to a close-up of Prez's notepad while he writes. Correspondingly, when Prez is instructed to record legal firms associated with B&B Enterprises, the camera cuts to a close-up of "Levy and Weinstein, Attorneys at Law," enlarged on the microfilm's magnifying screen. Freamon then instructs Sydnor how he will cross-reference

Prez's discoveries in the city land records. The camera observes files being brought to Sydnor in the future as Freamon continues to narrate the montage of images. Sydnor is instructed to note down the names of all the corporate listings who own multiunit properties and call that list over to Prez, who can look for further connections in the charter papers. Freamon uttering "note" and then "call" prompts the camera to cut to Sydnor taking notes and then removing a phone from his pocket. This scene does not simply expedite narrative. Freamon's assured, calm, and dispassionate instructions emulate the narrated montages replete through *Dragnet* where Friday curates the images on-screen to teach viewers the efficiency of rigorous desk-based detective work.

Utilizing recordkeeping to locate criminality is central to *Dragnet*'s and Freamon's detection. As Freamon concludes his lesson to both rookie detectives, the Pawnshop Unit veteran states that "in this country somebody's name has got to be on a piece of paper." Such wisdom dispensed by Freamon could quite easily be spoken by Friday during the opening montage to "The Big Cast" (1952). Here Webb's dialogue walks viewers through the records held in business, industry, government, households, and the police. Like Freamon, Friday's explanation of different filing systems directs the camera's gaze to reveal that everyone leaves a paper trail that can be unearthed by a skilled detective. Similarly, in "The Big Boys" (1954), Friday narrates a scene in the LAPD's "stolen property pawnshop files." A long shot surveys a big room full of paper records being filed by a busy workforce while Friday discloses that "there are thousands of cases that never get space in daily newspapers." Then a close-up of one of the files being checked uncovers the names of the four hoodlums Friday is pursuing. Therefore, both shows share the same ideological view that successful detective work demands the methodical investigation of written records. Freamon's adage that "all the pieces matter" works as a contemporary version of Friday's catchphrase, "just the facts, ma'am."

Dragnet's four central conventions can be found in *The Wire*. The latter also utilizes a slow pace and a documentary-level attention to detail to subject viewers to (1) a pragmatic obsession with what's enough to charge their prime suspect, (2) an emphasis on official terminology, (3) a distinctive editing rhythm that privileges close-ups between characters working through evidence bookended by long shots, and (4), by episode 9, narration is used to walk viewers through Freamon's investigation into Barksdale's business interests. Ultimately, *The Wire* has a passing reverence for BPD insignia, a stark contrast from *Dragnet*'s overwhelming faith in anything associated with the LAPD's infrastructure from its grand architecture right down to its badge design. Ideological faith in the institution of policing has been watered down by *The Wire* because the detective work revered by both shows has been sabotaged by the BPD's institutionalized prioritizing of keeping case clearance rates high. Therefore, detectives are concerned only with meeting their workload targets. Through the course of the Barksdale Detail, however, Freamon's character provides a vision of how detectives *could* work together across departments, a view that Joe Friday of *Dragnet* reassures viewers is how detectives *already* work.

NAKED CITY (1958–1963)

In addition to sharing *Dragnet*'s vision for what constitutes effective detective work, *The Wire* is admired for the way it examines what compels and motivates civilians to commit crimes. In direct contrast to the internal politics of the BPD, a viewer regularly witnesses Barksdale and Bell conversing with their soldiers in the back office of Orlando's strip club, a business they use to launder their drug money. Here they make decisions on increasing their profits, keeping ahead of the BPD's investigation, clamping down on police informants, and protecting themselves from Omar robbing their stash houses. Beneath the heads of the Barksdale operation is Avon's nephew D'Angelo, a lieutenant who supervises drug dealers stationed in a low-rise housing project. D'Angelo is demoted to "the pit" at the start of the season as punishment for carelessly killing a security guard. Soon, D'Angelo tightens the pit's operations and increases its profits in the hope he will be promoted back to running a Franklin Terrace tower, although over time, D'Angelo grows increasingly disillusioned with the drug trade following philosophical discussions with lower-ranking drug dealers Malik "Poot" Carr (Tray Chaney), Justin Wallace (Michael B. Jordan), and Bodie Broadus (J. D. Williams).

Many have praised the equal amount of screen time devoted to key characters within the hierarchy of Barksdale's gang in relation to the police. But this is nothing new to American cop drama. *Naked City* was a popular yet critically acclaimed program that also sought to uncover the harsh socioeconomic inequalities at play in American cities. ABC, having badly trailed behind NBC and CBS audience numbers, used *Naked City* to claw back viewers. Inspired by the 1948 film noir of the same name, producer Herbert Leonard envisioned an anthology series whereby viewers would learn the new story of a citizen drawn into crime each week. Conversely, producer

Screen Gems felt that the program should be another clone of *Dragnet*'s established formula. As a compromise, the resulting program opens with a guest star committing a felony with a pre-credit prologue explaining and rationalizing why the crime is to be committed. Then the detectives appear after the first commercial break. This balance helped move ABC toward "a position of prominence in prime-time viewing," as the show won a 1959 Emmy for the best dramatic series of less than one hour. In 1960, the program was extended to hour-long episodes. Detective Adam Flint (Paul Burke) is a different type of detective compared to *Dragnet*'s Joe Friday. He reaches out to criminals as an unofficial social worker, parole officer, careers adviser, psychiatrist, and friend. Flint is interested more in the motivation for committing crime than in dispassionately amassing enough evidence to arrest criminals.

From episode to episode, viewers are exposed to characters suffering from varying degrees of "psychological and/or sociological deficiencies," as crime is symptomatic of loneliness, alcoholism, mental illness, or an inability to afford essentials. Philosophically, then, *Naked City* shares an affinity with *The Wire*, as both programs treat morality as relative. Both believe that "moral standards of any one culture are different from those of any other culture" and that "no one set of cultural moral standards is superior to, or more true than, another."[14] *Naked City* unearths how Chinese and Romanian communities settle their disputes in a way that is not compatible with American law. *The Wire* provides comparisons between the structures, standards, and values of the Barksdale crew and the BPD without casting judgment over one at the expense of the other. D'Angelo Barksdale is regularly juxtaposed with McNulty for being of equivalent rank within his organization. When McNulty is disciplined by Rawls for having encouraged Judge Phelan to set up the Barksdale Detail, a contrasting scene unfolds between Avon Barksdale discipling his nephew D'Angelo for having acted emotionally and killing a security guard. Simon constructed this scene and others to observe competing operations with different standards of professionalism. In this instance, both characters must take their disciplining with a similar degree of humility so as not to upset their superiors further and face additional punishment. Both are being demoted for acting emotively, as Rawls feels inconvenienced having to resource a new case, as does Avon for having concentrated his resources on keeping D'Angelo out of prison.

Similarly, D'Angelo's court case at the start of the first episode stands in deliberate contrast to drug addict Johnny Weeks's (Leo Fitzpatrick) fate at the episode's conclusion. Bodie catches Weeks red-handed when the heroin

user attempts to scam the dealers with counterfeit money. Court is effectively held in the form of a housing project trial with D'Angelo sitting as the
judge. In the opening courtroom scene, D'Angelo faces a murder conviction.
The camera has freedom to move seamlessly yet assuredly so that viewers can take into account the looks and reactions of Barksdale's enforcers
in the back intimidating witnesses, D'Angelo at the defense table, prosecutors, the judge, and rivals Bell and McNulty goading each other. In contrast,
Weeks's makeshift trial is much smaller in scale, unfolding on a spot of
pavement between three characters, each occupying a static facial close-up.
Bodie wants to kill Weeks so that others will be deterred from undermin-
ing their profits. Weeks tearfully pleads for his life. D'Angelo is afflicted
and cannot live with another death on his conscience. As D'Angelo opts
to leave the scene, the camera observes Poot, Bodie, and Wallace severely
beating Weeks. While this smaller impromptu street trial is viscerally more
violent than the trial at the start of the episode, the official courtroom scene
is not treated as inherently morally superior. Both processes have their flaws.
Judge Phelan is powerless to clear the court and so cannot prevent Barksdale's enforcers from intimidating a state's witness into withdrawing their
statement, meaning that D'Angelo evades punishment. In contrast, Weeks
receives harsh retribution that does not necessarily match the severity of his
crime. Despite the vast differences in scale and resources, underscored by
the camera's maneuverability (or lack thereof), both trials seek an equitable
and logical outcome.

Shooting on real locations was also central to *Naked City*'s authenticity. It went on to win an Emmy for editing in 1962, and Jack Priestly won
two more for cinematography in 1962 and 1963. Rather than being reduced
to interior sets, 75 percent of all shooting was carried out on the real streets
of New York. *The Wire* occupies a similar social realist inclination to
capture how real-life environments impact characters. Bubbles's ongoing
attempts to kick his drug habit and occupy his time with meaningful activity could be its own *Naked City* episode. "The Face of the Enemy" (1962),
for example, follows World War II veteran Cornelius "Neil" Daggett (Jack
Warden) attempting to reacclimate to society by numbing triggers of his
posttraumatic stress disorder with alcohol. Similarly, episode 10 of *The
Wire*, "The Cost," sees Bubbles trying to avoid the temptations that surround him throughout Baltimore City. Following an establishing shot of a
park, we share Bubbles's point of view (POV), where he observes a drug
deal taking place nearby, so he then averts his gaze to stare at leaves on a
tree. Bubbles then hears his name and looks around and, in another POV, a
dealer walks past the bench, recognizing him. The dealer asks how Bubbles

is before walking to the exact same spot where we previously saw a different drug dealer standing who has now disappeared. In essence, a viewer is aligned with Bubbles's perspective, and a great deal of time appears to have passed in this opening three minutes. Viewers share Bubbles's sense of déjà vu and confusion as two men stand in a spot under a tree to conduct drug deals in the exact same shot composition a few seconds ago. Bubbles does not know how much time has passed because he has no control over his surroundings given his physiological dependency on heroin and sociological deficiencies. He does not have a home or a job to detract him from the drug abuse riddling the city.

This direct occupying of Bubbles's POV occurs in the same vein as *Naked City*. In the episode "To Dream without Sleep" (1961), Fran Burney (Lois Nettleton) has been conned by an escort service into dating a married man. On learning this news, Murray stabs her suitor in a crime of passion before proceeding to spend time in the local park. Like Bubbles, Murray sits on a bench, rocking backward and forward and wringing her hands, contemplating her previous actions. As the episode progresses, the camera then visualizes Murray's memories of her joining the escort service through a flashback unveiling how she was persuaded to change her appearance for the agency's books. Across both shows, viewers are given direct access to at-risk characters whose perspectives are triggered by their surroundings. On this occasion, Murray's talking to a phone operator and the act of reaching out for help bring this memory to light in the same way that Bubbles's seeing his former dealer stifles his perception of time. The message of each show is the same; as Bubbles's sponsor later informs him, vulnerable members of society are "not strong enough to do this on your own." Unlike *Naked City*, however, there is no heroic savior. Detective Adam Flint can prevent Murray from committing suicide, secure the alcoholic Dagger a job, and, in "Portrait of a Painter" (1962), help Roger Barmer (William Shatner) figure out how his wife came to be murdered during his psychological blackout. *The Wire*'s Baltimore is a harsher environment, as characters seeking recovery cannot turn to a white knight for help. Bubbles's relationship with detectives Greggs and McNulty remains transactional. Rewarding the addict with small amounts of cash only jumpstarts his relapses into drug addiction. Like *Naked City*, Bubbles's reversion to crime is in part due to biological need, lack of social protections, and the uncaring nature of a city environment, all of which are observed in a morally relative light. The key difference here is that even the most sympathetic of detectives cannot instigate meaningful change to a vulnerable person in the wake of larger societal forces.

KOJAK (1973-1978)

No discussion of *The Wire*'s chief influences can omit the leading man of season 1. McNulty is undoubtedly the principal protagonist, as he has the most screen time and sets the narrative in motion by appealing to Judge Phelan. He clearly operates in the mold of the rogue cop of the 1970s who questions the efficacy of procedures so revered in the 1950s. The protagonists of *Columbo* (1968–2003), *Police Story* (1973–1987), *Ironside* (1967–1975), *The Mod Squad* (1968–1973), *Kojak* (1973–1978), and *Baretta* (1975–1978) all solve crimes idiosyncratically by rejecting procedure and battling the bureaucratic systems that seek to constrain them. While many praise *The Wire*'s cynicism toward traditional heroism, McNulty achieves meaningful change by relying on the same foundations as the Kojak archetype.

Kojak was a new kind of cop show for new post–civil rights age. While NBC was too scared to green-light the format, CBS picked up the character as part of its initiative to capture city audiences. Critics instantly praised the *Kojak* pilot for its unrelenting focus on the unremitting ugliness of Spanish Harlem and the Brownsville section of Brooklyn, all of which were shot entirely on location. Setting the tenor of the show that followed, *The Marcus Nelson Murders* (1973) dramatizes the real "Careers Girls Murders" of New York 10 years previously, where two young white middle-class women, Emily Hoffert and Janice Wylie, were slain in the flat they shared. The television film details how eight months later, with pressure mounting on the police, a young black Brooklyn man with learning difficulties named Lewis Humes (Gene Woodbury) is arrested on suspicion of two unrelated attempted rapes and is charged with the Hoffert/Wylie murders. Throughout, Manhattan detective Lieutenant Theo Kojak (Telly Savalas) remains suspicious. His own personal investigation reveals that a murder confession was beaten out of Humes. With the help of a seasoned defense lawyer, Kojak secures Humes's acquittal. But when Humes is later convicted for the attempted rape of Mrs. Alvarez, Humes receives an overzealous 5- to 10-year sentence despite being a first-time offender. Kojak's first outing concludes with his narration informing viewers that the Humes case "was cited in the *Miranda* decision of the Supreme Court, which demands that his constitutional rights be read to a man under arrest." From the outset, Kojak is on a personal crusade to improve the justice system one small step at a time. In so doing, he repeatedly experiences institutional injustice over five seasons and 118 episodes. The only guarantee is that the cyclical nature of crime will forever continue.

The first key characteristic that McNulty shares with Kojak is his "world-weariness." Kojak pursues criminals repeatedly relying on a signature catchphrase. He asks detectives, witnesses, informants, and suspects, "Who loves ya baby?" Posing this question is a deliberately rhetorical device to infer that while he may care for his compatriots, the "social forces" that conspire to maintain "racism, criminal rights, civic corruption . . . and the social determinants of poverty," who also block meaningful attempts to reform accountability, do not.[15] Kojak redefines American police work as having to contend with a huge set of formidable social forces that inhibit yet motivate him to deliver justice. Kojak's rhetorical catchphrase is matched by McNulty's repeated question, "What the fuck did I do?" McNulty first poses this question in a bar toward the end of the first episode when decrying how Daniels is seeking to make low-level arrests. McNulty informs Bunk, "I feel like that motherfucker on *The Bridge on the River Kwai* [1957], 'what the fuck did I do?'" British prisoner of war Colonel Nicholson (Alec Guinness), whom McNulty refers to, is forced to build a bridge to aid the Japanese military only to see it destroyed by the Allied forces. McNulty reappropriates the colonel's final words "What have I done?" to come to terms with how a big project that he instigated has snowballed into something likely to consume his sanity and professional reputation. Then in episode 2, "The Detail," McNulty uses the same phrase to protest his innocence, feign naivety, and defend himself. Here Daniels corners McNulty in Homicide's interrogation room and cautions him for breaking the chain of command. In episode 9, "Game Day," Daniels is also annoyed that McNulty requires a fresh affidavit to monitor a new cell phone, as it will prolong the case by another 30 days. After the lieutenant slams his office door, McNulty asks, "What the fuck did I do?" Freamon points out that Daniels's career is "hanging in the balance" on producing quick results. Finally, in episode 11, "The Hunt," when Greggs lies in critical condition, a tearful McNulty experiencing shock mournfully asks Rawls, "What the fuck did I do?" as he struggles to comes to terms with the guilt of putting an officer in terminal circumstances. Like Kojak's "Who loves ya baby?" McNulty's "What the fuck did I do?" is an existential question. McNulty also repeats it to contemplate why colleagues are against his unorthodox methods and attempts to produce meaningful change while simultaneously vocalizing his frustrations with the police hierarchy.

Underpinning Kojak's and McNulty's browbeaten disposition is their nonchalant ability to confront their colleagues and superiors. Although the inspiration for Kojak's pilot was a case from the late 1960s, the problem of police corruption was very much in the air in the 1970s. Writer/producer Abby Mann was an Academy Award–winning film writer known for his liberal politics and a close friend of Martin Luther King Jr. In an era when the *New York Times* regularly exposed police corruption on its front pages, Kojak was deliberately written as a *Serpico* (1973) figure, an "honest man among dishonest men" whom he is willing and able to heroically confront.[16] In the pilot, when viewers are first introduced to Kojak's character, he is informed by Inspectors MacNeill and Hoffstetter that 100 men will be issued to investigate the Marcus Nelson murders. Kojak protests that "you're going to have 100 detectives falling all over themselves for promotion," inferring that the most ambitious rather than the most adept detectives will put themselves forward for a high-profile case. MacNeill defends the decision, reminding Kojak that "it's not your business to determine policy" before the camera cuts swiftly back to Kojak, who immediately retorts, "No that's your department" as the two men leave. Kojak backchats to defiantly have the last word and bruise the ego of his superiors. It is Kojak who hauls Detective Dan Corrigan (Ned Beatty) before Assistant District Attorney Goodman (Robert Fields) demanding that the recently promoted detective provide cast-iron answers as to why there are inconsistencies in his evidence on Humes. After Corrigan leaves, dismissing Kojak's accusations, the protagonist concludes the scene demanding to know what "you [the assistant district attorney] are going to do about it." McNulty equally relishes the opportunity to backchat and challenge authority. When the Barksdale Detail is first established, Lieutenant Daniels's first briefing is interrupted by McNulty vying for sustained surveillance. Daniels overrules him, stating that there will be no mics and no wires, as "we do this fast and clean and simple" to conclude the meeting. As Daniels walks to his office, McNulty undercuts Daniels's closing message, confirming, "Then you don't do it at all," visibly enraging Daniels. Pearlman exclaims, "You could have had this fight between yourselves before calling the state attorney's office." Like Kojak, McNulty actively humiliates senior ranking officers in front of legal representatives within formal settings by having the last word on matters. In light of McNulty's dogged determination, Daniels succumbs to McNulty's view that long-term surveillance and wiretaps are worthwhile and capable of securing high-level arrests. In both shows, a lone detective crusading against immediate authority figures across a number of departments can produce a change in wider policing culture, be it the introduction of *Miranda* rights or a new detail that convicts the elusive Barksdale.

Finally, in challenging their colleagues, both Kojak and McNulty can appear more sympathetically aligned with criminals. Kojak utilizes his Greek ancestry and McNulty his Irish routes to successfully operate as a "mediator between the white and black" cultures.[17] Both can frequent black communities and speak the language of the street in a way their colleagues are unable. In the episode "Bad Dude" (1976), for example, Kojak and bounty hunter Salathiel Harms (Rosey Grier) negotiate who gets to apprehend mob boss Sylk (Bill Duke). Initially, Harms protests that he'll lose a lot of money if he can't take Sylk back to California, to which Kojak replies, "It's all in the breaks of the game baby." As the only witness, Harms asserts that he has leverage over Kojak and can testify that the detective busted in without identifying himself and assaulted Sylk's secretary and chauffeur before illegally planting a firearm on the suspect. Although Kojak points out that Harms still cannot apprehend Sylk, as the bounty hunter is a private citizen, Harms utilizes a legal loophole by having Sylk ask Kojak that he be escorted back to California by Harms. Impressed as well as amused, Kojak relents and offers Harms a squad car to escort them both to John F. Kennedy International Airport to catch their plane. Similarly, during the hostage negotiations of "Siege of Terror" (1973), it is Kojak alone who appeases the Talaba gang by asserting, "Frankie baby do I have a deal for you . . . you're going to tell your brother to give himself up," the ultimatum being either "we cut him up for dog meat or he goes into the slam for keeps." In both instances, Kojak can reach an agreement with those operating illegally by using colloquialisms of black subculture in an accurate yet confident tone alongside respecting their predicament, appreciating their intelligence, and giving in to certain demands to cut deals. "Bad Dude" ends poignantly, as the final shot is of Kojak and Harms holding hands in the air in a manner similar to a high five. The camera zooms in on their black and white clasped hands together in a freeze-frame. Both men share a kinship; despite their ethnicity, they can confidently express through a gesture traditionally exchanged at that time between black Americans.

Similarly, McNulty can converse directly with members of the Barksdale crew on their level and placate them into giving information in a way that other detectives cannot. In the same manner that Kojak talks down Talaba's gang, McNulty does not raid the pit as his colleagues have prematurely attempted. In episode 2, "The Detail," McNulty instead casually walks into the pit in civilian clothing and sits alongside D'Angelo and Bodie by pulling up a stool alongside their orange sofa. Says McNulty, "Let's understand each other; I'm not western district . . . I don't give shit about a possession charge." Interested in obtaining intel on the drug-dealing hierarchy, he exclaims, "Fuck the jury" and instead offers an opportunity for "sharing our thoughts." It's here that McNulty first finds D'Angelo's pager, which serves as a breakthrough. Now the detectives have a means of tracking how the dealers contact one another. Furthermore, McNulty convinces

Omar to snitch on the Barksdales by encouraging the lone scar-faced bandit to "pay it back" as vengeance for the brutal killing of his lover. McNulty equates the Barksdale Detail's predicament to Omar's situation, suggesting, "We're out here on our own playing the game for ourselves just like you." Then later, when Omar starts targeting Barksdale's crew, executing Stinkum (Anton Artis) and maiming Wee-Bey (Hassan Johnson), McNulty convinces Omar to "hang back" because "dropping Stinkum fucks us on our thing." In each of these scenes—in episode 6, "The Wire," and episode 8, "Lessons"—McNulty is the only white character negotiating with black criminals on their own terms, reaching agreements, and progressing the case. It has been argued that the McNulty character exists as a "roguish, talented Irish-American cop," simply providing "an easy 'in' for the viewer, a recognisable character you could latch on to in the first series as you got used to the unfamiliar settings and dialect and the relatively demanding style of writing."[18] However, examining McNulty's similarities with the 1970s rogue cop tradition in closer detail, it is clear that McNulty's cynicism toward hierarchical procedure, determination to challenge authority, and ability to converse with black gangsters on their own terms are three vital foundations to his and Kojak's characters. McNulty is unafraid to step on the toes of Major Rawls, Lieutenant Daniels, and Assistant State Attorney Pearlman; engage in a dialogue with Omar; and negotiate Barksdale

Figure 3.2. McNulty is the only white character who is at ease sharing frank exchanges with black criminals. HBO/Photofest © HBO.

enforcer Savino Bratton's (Chris Clanton) eventual surrender. It is by specifically operating in the Kojak mode of the rebellious detective archetype that McNulty can overcome critical impasses in the Barksdale investigation.

STARSKY AND HUTCH (1975–1979) AND THE BUDDY GENRE

McNulty's rebellious nature manifests successfully, in part, through interactions with his Homicide partner and best friend, Bunk Moreland. Bunk prevents McNulty from acting too destructively and convinces him to use his frustrations productively. Together, both characters abide by the conventions of the buddy cop film genre that Spelling-Goldberg Productions first brought to the small screen. The hugely successful *Starsky and Hutch* captured the emerging younger breed of cop whose formative experience was informed by either military service in Vietnam or college campuses. The impulsive former soldier David Starsky (Paul Michael Glaser) bounces off the intellectual college graduate Kenneth Hutch (David Soul). Scriptwriter William Blinn deliberately challenged the dynamic of established cop shows whose middle-aged heroes occasionally defer their wisdom to a younger subordinate. The upcoming generation of the 1970s and their exposure to drugs and counterculture provides further disdain for superiors and the rule book. Actors Glaser and Soul were young actors in peak physical condition, permitting a faster tempo of events whereby clues are no longer puzzled over or suspects reinterviewed. Instead, the show favors short scenes that principally link together a series of action sequences and choreographed car chases in a speeding Torino. Unlike their suit-wearing forebearers, Starsky and Hutch are fiercely loyal and physically express their mutual affection through endless shoulder squeezing, back-patting, and locker-room horseplay, so much so that a senior ABC executive dubbed them off the record as "French kissing primetime homos."[19] While McNulty and Bunk are not fashionistas in peak physical condition forever embroiled in car chases and gunplay, what they do share is a focus on male friendship at the expense of traditional heterosexual romance.

The dynamics of Starsky and Hutch's friendship comes directly from the buddy film genre. *Butch Cassidy and the Sundance Kid* (1969), *Midnight Cowboy* (1969), *Thunderbolt and Lightfoot* (1974), and later the blockbuster series *Die Hard* (1988) and *Lethal Weapon* (1989) are all variations on principles established by *Easy Rider* (1969). Through all these films, men bond through being released from their repressive relationships with women and the domesticity that they represent. The way that McNulty's and Bunk's friendship blossoms perfectly aligns with film critic Robin Wood's six-step journey of protagonists belonging to the buddy genre. First, the journey the two men embark on has "no goal or its ostensible goal proves illusory." This is clear from the outset. When McNulty drinks with Bunk after the first day that the Barksdale Detail has been established, he complains to his friend the career-focused Daniels is going to "fuck this Barksdale thing up." Bunk's counterclaim that "you already fucked it up Jimmy, you made it happen" means that McNulty has kick-started a unit that is guaranteed only to demote McNulty, having aggrieved too many superiors. Second, the buddy genre marginalizes women, who are "merely present for casual sexual encounters" and can be easily picked up and disposed of to favor the male friendship.[20] The divorced McNulty visits Pearlman, the mistress throughout his marriage, only when he needs legal or professional advice. Sex between McNulty and Pearlman is purely transactional, whether it is using her knowledge to clone a beeper or seeking comfort having learned the extent to which his superiors are trying to "fuck" his career.

The third stage of the buddy genre is "the absence of [a] home." Both McNulty and Bunk regularly drink together in dive bars and then through the night propped up against the hoods of their cars, as they do not want to return home. In the first episode, McNulty even begins work immediately after one of their drinking sessions. Furthermore, the divorced McNulty does not have a familial home to return to. For him, "home" is an unfurnished apartment where he sleeps in a mattress on the floor surrounded by empty beer bottles. It could easily stand in for the squats of West Baltimore that Bubbles occupies. We never actually see Bunk's home either. In keeping with the fourth stage of a buddy story, their "male love story" is the "emotional center and charge" of the series at the expense of any heterosexual union. The most tender exchange of the season occurs in episode 7, "One Arrest." Two over-the-shoulder close-ups isolate both teary-eyed men from the wider bar area that is kept in soft focus. Framed as if two people on a date are about to exchange a kiss, McNulty thanks his work partner because "when it came time for you to fuck me, you were very gentle," to which Bunk replies, "It was your first time, I wanted to make it special." The fifth stage of a buddy film that *The Wire* adheres to is "the presence of an explicitly homosexual character" to "guarantee the heroes' heterosexuality." Omar provides this function through the scenes in which he has sex with Wright. Finally, the sixth stage of a buddy narrative is some form of death so that "the male relationship must never be consummated." While neither Bunk nor McNulty dies, death itself has a continual presence. In their first drinking session, McNulty urinates in the center of a railway track as he confirms that he is going to do the Barksdale case to the best of his ability. This moment of affirmation comes as McNulty drunkenly stumbles off the track just in time to avoid being hit by freight train. Like the buddy genre, *The Wire* is forever

Figure 3.3. McNulty and Bunk's friendship represents the most tender and mutually appreciative relationship throughout all five seasons. HBO/Photofest © HBO.

duplicitously "suggesting a homosexual relationship" might emerge while "emphatically disowning it."[21] The men's relationship is the emotional core of the investigation, as their affectionately frank reciprocations can drive the case forward, especially when McNulty's personal protestations are insufficient. It is Bunk who dissuades McNulty from confronting Rawls when they get word that the Barksdale Detail is being closed. McNulty's buddy convinces him to defer his frustrations to Daniels, who can persuade the higher-ups to keep the wiretap going. These male buddies provide the first season's only reciprocally tender, affectionate, and loving relationship. Without it, the Barksdale Detail would have ended in episode 6, "The Wire."

HILL STREET BLUES (1981–1987)

It is difficult to imagine a world in which *The Wire*, with its vast range of 13 regular fully fleshed-out characters, could exist had *Hill Street Blues* not been commissioned 20 years previously. While the series shares very little thematic and visual similarities, its approach to narrative provided a template for *The Wire*. *Hill Street Blues'* pilot script contains 120 scenes over 59 pages and 13 principal characters with a further 18 speaking parts. For the first time, the American cop show now had story lines that could overlap, interweave, and sometimes be dropped altogether to either reemerge later or completely disappear. It was not uncommon for a single episode to follow threads from more than a dozen stories: a flexi-narrative.

Head of NBC Fred Silverman, in anticipation of the feature film *Fort Apache, The Bronx* (1981) being released, decided that NBC needed a realistically urbane, gritty police series to occupy a space in the zeitgeist. Michael Zinberg, vice president of comedy development at NBC, then implored Steven Bochco and Michael Kozoll to write the show. Having seen their detective dramas *Delvecchio* (1976) and *Paris* (1979) crash and burn after one season poised both writers to transform the genre. Both men drew their visual and aural cues from the U.S. direct cinema documentary *The Police Tapes* (1977) utilizing handheld cameras to give the impression of unrehearsed action occurring in real time. *The Wire* is a lot less chaotic than *Hill Street Blues* both aesthetically and thematically, as Baltimore has reached a level of acceptance that the drug trade has taken over large swathes of the city. The understaffed police force's priority in its quiet, calm, isolated, serene skyscrapers of the downtown area is to keep the homicide clearance rate down as individuals vie for promotion. This is a far cry from *Hill Street Blues'* depiction of a modern nightmare whereby Hill

Street station provides the last modicum of defense in an urban war zone. All around Hill Street, cars break down, paint flakes off the precinct walls, and the pipes and boilers are forever leaking. In better times, staff might strive for justice; for now, all are simply "trying to live through it, survive, keep the lid on" violence that lurks around every corner.[22] Comparatively, in *The Wire*'s episode 2, "The Detail," Daniels and his Barksdale Detail detectives first enter the basement room that they have been assigned below City Hall's police offices. Our introduction to this makeshift space works as a nod to the chaotic imperfections of Hill Street station. The detectives walk through an echoing, shadowy corridor. An iron grate is pulled back to reveal a dungeon-like room where the lightbulb doesn't work, pipes are exposed, and tapping sounds percolate through the network of old, leaking lead pipes. Daniels's first briefing in this office space mirrors Esterhaus's chaotic Hill Street station roll calls. Daniels is interrupted by the sound of a flushing toilet and plumbers banging pipes, shouting to one another and walking into their office. The pacing of the scene is slow, and the camera is largely still compared to the freneticism of the Hill Street roll calls because the Barksdale Detail has been deliberately left in a form of purgatory. No detective, at the level of major and above, wants the detail to go ahead. Nonetheless, *Hill Street Blues* established a formula comprised of a large ensemble cast featuring women and minorities, gritty urban settings, a documentary aesthetic, and dark humor, all interweaved through flexi-narratives. This recalibrating of the foundations of the American cop show informed successes through the 1990s that in their own way have also influenced *The Wire*.

HOMICIDE: LIFE ON THE STREET (1993–1999)

Hill Street Blues expanding the range of character types appearing in cop shows opened up a possibility to have different discussions about crime and its impacts. Following this shift toward seriality and melodrama, series in the 1990s focus largely on "the private, intimate, and often intense interpersonal relationships among detectives, victims, and suspects." Seven seasons of *Homicide: Life on the Street* focus on a group of detectives working in the BPD's Homicide Unit. Compared to the drama's chief inspiration, Simon's book *Homicide*, detectives' personal dilemmas take precedence. John Munch (Richard Belzer) has been married three times. Tim Bayliss (Kyle Secor) was molested as a child. Meldrick Lewis (Clark Johnson) survives a series of dead detective partners. Frank Pembleton (Andre Braugher) suffers a debilitating stroke. In this Homicide Department, detectives spend more time in the interrogation suite, "the box," than they do on the street. The narrative aim of each episode lies in securing confessions from their suspects.

Homicide aired on NBC's prestigious "must-see Thursdays" at a time when network television was distinguishing itself from the competition of emerging cable channels. So the show adopted a unique visual style to underscore its dialogue-heavy scenes. Executive producer Barry Levinson demanded that "editing techniques like jump cutting or repeating the same shot three times give the audience the same sense of stimulation as gun battles and car chases, but more in line with the kind of stories we were trying to tell."[23] This flashy visual approach added the energy and dynamism of action-oriented cop shows to highlight key details of investigations for viewers to evaluate.

Homicide's repetition of shots and the use of slow motion in particular draw attention to the ugliness and wide-ranging impact of violence. In "The City That Bleeds" (1995), Munch, Howard, and Beau Felton (Daniel Baldwin) approach an apartment to serve a routine warrant. Immediately, they are critically wounded when a gunman opens fire with two pistols from the floor above. In among the panic and chaos, slow-motion close-ups and mid-shots are used to isolate the bullet entering Howard's chest, Felton's leg, and Bolander's back (and the blood that protrudes from each character) and elongate the expressions of pain and shock on their faces as they fall to the ground. When the guilty suspect Gordon Pratt (Steve Buscemi) is eventually apprehended in the episode "End Game" (1995), Pratt lies on a massage table. The camera focuses on his face as Pembleton's gun enters the frame and is inserted into Pratt's cheek so hard that he flinches backward and opens his mouth in pain as the detective states, "Do not move or I will shoot." This shot is repeated two more times in slow motion to replicate Pembleton's cathartic retribution for the pain his detectives have experienced.

Slow motion's synonymy with violence also intersects with racial politics. In the episode "Every Mother's Son" (1995), 14-year-old Darrel Nawls has been shot to death by Ronny Sayers, of the same age, in a case of mistaken identity. In a key scene, Patrice Sayers (Rhonda Stubbins) and Mary Nawls (Gay Thomas) wait in the Homicide Department's waiting area (fishbowl) not knowing that their circumstances are connected. The two women concur that their families are trapped in a cycle of violence and relative poverty given the deteriorating neighborhoods they live in without strong male role models. Sitting together on a bench facing forward and framed in matching close-ups effectively layers the two women's faces onto one

another to accentuate the commonalities between them. As both unsuspecting women find kinship, the camera cuts to a shot of Darrel Nawls's body
still laying down headfirst in the bowling lane, his arms outstretched with
a large amount of dried blood protruding from his head having stained the
floor. The camera observes the scene in slow motion, rotating 360 degrees
above the head of the body. The flashing cameras of forensics at the crime
scene eventually brighten the scene into a blinding white light for a commercial break. The purpose of this shot's interjection is to confront viewers with the grisly nature of the murder committed that has brought these
well-mannered women together, bring to light the type of trauma they will
become burdened with, and demonstrate the risks that come with living in
their neighborhoods.

According to Simon, *The Wire* utilizes *Homicide*'s showy style of film-
making only once. In the very first episode's conclusion, *Homicide*'s visuals
are utilized to demonstrate that William Gant's (Larry Hull) identification
of D'Angelo Barksdale in court results in the maintenance man's murder.
While Bunk examines a cordoned-off murder scene outside the McCullough
Homes, a crowd emerges on the other side of the police tape. When Bunk
instructs the officers to turn over the body, the camera cuts to a close-up of
Gant's face as it vacantly looks up at the officers. This turning over of Gant's
body triggers a flashback in the onlooking D'Angelo. The drug-dealing lieutenant replays the episode's opening scenes from the courtroom in his mind.
Viewers hear the exact same audio from the beginning as the prosecuting
attorney asks Gant, "Do you see the man identified as D'Angelo in the courtroom today?" The camera then cuts to the exact same shot at the start of
the episode, this time tinted blue, as Gant again raises his finger, points at
D'Angelo in the face, and states that "he's right there," this time at a slightly
slower speed. As the episode replays this answer that sealed Gant's fate, the
camera zooms in closer to Gant's face through five static jump cuts. Just like
Homicide, this use of jump cutting, slow motion, scene repetition, and color-
ing are designed to momentarily interrupt a viewer's suspension of disbelief
and highlight the narrative significance of what they have witnessed in a
more impactful way. Simon claims that D'Angelo's flashback was imposed
on them by HBO; worried viewers would forget that Gant was the witness
from the earlier trial.

Simon asserts that D'Angelo's flashback was a one-off, as there was "no
other way to explain the narrative to viewers being asked to absorb detail in
a different way people did normally."[24] However, a *Homicide*-style use of
slow motion occurs on three further occasions. When Barksdale and Bell
visit the pit in episode 6, "The Wire," both characters walk across the pit in

slow motion. As the men reach D'Angelo, they all hug, and the scene speeds back up into real time. While Bell and Barksdale are visiting to financially reward D'Angelo's men for successfully identifying Wright for robbing their stash house, whom they have since brutally murdered, they also use the opportunity to question D'Angelo about a potential informant. The slow motion is used to emphasize how Barksdale and Bell's presence slows down time for those working in the lower end of their organization. Waiting for their bosses to walk across the pit takes longer than real time, as the Barksdale subordinates remain fearful of what punishment could await them at any moment. Their fate and the nature of their existence is wholly dependent on the discretion and whims of their two leaders. This link between slow motion and violence is further underscored when McNulty later takes Omar to see Wright's body in the morgue. As a bedsheet is pulled back in slow motion, Wright's face is framed upside down in a black-and-white close-up filling the screen in a freeze-frame. Here viewers take in the cigarette burns on Wright's face, the blade mark in the corner of his mouth, and his crushed eye socket. Then in episode 9, "Game Day," the Barksdale Detail attempts to take a photograph of Avon following Sydnor's positive identification. As Avon's car leaves the community basketball game, Daniels, Sydnor, and Herc with Carver follow him in three separate unmarked police cars. Avon jumps a red light and turns around to lose them all. Avon's car then emerges before an unsuspecting Daniels driving in the opposite direction. As Daniels sheepishly looks out of his side window, Avon looks directly back at him. Assuming Daniels's POV, Avon waves his finger from side to side as if reprimanding Daniels for attempting to follow him. Crucially, Avon is filmed in slow motion while he coolly issues Daniels with this warning. While Simon is right to point out that flashbacks were not used again, three further scenes have emulated *Homicide*'s visual style but to a different end. In *Homicide*, slow motion frames violence either to accentuate the catharsis and frustrations experienced by warring detectives and criminals operating on either side of the law or to confront viewers with moments of trauma imposed on unsuspecting victims as a springboard for searching for the commonalities that exist between the subjective experiences of black citizens living in dissimilar yet impoverished areas of Baltimore. In *The Wire*'s Baltimore, however, slow motion demonstrates how power—and power to dispense violence—has been concentrated into two powerful individuals. Framing Barksdale and Bell walking across the pit, Wright's injuries, and Barksdale outsmarting Daniels in slow motion imitates the shock, awe, and terror both men can provoke in the outsmarted perspectives of D'Angelo, Omar, Daniels, and others.

NYPD BLUE (1993–2005)

Nine months after *Homicide* hit American screens, *NYPD Blue* arrived. Cocreators Steven Bochco and David Milch made headlines before the program aired, as television's first R-rated series was set to regularly include explicit violence, language, and sex. The growing controversy was instantly quelled by its success. The first episode commanded a 27 percent audience share, which it would largely retain throughout its first season. By the end of the year, it commanded the second-highest number of viewers for an hour-long drama just behind *Northern Exposure* (1992–1995). Being set in New York but filmed in Los Angeles produces a focus on interior settings. Like its rival *Homicide*, the show builds on Bochco's previous creation *Hill Street Blues* as moral concerns play out through its flawed protagonists. Detective Andy Sipowicz (Dennis Franz) lies on the stand, verbally abuses lawyers, struggles with his health, physically assaults citizens, and survives an attempted murder, and that's just in episode 1! Initially, Sipowicz is a loose cannon, a violently temperamental racist, sexist, and alcoholic whose redemptive journey guides *NYPD Blue*'s overall narrative arc, one that sees Sipowicz lose his eldest son, a wife, and two partners. To Milch, *NYPD Blue* "is intensely about the question of how to be and that's what governs all the stories."[25] Unlike *Homicide*, *NYPD Blue* provides an image of the model citizen: disciplined and self-reliant but also open and empathic. All characters, whether detective, lawful citizen, or criminal, must learn their weaknesses and help others.

In a similar vein to *Homicide*, the interrogation room is again the crux of all police work. The most successful form of confession on *NYPD Blue*, according to Nichols-Pethick, is the "negotiated" confession obtained through either "coercion" (a physical beating) or "consent." The consensual confession is offered by suspects to provide excuses for their actions and absolve themselves of some responsibility. In "Twin Petes" (1998), for example, a drug addict suggests that he suffers from blackouts and seizures and therefore isn't responsible for robbing two ATM machines. In "NYPD Lou" (1993), Freddy (John Fleck), who has raped and killed a small boy, comes to the conclusion that he needs "treatment" for his actions and impulses. In "Simone Says" (1994), Arthur Davis (Charles Lanyer) admits to abusing his daughter only after Detective Gregory Medavoy (Gordon Clapp) feigns empathy with him: "I'm a family man. I know how important it is to keep families together . . . your coming forward is the best chance at keeping this situation under control." Each suspect places the "blame for their crime on their own lack of self-control." They also shirk responsibility for feeling unable to control their environment. In "Heavin' Can Wait" (1995), a young drug addict admits to killing two young children during an armed robbery, insisting that the gun went off virtually by itself. In "Hammer Time" (1998), a crack-addicted woman brutally murders her own daughter, blaming her offspring's inability to control her bladder. What separates the detectives as model citizens from the suspects is their ability to gain and maintain control in the midst of personal and professional chaos. The lack of control exhibited by the guilty suspects identified is directly opposed to the detectives' efforts. If Sipowicz is a character on the path to redemption, then the suspects he encounters provide a mirror-image reminder of just why his recovery is so important. The characters of *NYPD Blue* are too complex to be easily positioned as simply "good" or "evil." Instead, "their virtue (or lack thereof) is marked by their ability to control their impulses and, paradoxically, to admit that they need help in learning that discipline."[26]

The acts of "letting go" and "reaching out" are key to *NYPD Blue*'s model citizen. While the detectives may be violent, they resort to violence only when it serves a purpose, namely, coercing a confession from someone they know is guilty. More importantly, the detectives know when to let go, surrender control, and learn from their mistakes and misfortunes. This importance is communicated visually. Much like Bochco's *Hill Street Blues*, *NYPD Blue* also obtains a moving camera and fluid shot composition. This time, however, Sachtler cameras were mounted to wheeled dollies to resist the jerky movements of Bochco's earlier program while still providing a restless camera that is regularly panning or tilting at speed albeit in a smoother manner. Bignell argues that *NYPD Blue*'s camera lacks "mastery over the fictional world" and cannot "deliver knowledge of that world confidently to the audience." Therefore, when the camera does stop moving, it serves to highlight the acts of characters reaching out or letting go. At the end of the pilot, a satisfying emotional encounter concludes the episode between Sipowicz and his detective partner John Kelly (David Caruso). Laying critically injured from a gunshot wound, Kelly stands over Sipowicz's hospital bed, where in a marked contrast to the rest of the chaotic episode, the camera remains unusually still with relatively long takes assembled in a conventional shot-reverse-shot sequence. Kelly informs Sipowicz that he is "like a father to me," and the scene ends with a long close-up of Kelly's and Sipowicz's hands in which the apparently unconscious victim appears to clasp his partner's hand, firmly suggesting that he is beginning a recovery. Bignell argues that the "camera's unusual effacement of its own agency in this scene clearly serves to prioritise the relationship of the two men."[27] Moments where characters are able to "reach out" to one another and/or "let go" are what the roving camera prioritizes. *NYPD Blue* holds the viewer at a distance from the fictional world by drawing attention to the camera's agency in presenting it. Ultimately, this gives extreme weight to tender moments of emotional connection.

The Wire equally values characters who can exercise discipline and "let go" of grudges and destructive behaviors when necessary. It also commends those who are openly empathetic with the capacity to "reach out" to others and bestow advice. There is room for emotional growth in *The Wire* even when an enveloping institution is set to consume an individual. However, *The Wire* turns *NYPD Blue*'s visual schema on its head to communicate the same ideological message. *NYPD Blue*'s camerawork is overwhelmingly restless and is forever searching for and clinging to emotional breakthroughs through momentary stillness. Instead, moments of emotional breakthrough in *The Wire* instigate camera movement as if the camera's agency is awakened and enthused by personal emotional growth. D'Angelo, Bodie, Poot, and Wallace regularly exchange heart-to-hearts in the pit, often when sitting on the orange sofa, acting as a surrogate family for one another. In episode 3, "The Buys," D'Angelo instructs Bodie and Wallace how to play chess. The establishing shot of all three characters sitting around the table remains still, as D'Angelo's offer to teach them chess is initially rebuffed. However, as D'Angelo begins teaching Bodie and Wallace how to play chess correctly, the close-ups of each individual's face tracks from left to right or right to left as D'Angelo dispenses knowledge and Wallace and Bodie process that knowledge. D'Angelo talks through different chess pieces and explains the moves they can make in terms that Bodie and Wallace understand. The lieutenant compares each piece to key players in the Barksdale hierarchy. The queen, says D'Angelo in a close-up, "she smart, she fierce, she move any way she want as far as she want and she is the go get shit done piece." This makes the queen the "Stringer Bell" piece, affirms Bodie in his responding close-up. Each restless mobile close-up contrasts sharply against the brief and still medium shots of the scene designed to simply spatially orient the viewer. What breathes life into the camera's movements is knowledge being imparted that academically and emotionally matures each drug-dealing character with a greater understanding of where they sit in the Barksdale organization.

Furthermore, in episode 4, "Old Cases," Bodie escapes from a juvenile detention center following the BPD's foolhardy raid of the pit. Bodie returns to the site and suggests that if the same had happened to D'Angelo, he'd still be down there. D'Angelo immediately retorts that he has already been inside a city jail before talking them through how Avon Barksdale's girlfriend

Figure 3.4. D'Angelo teaches his workers how to play chess. HBO/Photofest © HBO.

Deirde Kresson was murdered. D'Angelo retells Bodie, Wallace, and Poot the story, working through the trauma that still haunts him, demonstrating to them the kinds of suffering that commands respect by those at the top of the Barksdale crew. Across three close-ups of the young men's faces, D'Angelo explains how he tapped outside the window of the unsuspecting woman at

3:00 a.m. and shot the naked, vulnerable Kresson through her window in a cold-blooded execution. As he walks his subordinates through the encounter, he chillingly repeats the phrase "tap tap tap," mimicking the sound the gun made on the glass that still reverberates in his mind. Revealing this personal information, which he has up to this point kept secret from others, brings the camera to life. When framing D'Angelo in close-up, it tracks from side to side as he reveals each detail as if confessing and coming to terms with the implications of his actions. In direct comparison, the close-ups of Wallace, Bodie, and Poot are still. The static close-up of Bodie in particular foregrounds a quizzical expression of his not quite believing D'Angelo's version of events. Later, it transpires that Wee-Bey committed the murder and that Bodie was right to remain skeptical, but the camera movements here value emotional authenticity. The camera is stimulated into movement by D'Angelo's confession as he is attempting to come to terms with the murder he witnessed—how it continues to traumatize him—and to relieve himself of the burden of carrying this knowledge—something Bodie is too closed-minded to comprehend at this moment. Within the pit, this moving camera highlights D'Angelo's acts of reaching out and letting go and his workers absorbing new knowledge through a journey of emotional growth. A camera that remains markedly still and askance from emotional breakthroughs, be it Bodie not accepting D'Angelo's trauma or initially rebutting D'Angelo's offer to teach chess, is a skeptically unhelpful one that stands as an obstacle to psychological development.

Conversely, within the offices of the Barksdale Detail, *The Wire*'s restless camera chooses to settle on significant breakthroughs that it wishes to draw the viewer's attention to. In this setting, *NYPD Blue*'s visual schema is turned on its head again, this time favoring technical breakthroughs in the case over the psychological growth of individual characters. In episode 5, "The Pager," once Wallace and Poot identify Wright for robbing their stash alongside Omar, the roaming camera in the detail's office settles on a fixed close-up of the office computer screen keeping a record of all the Barksdale crew's messaging that ensues. The computer monitor fills the camera's frame to clearly display either phone numbers used to message cloned pagers and the accompanying six-digit codes sent to them or the numbers dialed from monitored pay phones. On three separate occasions, the camera patiently observes each individual digit appearing on the computer screen over 10 seconds. Additionally, after viewers witness the spoken phone calls unfolding between members of the Barksdale crew, a following close-up of the computer screen reveals the duration of each phone call, ranging as they do from 3 to 17 seconds. While *NYPD Blue* uses a still camera to highlight moments of emotional connection between detectives, *The Wire* uses a still camera to contemplate the ruthless efficiency of Barksdale's communication model. The painfully slow duration of each shot of the computer monitor evokes the sheer amount of time, patience, and focus required of detectives to sift through all their recorded communications and make sense of them.

Within the confines of the Barksdale Detail office, the camera is regularly drawn to and remains fixated on the computer screen. Earlier in "the pager" episode, the camera enthusiastically pans between Herc, McNulty, Carver, and Prez, emulating their childish glee as they giggle in response to Poot having phone sex over a monitored pay phone. But then as the phone call begins to dispense important drug-dealing intel, a still close-up of the sound waves being displayed on the computer monitor anchors the scene four times. Furthermore, in episode 8, "Lessons," the detail office is introduced by a mobile camera that moves down from the detail's office window before tracking through to the listening equipment and resting on a PC screen as detectives listen to Bell confirming that a drug shipment is being delivered to the towers. In the same episode, the camera then later rests on the same computer screen for 13 seconds as detectives listen to Barksdale crew members discuss how Omar shot Stinkum, promptly ceasing their line of inquiry into Barksdale's enforcer. Although producer Bob Colesberry purposefully rejected the "self-conscious flashiness" of 1990s American cop shows, *The Wire* does not completely abandon their visual logic.[28] Slow-motion shots akin to *Homicide* demonstrate the underlying brutality of Barksdale's and Bell's power that strikes fear into individual perspectives within their workforce. Similarly, a smoothly moving yet restless camera akin to *NYPD Blue* is energized by the intellectual and emotional growth that low-level drug dealers can experience. This 1990s visual discourse adds a degree of humanity and sustained interest in the personal circumstances of criminals, building on the precedent first set by *Naked City*. Finally, after 40 years, the pendulum swung back to uncovering the human interest stories underlying acts of criminality. Lawbreakers are no longer a yardstick against which the rectitude of detectives is measured. In response, however, scenes unfolding within the detail office follow this same 1990s visual schema to privilege a closer thematic affinity with *Dragnet*. On this side of the law, the focus, patience, and resourcing required to successfully monitor communication records are prioritized by the camera over the well-being, human interest stories, and tender connections underpinning the detective characters. Ideologically, *The Wire* believes that adherence to traditional detective work is what leads to meaningful change over individual detectives seeking redemption and maturing into model citizens.

ALL THE PIECES MATTER

As the first season of *The Wire* draws to a close and key players within the Barksdale crew are successfully convicted, the conclusion affirms how *The Wire* has borrowed from 50 years of American cop show conventions. In a nod to *Naked City*, McNulty hands Bubbles money on his park bench to steer the addict clean of drugs. Herc stands before new police recruits sitting behind their desks and instructs them to use their heads in a scene derivative of Esterhaus's roll calls at Hill Street station instructing his staff to "be careful out there." Wee-Bey is arrested by a mixture of BPD detectives and uniformed Philadelphia police officers. As Wee-Bey is driven away in handcuffs, the scene's penultimate parting shot is of the Philadelphia Police Department badge logo affixed to the side of a patrol car, mimicking the way that *Dragnet* displayed the LAPD badge. Similarly, the court case sees each member of Barksdale's crew sentenced. Emulating a typical *Dragnet* conclusion, where the convicts standing before the camera have their prison sentences read aloud by a narrator, Assistant State Attorney Pearlman details before the court and viewers each charge as the camera focuses on the apprehensive-looking accused in close-up. Barksdale receives "a maximum of seven years for procuring one kilogram of heroin," and for D'Angelo, "the state is offering only the maximum allowable 20 years" for his transporting of the heroin across the state border in light of his "previous distribution charges" and "refusing to help the investigation." As the court session concludes, Barksdale catches McNulty's eye on the way out, and through McNulty's POV, Avon nods at him in slow motion, grinning as a mark of respect for what McNulty has achieved. Simultaneously, this slower speed draws attention to the menacing quality of Barksdale's grin given that, as in *Homicide*, slow motion is synonymous with the scale and brutality of the violence he has inflicted. Once the court is cleared, McNulty stands alone, existentially remarking, "What the fuck did I do?" as his Kojak-style catchphrase comprehends the scale of what has been achieved. Bunk then passes McNulty on his way out and rhetorically asks, "You happy now? You bitch" before Pearlman then strokes McNulty's arm when exiting. As per the buddy genre, both McNulty's male workplace partner and private female partners are equated with one another. In keeping with the genre, Pearlman is second in the pecking order, able to affectionately congratulate the show's chief protagonist for his heroic efforts only after his male best friend already has. Like *NYPD Blue*, here the camera admires and takes in these tender exchanges of McNulty "letting go" of his obsessions with the case and Bunk/Pearlman "reaching out" to offer their partner emotional support now that the case is over.

Overall, utilizing familiar conventions of the cop show genre enables viewers to make sense of the first season's critique of the legal system. Here they learn that the BPD is so dictated by promotions and targets that securing easy low-level arrests has taken precedence over sustained investigations into those overseeing drug-dealing organizations. Having made this argument, Simon already had plans to expand *The Wire*'s universe across season 2 to further critique how law enforcement's attitudes to drug dealing have even wider implications to citizens living throughout American cities.

CHAPTER 4

SEASON 2

The Port of Baltimore

"**W**hat the fuck is this? What happened to our drugs?" Clarke Peters chuntered to himself while reading through his fresh season 2 scripts. Pivoting from gritty crime drama with a mainly black cast to the trials and tribulations of white dockworkers shook the actors to their core. Green-lighting season 2 had not been seamless. It was only after episode 5 was cut that Chris Albrecht called Simon to inform the writer that they were renewing the show. "It's getting better with every episode," hailed Albrecht. Simon didn't appreciate the backhanded compliment. Had Albrecht not understood the concept of a visual novel from his pitches? Had Albrecht not enjoyed the first four episodes? Nevertheless, a less-than-sympathetic commissioner could have easily canned *The Wire*, so Simon took Albrecht's praise. But the regular cast still felt excluded. Michael K. Williams confronted Simon in his office on behalf of his actors. He asked, "Why are you running away from the show we were building for a season?" Initially, Simon misread Williams, thinking that the actor was annoyed at having less screen time. Williams retorted, "I don't care about the number of lines. I want to know what you're doing,"[1] so Simon explained.

He, Ed Burns, and Bob Colesberry were broadening the scope of the show. They were building a city by focusing on a different institution in each season and how it is impacted by the drug trade. Season 2, then, is about the last days of being able to follow in your father's footsteps and make a living on Baltimore's diminished waterfront, a project that Simon was all set to develop as his next book had season 2 not been green-lit. Satisfied, Williams went back to all the other actors and reassured them that Simon and his team knew what they were doing. Simon and Williams would then repeat this practice before every season to talk through the major thematic developments and general direction of the program. Williams effectively became an ambassador for the show. Accordingly, Peters soon came around, realizing that season 2's change of focus "was a way of saying: this isn't about you. This is about the city of Baltimore. It was necessary."[2] Therefore, this chapter is the first time a chronological history of the Port of Baltimore and its industrial development are explored to determine how characters belonging to contrasting subcultures, generations, and lineages interact differently with the landscape and its industrial heritage. It then compares how these perspectives sit with the Barksdale characters' continuous combating of prominent racial stereotypes.

SEASON 2 ENTERS PRODUCTION

To understand the plight of dockworkers, Simon hired scriptwriter Rafael Alvarez, a former *Baltimore Sun* journalist begat by three generations of maritime laborers. Alvarez had enjoyed a middle-class suburban upbringing off the back of his father's tugboat wage. But when Bethlehem Steel went bankrupt in 2001, Alvarez was the first in four generations who had to find work elsewhere. Nevertheless, the wider Alvarez family provided Simon and Burns with access to stevedores, immigration officials, port personnel, customs inspectors, and steamship agents whom the writing staff interviewed before filming began in 2003. Chief clerk of the Seagirt Marine Terminal, Walt Benewicz, and his union brothers provided many of the anecdotes used to underpin season 2's authenticity. Ziggy Sobotka, for example, was based partly on Pinky Bannon, who wore a tuxedo to the docks and brought his pet duck dressed in a diamond-studded collar to various Locust Point bars where the bird sipped beer.

Having developed the second series and eased his cast's initial fears, another snag soon presented itself. As the crew began filming, Simon discovered that the city was not renewing his team's permits. While the state of Maryland had okayed filming on Baltimore's state-owned port, Baltimore mayor Marty O'Malley had blocked HBO's permits to film in the streets. Sure, season 1 had had its teething problems. The Ritz Cabaret club was seized by the feds, as the real owner of Orlando's had been laundering drug money. Wardrobe assistant DaJuan T. Prince was locked in police cells overnight despite an HBO supervisor verifying his reasons for driving around at

night with 10 police uniforms in his trunk. One day, a mugger accidentally ran onto the set, saw uniformed police officers, and lay down on the
ground to give himself up. Another day, everyone was held back from filming because there was a sniper on a roof. Another time, a dead body was
removed from the block that they were due to film on. From the resentful
drug dealers who lost earnings from film crews locking down their corners to
Baltimore's elected leaders who facilitated television ads that directly challenged *The Wire*'s "negative" depictions of Baltimore, the production had
ruffled feathers. With production gridlocked, Simon finally plucked up the
courage to call up O'Malley. Armed with fellow writer George Pelecanos,
the future of the show rested on this phone call. It didn't start well: O'Malley
was mad. Screaming into the phone, O'Malley demanded that Simon make
a show about all the good things he was doing for the city. Simon reminded
O'Malley that the mayor and his chief of staff had agreed to filming permits
over lunch prior to season 1. The show could have been made in any rustbelt
city: Philadelphia, Cleveland, or St. Louis. But the mayor, reassured that the
program was antidrugs, opted to have the production on his turf given its
economic benefits. Despite being reminded of this gentleman's agreement,
O'Malley stood firm, maintaining that "we want to be out of *The Wire* business." "Okay," said Simon. Taking a harder line, he explained, "They've got
row houses kind of like West Baltimore's in Chester, Pennsylvania, and in
Wilmington, so I'll figure out a way of doing this regardless." Looking to
cut all ties with Simon, the mayor clarified, "It'll say Pennsylvania or Wilmington on the police cars, right?" "No," Simon snapped back, "we already
started the story." "Let me understand this," said the mayor. "You'd film it
in Philadelphia or Chester, they'd get the money, and yet it'd still be a story
about Baltimore?" "Yes, Marty," verified an irritated Simon. "Well," said
O'Malley after a pause, "we'll reconsider your request for permits" before
slamming down the phone. Simon pocketed the cell phone and exhaled
loudly. "Well?" asked Pelecanos.

The filming permits were renewed later that week.[3]

The plot of season 2 arises from an ego-driven pissing match between
a pair of Locust Point Polish Americans. Major Stan Valchek (Al Brown),
commander of the Southeastern District, donates a stained-glass window to
his local Polish Catholic church. On personally delivering the window design
honoring police officers, he is incensed to find that longshoremen union boss
Frank Sobotka (Chris Bauer) has already installed a window that features
men unloading a ship. Valchek promptly reassembles season 1's Barksdale
Detail to uncover Sobotka's funding sources. Patrolwoman Beadie Russell
(Amy Ryan) is added to the team on finding 14 dead women in a shipping

container among Sobotka's cargo. As secretary treasurer of the International Brotherhood of Stevedores union, Sobotka channels his profits from smuggling to buy votes in the state legislature to facilitate overdue port improvements. Concurrently, his son Ziggy Sobotka (James Ransone) and nephew Nick Sobotka (Pablo Schreiber) turn to selling drugs. Again, the team of detectives uses wiretaps to infiltrate the crime ring and slowly works its way up to "the Greek" (Bill Raymond), a mysterious man overseeing smuggling operations. As the Greek orders more dangerous contraband, his Sobotka arrangement spirals out of control. Tipped off that Sobotka has become an FBI informant in exchange for his son's lighter prison sentence, Sobotka is lured to a meeting by the Greek's men where he is executed. The investigation ends with the 14 bodies attributed to the Greek's sex-trafficking operation. Drug dealers and mid-level smuggling figures tied to the Greek are arrested, but the chief smuggler escapes uncharged. Sobotka is reelected as union treasurer posthumously before the union branch is dissolved.

A HISTORY OF THE PORT OF BALTIMORE-COURTESY OF MCNULTY

The pre-credit sequence to episode 1, "Ebb Tide," tours viewers across the Port of Baltimore alongside McNulty's perspective of a day on harbor patrol. Here an audience is geographically oriented in the southeast area of the city through a visual history of the port's industrial development and socioeconomic decline. On hearing a lone seagull, the camera slowly fades from black to reveal a police boat atop the harbor's water. The camera steadily tracks with the slow-moving boat for six seconds. Cut to inside, and McNulty is standing with his head down, arms crossed, "freezing his balls off" in a small, restrictive space alongside the driver, Officer Claude Diggins (Jeffrey Fugitt). The slow fade-in and natural sounds of the seagull (that we do not see), bobbling gray water, and unending ringing of a buoy's bell encourage viewers to share McNulty's perspective of the port as a desolate location where officers go for their career to die. "It ain't so bad," Diggins attempts to reassure McNulty, "in a couple more months it's going to be spring," as if a variation in the temperature is all they can look forward to. Despite being in an open area, three huge cranes stand in the background of the shot, occupying two-thirds of the overall frame and making the long shot of the harbor feel constricted. Akin to Dickens's *Our Mutual Friend* (1865), the Patapsco River stands in for the River Thames as McNulty, like shivering solicitors Wrayburn and Lightfoot boating across London, experiences a "sense of menace" and engulfment from the "iron immensity and decaying jumble of the cityscape."[4] Yet given Baltimore's deindustrialization, these remnants of the industrial age lack the kinesthetic immediacy that they would have occupied during Baltimore's and London's industrial peaks. McNulty's perspective is tinged by Greek mythology. He has been sentenced by his demigod superiors to spend the rest of his career in this freezing underworld. Completely removed from the land of the living, the buoy's consistent ringing is the death knell to McNulty's career and joie de vivre.

Chesapeake Bay, which links Baltimore to the Atlantic Ocean, is an enclosed, long, and shallow body of water limiting the speed and efficiency with which containers can move cargo in and out of the docks compared to nearby Virginia; Newark, New Jersey; or Philadelphia. While this has frozen the port out of contemporary shipping markets, as emphasized by the deadened atmosphere of the opening shot, historically, it worked to the city's advantage. The Port of Baltimore was established at Locust Point in 1706 to trade tobacco. Its growth accelerated during the American Revolution (1775–1781), as Fells Point shipyards assembled America's first warships to fight the British. There were no large ships to match the British navy, so American vessels were designed to be fast and maneuverable to overtake, capture, and seize goods from slow-moving British cargo ships. Nimble vessels known as "schooners" could prove temperamental, as the hull's design, tall masts, heavy spars, and large sails left the boats liable to capsize bow first. But this did not deter the fearless crews. In 1776, the British ship *Otter*, armed with 16 guns and 130 men, was sent up Chesapeake Bay from Norfolk, Virginia, to neutralize Baltimore's shipbuilding trade. As the warship approached, hundreds of volunteers gathered on Fells Point, hurriedly mounting cannons to their new creation, *Defence*, ahead of schedule. The quick mobilization of the people of Baltimore and narrow yet shallow Chesapeake Bay ensured that Britain's *Otter* was grounded twice, forcing the fleet into retreat. Soon, a surge in the wealth and population of craftsmen, manufacturers, entrepreneurs, and apprentices increased Baltimore's population from 6,000 to 9,000 people. This was due in part to Baltimore being the only major American port to escape British depredations. It even briefly served as the nation's capital from December 1776 to February 1777. By the time of the Napoleonic Wars (1806–1815), one-fifth of the city's population had investments or livelihoods in legal piracy, as more privateers were commissioned in Baltimore than any other port. Another British attack of 3,270 men on September 12, 1814, the Battle of Baltimore, was forced into retreat when Major General Robert Ross was shot dead as his troops attempted to land.

The hostility that comes with a decidedly long, shallow, and enclosed Chesapeake Bay, evoked by the confined nature of the two opening shots, is precisely what protected Baltimore from external threats and enabled it to thrive economically during times of hardship. Baltimore's fortunes ran against the state of Maryland, as it was able to capitalize on worldwide conflicts by flooding the Atlantic marketplace with cheap grain while Greek, German, and Scottish refugees flocked to establish the country's first shipbuilding industry, exploiting the American need for a naval fleet. Diggins tries to dissuade McNulty from his pessimistic outlook, affirming that "your bosses did you a favor," but he is interrupted by a call from the boat's radio. Both men are informed that a 60-foot-wide private vessel's engines have died and that the vessel has made a distress call. While Diggins is given these details, the camera occupies McNulty's POV as he looks to the Lazaretto Point lighthouse beside small but prominent American flags blowing in the wind. In response, McNulty's face displays ambivalence toward this relic. The replica of the former lighthouse symbolizes how watchtowers and forts were able to repel British attacks, as citizens could spot approaching vessels. On the other side of the Patapsco River, running directly parallel to the lighthouse, is Fort McHenry, where the 1814 Battle of Baltimore took place. This heritage site of successful combat that founded and preserved the sovereignty of the United States is not appreciated or acknowledged by McNulty's unmoved expressions. The secluded port area, useful during war, has little use for a twenty-first-century economy and job-seeking Baltimoreans.

The Port of Baltimore did, however, continue to modernize through the 1800s and 1900s. Beyond offering fortitude against foreign invaders, its unique location and topography invited industrial innovation. The Baltimore and Ohio Railroad made Baltimore a major shipping *and* manufacturing center. By 1820, its population had reached 600,000, and its economy shifted from its primary base in tobacco plantations to sawmilling, shipbuilding, and textile production. Heavy investments in transportation provided Baltimore an exceptional efficiency for several lines of reciprocal trade involving new steam-powered mills and factories lining Chesapeake Bay that could produce, grind, and refine sugar, flour, wool, plaster, chocolate, mustard, and castor oil. In 1881, there were 39 corporations, and this grew to more than 200 within 14 years. Having been informed of the distress call, Diggins radios for the location of the stranded vessel. On-screen, accompanying this dialogue, the camera cuts to reveal the grain elevator through McNulty's POV. Built in 1923, the Baltimore and Ohio Railroad–owned elevator, or grain pier as the longshoremen call it, is a 24-story, 300-foot-tall building that had a capacity for 3.8 million bushels of grain. This grain elevator has a peculiar design compared to others, as it is divided into two different massing components. Within a conventional steel tower, vertical distribution of grain occurred through a network of octagonal-shaped storage bins to load ships. But next to this tower are six cylinder-shaped silo bins made from reinforced concrete used for mass grain storage before being circulated through the adjacent tower. Combined, the unusually external silo bins with the adjacent elevator tower could store and load grain onto outgoing ships in huge quantities at a faster rate than others, making it one of the primary sources of grain for the whole world. The shot of this imposing structure fills McNulty's POV with the harbor water barely visible in the bottom one-tenth of the frame. The camera then cuts back to a close-up of McNulty, who, having taken in the splendor of the grain elevator, lets out a sigh and directs his gaze elsewhere. The structure is a rusting reminder of when Baltimore was a world-leading beacon of manufacturing and shipping. McNulty feels deflated by the impressive feat of engineering that it once represented compared to its current state of disrepair.

Following the grain elevator's construction, between 1920 and 1926, Baltimore rose from the seventh to the third most attractive port in the nation due to large investments made in transporting coal. All three major railroads built coal piers, plying the harbor with freshly mined Appalachian coal direct from their mountainous railways. The world's largest copper refinery in Canton depended on these regular coal deliveries to meet the plant's appetite for electricity. Coke ovens producing Bethlehem steel at Sparrows Point also consumed mountains of coal, and the methane generated was piped to local gasworks. "Geographically, the coal metabolism and the triangular trade of gas, electricity, and steel defined a potential in Baltimore that would be developed rapidly in World War I."[5] In five years (1914–1919), Baltimore's manufacturing labor force had increased by one-third, its manufacturing capital doubled, and the value of manufactured products and exports tripled. The city emerged from World War I as a modern industrial complex underpinning America's newfound status as the world's largest superpower. The radio then informs Diggins that the stranded boat has a location of 2,000 yards off the Armistead pier (named after George Armistead, who successfully commanded the Americans in the 1814 Battle of Baltimore). Simultaneously, McNulty's POV captures discarded steel foundations in the bay. He opens his mouth in awestruck disbelief, as looking at the imposing relics of Baltimore's World War I modernization illuminates the sheer scale of the former world-leading industries. As the boat turns course to locate the stranded vessel, the words "Canton marine terminal" are clearly displayed behind it, referencing where the world's largest copper refinery was once located. Changing direction, the boat approaches Bethlehem Steelworks. The steelworks first occupy the skyline in the distance as both characters look out over the railings at the front of the boat, and the viewer occupies an approximate point of view. McNulty informs Diggins that "my father used to work there" before Diggins reveals that he had an uncle who was a supervisor there. The camera then cuts to a shot of the boat right in front of the structure as we are told that Diggins's uncle "got laid off in 78." The huge bronze rusting structure dwarfs the tiny-looking boat and cuts out the sky. As the boat steers left of the old steel site, McNulty explains that his dad was "let go in 73." The cinematography of this sequence replicates how both characters were heading for that trade but have had to take a different direction in life from the pull that the huge structure once drew for able-bodied men.

The direction of the U-turning police boat symbolizes that rather than the 1920s heralding a new era of industrial expansion, as was promised, time has proven the 1920s to be Baltimore's final industrial swan song. The boat has circled the canton area as if replicating the plethora of major industries that previous generations of blue-collar tradesmen could choose to work in. Then the boat is drawn to Bethlehem Steelworks, where jobs were later concentrated. As children, the steelworks was a viable career prospect on the horizon of Diggins and McNulty but has become an imposing fork in the road that they and subsequent generations have had to avoid. From 1970 to 1995, Baltimore lost more than 95,000 manufacturing jobs. The port's railway infrastructure was built around bulk cargoes of coal and grain but could not facilitate new worldwide demand for shipments that trucks carried for more personal consumption—everything from textiles to shoes. At this crossroads, political leaders concentrated capital into redeveloping the inner harbor area into a new entertainment district consisting of shops, restaurants, hotels, the national aquarium, Orioles Park, and a convention center. But jobs for locals were disappearing. General Motors and Bethlehem Steel, the biggest employers, closed in 2001 and 2003, respectively. During filming in 2004, the Port of Baltimore was ranked twelfth for imports and twentieth for exports within the United States alone. The port remains operational, employing 15,300 people who specialize in offloading vehicles and farm equipment in much smaller quantities. Workers can also be found in waterfront distribution centers owned by the likes of Amazon for lower pay and less secure working conditions than their seafaring ancestors. The port has become an area of tourism, recreation, and entertainment for visitors, as 213,000 residents would migrate from Southeast Baltimore to the outer suburbs.

McNulty and Diggins's police boat, then, replicates Baltimore's economic journey, moving as it does from the area of the canton refinery toward the steelworks only to veer off to assist a stranded luxury yacht underneath the Francis Scott Key Bridge, named after the author Francis Scott Key, who wrote "Defence of Fort McHenry," a poem inspired by the bravery he witnessed at the Battle of Baltimore. Its words are better known as the lyrics to the American national anthem, "The Star-Spangled Banner." The bridge itself spans the whole Port of Baltimore and was opened in March 1977 to provide a route across Baltimore Harbor for vehicles transporting hazardous materials (prohibited from both the Baltimore Harbor and the Fort McHenry tunnels). It has since come to be used by commuters utilizing I-695, an auxiliary interstate highway that loops around Baltimore connecting suburbs and business parks outside the city with one another. Unfortunately, the name Scott Key, who was inspired by the forts, battles, and bravery he witnessed firsthand in Baltimore Harbor, became synonymous with the thousands of commuters passing through the port as quickly as possible every day before the bridge collapsed on March 26, 2024, after it was hit by a container ship. Juxtaposed with this location, the stranded yacht represents the primary source of revenue that the port now attracts: tourism and leisure.

As McNulty and Diggins approach the yacht located under the bridge, in an apparent state of distress, viewers immediately witness a montage of people dressed in dinner jackets dancing to a live band and being waited on by smartly uniformed staff. As the police boat nears, we see that this ship is called *Capital Gains*, from Washington, D.C. The boat represents the future direction of Baltimore's economy. As the country has now opted to import cheaper materials from abroad, the port has had to repurpose itself as a recreational harbor for out-of-town tourists and investors making capital gains. The harbor has become a plaything for the rich and powerful who in this instance party on board unaware that their ship has come into any trouble until the police boat arrives. On board, McNulty offers the boat a towline to Henderson's Wharf in Fells Point, a spot where ships used to be built and that is now a place where people dock their vessels to enjoy the shopping and leisure facilities. However, the party's host offers McNulty money to tow them somewhere out of the way to keep the party going. The shot then fades to McNulty's POV of the party boat tied to the back of the anchored police boat at nighttime alongside a freight carrier. From the dock McNulty listens over the loud music, and partygoers drunkenly enjoying themselves into the small hours of the night. McNulty watches the revelers from a distance with the same body posture from the start of the sequence, his arms crossed again, visibly annoyed at the amount of time that has passed. His role as a policeman is now serving the haves rather than protecting the have-nots, who simply wish to not be inconvenienced. Academic Lucasi describes the villainous Greek and his allies as people who claim "no allegiance to the city" using Baltimore "only as a market for their traffic in" goods.[6] This could quite easily describe the partygoers, whom McNulty looks on with the same level of disdain he has for the port's present condition. As urban historian Marc Levine has argued, "The chief beneficiaries of Baltimore downtown inner harbor development have been developers, financiers, real estate speculators, suburbanites, a few affluent condo dwellers, and tourists whilst Baltimore natives sank deeper into poverty."[7]

A viewer is introduced to season 2 through a journey of the port's history, first through the remnants that signify the battles and privateering that founded its shipbuilding industry and war of independence. Then viewers journey through former sites of industrial innovation and modernization that once loaded grain, refined copper, produced gas, and built steel for the rest of the world through coal power. Now the harbor exists to serve the tourism and leisure industries that are occupied by unappreciative figures using the port on a temporary basis to enjoy the views of the Chesapeake Bay far removed from Baltimore's industrial heritage. McNulty is visibly annoyed contemplating the descent that the port has endured from being at the forefront of founding a world superpower to being stripped of assets and serving no economic purpose for the country's future economic direction. McNulty's perspective that has grounded a viewer's perception of the location for the second season is completely removed from the Sobotka family, who proudly hail from Polish immigrant dockworkers and so have a different relationship with the port that they seek to maintain.

THE SOBOTKAS

The Wire is a work of social realism for being attuned to the way that "environmental factors" can impact "on the development of character."[8] Therefore, different characters occupy contrasting connections with the port's landscape. Compared to McNulty, Frank Sobotka is a cargo checker and union treasurer brought up by successive generations of dockworkers. He is energized by and finds purpose in the same structures that alienate McNulty. We are first introduced to Sobotka in his office as he argues with Nathanial "Nat" Coxson (a cargo handler), who wants to consolidate union resources into upgrading the grain pier. Frank has a more ambitious plan that would also involve the union buying political support to also have the canal dredged. Both men reach an impasse. Coxson is frustrated that Frank will not listen to pragmatism, which might lead to "actually come away with something." As Frank leaves his office, he walks among the shipping containers in an expansive long shot, basking in the bright sun. We occupy his POV as he looks up at a seagull flying in an open, unblocked shot of the sky, majestically gliding over the stacked containers before the camera cuts back to his face in close-up, where his sunlit face smiles in response. The camera then tracks around Frank 360 degrees as he breathes in huge amounts of air, continuing to smile at sights of the operational cranes and trucks moving shipping containers around him. The lone seagull and cranes that are used to evoke McNulty's isolation put a spring in Frank's step, instilling him with purpose. However, this serene and idyllic camerawork is mismatched with the drama that unfolds through the course of Frank's working day. He learns that his nephew Nick is working his first shift in two weeks and that Otto still owes him money, and he is forced to fire his son Ziggy from a day's work for losing a client's container before sending Nick to the Greek to negotiate more imported contraband. McNulty finds the landscape cold, haunting, shockingly unattained, and restrictive of his movements. In comparison, Frank is framed by a free-flowing camera that kicks into action once he has optimistically fought for ambitious dock expansions. The sight of the blue sky, cargo machinery, and a flying bird imbue Sobotka with enough reassurance to distract him from his day-to-day reality replete with operational problems. He feels that he can personally spearhead another comeback from adversity, as has defined the Port of Baltimore for centuries through more adverse depressions and worldwide conflicts, via his own modern form of privateering. Initially, in line with Williams's definition of social realism, Frank's perspective offers a politically imagined possibility as to how the docks can be modernized yet preserved. While a decidedly nostalgic perspective suffused with pseudo-memories of an idealized past motivates Sobotka, some academics have concluded that the smaller spaces that his character occupies, including offices, shipping containers, trucks, cafés, bars, and his home, at least offer some kind of counterforce to the dogma of neoliberalism and rampant global markets.[9]

For the generation beneath Frank, however, even these signifiers of Polish working-class life remain "tantalizingly visible but out of reach."[10] All the Sobotkas are descended from Polish immigrants and live in the Locust Point neighborhood. The grain elevator (grain pier) stands prominently at the end of their street. In 1914, these Polish homes were notorious among the first generation of immigrants for being the most overcrowded and filthiest and having the highest rate of infant mortality. As the influx of Polish people came after the Germans, Irish, and Lithuanians, they were left with the less well-paid shipping jobs and experienced much higher mortality rates than other immigrant workers unless they could speak German. These first Polish settlers, however, managed to pool together savings to collectively buy whole neighborhoods. In 1914, there were 20 Polish building and land associations. By 1970, there remained seven with more than $25 million in assets. This is the neighborhood that Frank and the generation before him were born into with the expectation that hard work directly leads to home-ownership. Nick, who still lives with his parents in his family-owned Locust Point house, has no direct connection to the generation of Poles who first settled in Baltimore to work on the grain pier and were able to own their own homes despite being rooted to the bottom of the social ladder.

To Nick, the looming decrepit grain pier structure at the end of the road has an engulfing presence that alienates him further from his heritage and parental expectations. Whenever the camera captures the grain pier as a backdrop behind the younger generation of dockworkers (Nick and Ziggy), it is associated with bad news. In the first episode, Nick walks to his car out in the front of the house. He has just been berated by his mother for not wak-ing up earlier to catch potential work. Having been denied breakfast and a maternal hug, he then fails to start his car. The scene concludes with a shot of the grain pier filling the camera's frame. We can barely see Nick in front of the overwhelming structure, making him look insignificant in relation to the tall cylinders of grain storage. In this shot, he admits defeat and opens his car door to commence walking to work, passing billboards for luxury apartments that his wage cannot afford. For his efforts, he discovers that there's enough work that day only for older union members. Then in episode 4, "Hard Cases," when Nick tries to rekindle his relationship with estranged girlfriend Aimee, she stays over in his bedroom without his parents know-ing. The scene begins with a long shot that pans down the top of the grain pier into the street of terraced houses. When Nick's mother upstairs bangs on the kitchen floor to awaken her son, the couple argue about how they will pick up their daughter. Aimee is insulted that Nick instructs her to leave via the back door to avoid his parents, as he sees them as "decent people." Despite having a child together, Nick is embarrassed that they are not mar-ried or own their own property and wants to avoid parental judgment. The grain elevator is again prominent in episode 5, "Undertow," when Nick tries to negotiate down Ziggy's debt with drug dealer Calvin "Cheese" Wagstaff (Method Man). Nick returns from an unsuccessful negotiation to his parents' house on Locust Point, telling Ziggy outside the house and grain pier behind that "they're still going to kill you." Similarly, in episode 11, "Bad Dreams," once the FBI has raided Nick's parents' house, he returns home, walking slowly up the street. The grain elevator fills the background of the shot as he crosses the road, aware that his neighbors are watching him. For the younger generations, the grain pier stresses the distinct lack of regular work compared to previous generations, who had it available right outside their home. Its towering structure claustrophobically exacerbates parental pressure to buy a home without the community support of housing associations that previous generations relied on. It is also synonymous with the impending fear Ziggy feels for his life and the shame Nick experiences following the police raid. At the end of the street lies a constant reminder that the neighborhood no longer provides possibility and security afforded to previous generations.

For Frank, however, the grain pier represents a different purpose. In episode 6, "All Prologue," Frank confronts his son Ziggy for burning a $100 note from the proceeds of trafficked goods in full view of union men in the Clement St. Café bar. Ziggy walks his father down to the docks in full view of the grain pier to manipulate his father's nostalgia into escaping further admonishment. Walking across the water's edge, Frank probes where Ziggy came by that money. Ziggy stops walking and instead regales his father with childhood memories of his uncles sitting around the kitchen table discussing work and dealing with "scabs" who worked through periods of industrial action. In comforting his father with idealized memories, both men come to stand in separate shots. Frank stands directly in front of the grain pier, bringing the structure into sharp focus, while Ziggy, in his own mid-shot, simply stands in front of a pitch-black background. For Frank, the pier has always offered stability that guides his union campaigning. But for Ziggy, it represents unfulfilled childhood promises of the past, leaving him shrouded in uncertainty. Both generations struggle to escape the pier's shadow. The older nostalgically associate it with memories of regular stable working conditions that they wish to pass on. For the younger workers, the grain pier represents the overpowering and unobtainable expectations of their parents.

Therefore, a sense of "doomed inevitability" does not necessarily color all the "long shots framing machinery looming over tiny human figures," as Vint has argued.[11] For McNulty, long shots of the harbor represent an already dead space; for Ziggy and Nick, it represents a lost future; but, for Frank, it offers reassurance, strength, and future possibility. Furthermore, characters' perspectives of their city environment are open to change. By episode 11, "Bad Dreams," the way that Frank is framed by structures suggests that a full shift in perspective has occurred albeit too late. Having been summoned to a meeting with the Greek where he will be executed, both Nick and Frank meet by a chain-link fence in front of the grain pier dominating

Figure 4.1. Frank Sobotka derives strength from surrounding port locations compared to the generation beneath him. HBO/Photofest © HBO.

the background of the shot. Both stand in front of the elevator structure, but as the camera pulls forward toward them, Frank comes to be positioned in front of the concrete cylinders. Here Nick informs Frank where the Greeks want to meet him as they discuss the scope of their criminal organization. A series of close-ups then ensue as Frank becomes more enraged about his son coming to be involved with smuggling heroin, which has led to Ziggy facing a life sentence for murdering the Greek's associate George Glekas (Teddy Cañez). We then occupy Frank's POV as he looks to the top of the elevator through the wire fencing in the shot's foreground and states, "Do you know what that is Nicky? . . . a condominium!" Coming to the realization that he cannot preserve a livelihood for the next generation or even leave them so much as a grain pier let alone a fully dredged canal finally stops Frank from pursuing his dream. He will go to the FBI to inform on the Greek for revenge to "do what those cocksuckers did to me." Nick attempts to deter Frank's new strategy, as the Greeks have suggested that they can lean on a witness to get Ziggy out of prison. Here the camera switches to the other side of the wire fence as the camera watches Frank grab it, shake it in frustration, and rest his head against it. For the first time, a barrier prominently stands between him and the defunct pier that he nostalgically idolized. Up until this point, the pier and other structures have been standing behind his figure unobstructed in sharp focus, imbuing him with confidence as he stands tall, dispensing his heady dreams of the future. Here he sends Nick home, aware that he is likely not to walk away from his meeting with the Greek alive. The final shot of the scene sees Frank stooping by the pier's empty storage cylinders, himself now also emotionally drained, unfulfilled, and devoid of a future like the younger generation has always felt. His perspective of the grain pier has altered to become aligned with his younger relatives.

In the final shot of the whole season, Nick stands against the same fence overlooking the pier in the rain before walking away. As the camera pans left with Nick down the street, for the first time, he is free and separated from the imposing grain pier structure and parental pressures it has come to represent. But it is hardly a joyous parting. Nick has evaded imprisonment but now lives in the federal witness protection program and is unable to work, and he sheds a tear for the complete death of blue-collar work for Polish Americans. For Williams, the family's fate was always a foregone conclusion, as season 2 is a modern Greek tragedy where Frank Sobotka "knowingly tempts fate and brings the tragedy down upon himself."[12] However, it would be more accurate to suggest that season 2 obtains a more complex social realist approach to character and setting whereby each of a multitude of perspectives has an unfixed, fluctuating relationship with industrial relics. From instilling Frank with purpose and confidence to dread and his impending sense of mortality, from an overbearing resentment stifling Nick's independence to a monument mourning his belonging to a family, the grain pier means something different to every resident of Southeast Baltimore, something beyond the comprehension of outsiders like McNulty, who can survey the industrial heritage with only a passing understanding and appreciation of its history, a set of perspectives that are now no longer possible to forge in real life. After filming, the abandoned grain elevator was turned into condos by the Turner Development Group. Now the Silo Point complex boasts 228 luxury apartments and 20,000 square feet of retail space, restaurants, spas and salons, and office space. Further gentrification of Southeast Baltimore continues to eviscerate the city's industrial heritage from generations of blue-collar Baltimoreans erasing all their contrasting and varying connections with it.

A HISTORY OF RACIAL DISCRIMINATION AT BALTIMORE'S DOCKS

Season 2 is not simply a tale of white blue-collar Americans struggling to make a living in a depleting industry. The continuing story of Barksdale's crew challenges a lot of enduring black stereotypes prominent since the

Civil War. I disagree with Vint's claim that there is a "lack of attentiveness in this season to the long tradition of racial discrimination in Baltimore that sits uncomfortably with its otherwise nuanced portrait of the community."[13] Racial discrimination is a central part of season 2's nuanced portrayal of Baltimore. Historians often gloss over the racial inequality that underpinned the port's formation. For example, many find virtue that in 1810, Baltimore held the largest concentration of free black people, and that by 1860, before President Lincoln had emancipated a single slave, 92 percent of all African Americans in Baltimore were free. Even decorated author and abolitionist Frederick Douglass, working as a ship caulker on Fells Point, observed that "white and black ship-carpenters worked side by side, and no one seemed to see any impropriety in it." However, tasked with finding his own work to pay his slave master meant that Douglass "endured all the evils of a slave, and suffered all the care and anxiety of a freeman," effectively shouldering the worst burdens of both worlds.[14] It was on Baltimore's shipyards Douglass fell afoul of four armed white carpenters who partially blinded him. After Lincoln's 1863 Emancipation Proclamation, which enshrined in law the ending of slavery, African Americans would continue to struggle for a piece of Baltimore's economic expansion. It was a time of opportunity mainly for the white immigrants, who benefited from an unnatural division of labor, exposing many black people to alarming vulnerability. In 1865, a few months after the Civil War's end, white workers at an East Baltimore shipyard went on strike to force the outright firing of 75 black caulkers. The yard's owner held out for more than a month but finally agreed to phase out the black workers. Every local newspaper sided with the black workers, but the weight of editorial opinion did not change the outcome. Between 1865 and 1867, white stevedores attacked black stevedores to force them off their jobs on at least four occasions. Interracial competition for waterfront work further intensified through Baltimore's industrial age. From 1910 to 1918, employers continued to exploit ethnic rivalries in labor disputes. When 125 Locust Point drivers ordered a strike demanding that the Baltimore and Ohio Railroad pay black workers $1.60 per day plus 20 cents for every hour of overtime, the railroad brought in 80 black workers from Philadelphia, paying them overtime to break the strike. As Baltimore's economy modernized through periods of hardship, the greatest adjustments and risks were shifted onto black citizens, who had the least power.

To reclaim their future, Isaac Myers assembled 15 African American entrepreneurs who helped to accumulate $40,000 so that the black caulkers could open a shipyard of their own on Chesapeake Bay. About $10,000 more was raised in black churches, and 300 black workers were employed.

Within five years, the company had repaid its entire debt. In 1869, Myers then founded the Colored National Labor Union. Six years later, he began the Colored Men's Progressive and Cooperative Union of Baltimore. Myers even founded a newspaper, *The Colored Citizen*. To an extent, Myers's efforts were largely unsuccessful, as the black-owned shipyard went out of business in 1884 after prolonged litigation. Nevertheless, it was an important moment in Baltimore's history. Amidst Myers's efforts, semiskilled black workers formed assemblies of the Knights of Labor union, comprised of workers across the port, including brickmakers, Fells Point wagoners, 300 grain trimmers, and the Montgomery Street stevedores. These assemblies would outlive the Knights of Labor to endure through the turn of the century, the largest black union being the Stevedores union with 1,300 members. While not always successful, such efforts demonstrated black Baltimore's capacity to generate autonomous institutions to tackle the challenges posed by white prejudice. Black people were continually modifying their vocations and unionized tactics, as modernization continued to alter industrial demand and employment patterns. Maintaining a regular wage required black workers to continuously adapt to change.

Season 2 acknowledges Baltimore's history of racial discrimination by demonstrating how black characters readjust to continually challenging circumstances. White dockworkers of Polish descent who feel entitled to a future of secure work have become nullified by relentlessly clinging to nostalgic expectations of the past. In comparison, black characters adapt. When we are first introduced to Frank Sobotka persuading Nathaniel "Nat" Coxson (Luray Cooper) to dredge the canal, Frank tries to appease his black colleague, stating that his plans will secure work for "your people" and "my people," alluding to their race. Nat, however, remains firm, as he realizes that Frank is asking for too much. Coxson pragmatically asserts that they should just try to secure grain pier renovations, as going for too much will result in coming back "with nothing but your shriveled ass dick in your hand." As Frank attempts to further patronize Nat about the advantages of a deeper canal, Nat talks over him, contending that he will go to the "district council" and tell them to "push for the grain pier." Visually, the racial dynamics of the scene are obvious for all to see. Nat the cargo checker stands throughout the scene in his Hi-Vis jacket overalls and helmet, while the three other characters from cargo handling sit back in their seats, dressed casually and surrounding him. The handlers comfortably own and have a greater stake in Frank's office setting and believe themselves to be in a more skilled profession. The pronunciation of Nat's surname is even identical to the term "Coxswain," a position that refers to somebody who steers a boat but the etymology of which literally translates as "boat servant." Significantly, it is the black dockworker who is perceptive enough to see what future challenges lie ahead and is trying to dispense some cold, hard truths so that the port can adapt. This goes over the head of Frank and his majority-white union reps, who still feel entitled and derive comfort from being in charge. Correspondingly, on leaving, Coxson demands that Frank "crawl back down those holds [to] remind yourself of who you is and where you come from." Coxson is referring to Frank's Polish ancestors, who would have been at the bottom rung of the social ladder when it came to securing seafaring work and would have competed with black citizens for the scraps of unskilled work available. Therefore, the scene establishes a difference of opinion between majority-white workers, who feel entitled to secure work, and black workers, who identify likely outcomes and realistically strategize accordingly rather than stubbornly chasing unobtainable dreams.

Beyond the docks, *The Wire*'s black characters have more of a propensity for adapting to sudden changes in the employment market. Despite Avon Barksdale being in prison and their principal drugs supplier cutting all ties, Stringer Bell keeps their organization profitable by selling weaker product and sharing territories with Prop Joe. Consequently, in episode 8, "Duck and Cover," Bodie lets his staff go because Prop Joe is taking over his tower. Asked whether the Barksdale crew will offer employees severance, Bodie simply retorts, "Get out of here." From top to bottom, the Barksdale crew pragmatically accepts (as with Coxson) that the labor market is susceptible to seismic shifts that they must tackle head-on as their ancestors have always done. Frank and his fellow white dockworkers of Polish descendancy, however, are experiencing precarious unemployment for the first time in generations and so measure success against idealized memories of the past that have long since been rendered obsolete.

THE BARKSDALES

While the Barksdale organization continues to be overseen by Bell, Avon and D'Angelo Barksdale serve prison time. D'Angelo decides to cut ties with his family after his uncle orders the killing of several inmates. Avon orders a batch of smuggled heroin to be lethally contaminated to frame prison guard Dwight Tilghman (Antonio D. Charity) as revenge for bullying Wee-Bey. Here a lot of black stereotypes prevalent in American mainstream culture are uncovered and challenged. Around the time of production, eminent black scholar bell hooks was analyzing enduring black stereotypes prevalent in U.S. culture since the Civil War, raising awareness of their continued harm to black men, and providing practical strategies to enhance the emotional well-being of black male readers. The most prevalent issue identified by bell hooks's study *We Real Cool: Black Men and Masculinity* is anti-intellectualism, something weaponized by black men who felt condemned to a meager existence, having not been educated. According to hooks, college-educated black men can feel alienated from their black roots. So when given the opportunity to socialize and bond with their community, educated black men are more inclined to "belittle education as a way of connecting with an anti-intellectual black world." Often, those who secure elite status "hoard the knowledge of the ways education empowers while pretending that it is meaningless."[15] This is how Barksdale and Stringer maintain power over their family and workers within their crew. They retain their knowledge and power by deliberately stifling intellectual progress for those beneath them.

D'Angelo is forever trying to break from his uncle Avon's shadow, combat his prescribed anti-intellectualism, acquire knowledge, intellectually mature, and live his own life on his own terms. Any attempt to engage with books in the prison library is obstructed by his uncle. In episode 3, "Hot Shots," Avon confronts D'Angelo. Working his prison job, D'Angelo and his colleague roll the book cart down an aisle, discussing the difference between Spider-Man and Ultra Spider-Man, signifying their love of reading. Avon appears at the end of the aisle, blocking D'Angelo's trolley in its tracks, prompting D'Angelo's friend to leave him alone with his uncle. Here Avon reminds his nephew that he works an easy job because of his uncle's power and influence. Avon proceeds to slap D'Angelo on the back while his nephew puts a book back on the shelf. Then as D'Angelo places another book on the shelf, the next camera shot views him from the other side of the shelving so that the books and shelves frame the edges of the immediate foreground of the shot and Avon's waist can be seen in the background leaning over D'Angelo. Here Avon tells D'Angelo, "Just shut your mouth and open your mind, you ain't going to be doing small piece of this 20." Visually, throughout this scene, D'Angelo is trying to break away from his uncle and set his own path, but whenever he manages to occupy his own close-up, the space becomes smaller as Avon corners him and restricts his movements further. Visibly constricting D'Angelo's space by using his body to press D'Angelo against the bookshelves functions as a constant reminder that D'Angelo enjoys relative freedoms only due to his uncle. To conclude the meeting, Avon turns D'Angelo back around to the bookshelves, forces his head down so that he is looking to the floor as Avon picks up a book, and leaves. This scene represents bell hooks's anti-intellectualism, as Avon does not want his nephew thinking for himself or acting independently. Any attempt to use the books for escape, intellectual maturity, or self-awareness must be suppressed.

In contrast, when free of his uncle, D'Angelo uses the library to grow intellectually and set a life path for himself. During a prison library reading class on *The Great Gatsby* in episode 6, "All Prologue," the teacher asks whether the pupils concur with Fitzgerald's view "there are no second acts in American lives." While the group agrees, D'Angelo interjects the group consensus. He feels that Fitzgerald "is saying the past is always with us. Where we come from what we go through how we go through it." Then as his teacher permits him to "go ahead," D'Angelo leans forward, prompting the camera to float freely around the table, moving closer to him. D'Angelo develops his point, suggesting that the boats and tides at the end of *The Great Gatsby* represent "how you can change up. Say you're someone new, give yourself a whole new story. But what came first is who you really are and what happened before is what really happened." As the camera sweeps slowly across all the other classmates' admiring facial reactions, D'Angelo concludes that "all that really matters is what you really do, what you go through." Essentially, D'Angelo brings the discussion alive. He jump-starts the camera's smooth, free-flowing movements. Freed from his uncle's grasp, he changes the dynamic of his environment with the intellectual capability to captivate the whole class. He empowers himself and his classmates to "get real with their own story" rather than just conceding to the fact that they are in prison and won't get another chance in life, as was originally interpreted by Fitzgerald's statement. D'Angelo is, as bell hooks's study advises, enabling himself and others to confront what they have been taught through life and how it has "affected their sense of themselves and others." Through this book club, as in hooks's teachings, "wounded black males can begin to heal the hurt to come out of isolation and let themselves live again."[16]

D'Angelo acts on his book club epiphany to confront his family. Another issue that bell hooks believes holds black men back, as propagated by historic cultural stereotypes, is the expectation that black men will "surrender their childhoods" in the "process of becoming." When D'Angelo's mother, Brianna (Michael Hyatt), visits him in prison in episode 6, "All Prologue," she repeats Avon's instructions demanding obedience and loyalty to the family instead of listening to his own thoughts and feelings. Further propagating anti-intellectualism, Brianna tells D'Angelo to "just show up and say what Levy tells you to." On refusing, his mother asks, "What's wrong with you?" to which he recounts a childhood incident. He explains that when living on Linden Avenue at age six or seven and playing on the porch, some twins from the neighborhood picked on him. D'Angelo remembers getting back into the house only to be told by his mother to "go back out there and fight." As the boys proceeded to beat D'Angelo, his mother refused to help, explaining, "I might have brung you into this world but you the one who have to live in it." D'Angelo then declares to his mother after reliving this traumatic memory, "Well Ma I'm still here, me. You gotta let me live like I need to live. Tell them all to leave me be." Following his prison education, D'Angelo has developed an ability to reflect on his childhood and use the past to mature on his own terms rather than allowing parental expectations to consume him. He seeks to break away from bell hooks's observation that black boys from impoverished areas "have been socialized to believe that physical strength and stamina are all that really matter . . . taught that 'thinking' is not valuable labor, that 'thinking' will not help them to survive." According to hooks's logic, D'Angelo is an example of one of the "wounded black males who must do the work of reclaiming their past in order to live fully in the present,"[17] something the white dock characters are unable to do, as they are guided and then consumed by their collective memories and expectations of the past.

This is not to say that the heads of the Barksdale organization who push anti-intellectualism on others are not themselves academically capable. *The Wire* is a very important text, as it rejects bell hooks's argument that prominent cultural representations of black leadership in the early 2000s solely reproduced a "motley crew of the narcissistic, the vaguely ridiculous, and the inept."[18] *The Wire* successfully combats this enduring stereotype by demonstrating how the likes of Avon Barksdale and Bell have much more control and agency over their environment than the white dockworkers. Regularly, scenes of Barksdale and Bell mastering their difficult predicament are directly followed by scenes of white dockworkers unable to do the same. When we first see Barksdale speaking to Bell in season 2, episode 1, Barksdale orders Bell within the prison's visitor center to see their supplier's lawyer in New York, as they have still not received their major drug package. He instructs Bell "to take it light but be firm" as they devise their strategy for continuing their drug-dealing organization's survival. Then in the very next scene, Nick Sobotka is unable to secure a day's work, as all the labor has gone to older union members. Similarly, in episode 2, "Collateral Damage," when Valchek ramps up his campaign to have Frank surrender his church window, he has all the dockworkers stopped, searched, and breathalyzed on their way to work as part of a police harassment campaign. Then in the very next scene, a guard brings Wee-Bey to Barksdale's cell as the camera tracks around the room to observe Barksdale relaxing and enjoying a Kentucky

Fried Chicken platter as both men discuss how to deal with Tilghman ransacking Wee-Bey's possessions. Here Barksdale promises, "Don't worry alright I'll take care of it." Despite being imprisoned, Barksdale is still able to run his drug-dealing operation on the outside and have any food or company he wants delivered to him. As chief inspiration for Avon Barksdale, Little Melvin Williams has claimed that "the way the script was written that is just the way it is . . . I've had some days in penitentiary that were so delightful I wouldn't replace them with nothing."[19] In direct contrast, the dockworkers have been harassed on their way to work after their breakfast was delayed, as the shop they purchase eggs from was closed. The white dockworkers are in a sense more imprisoned by their diminishing working-class community. Despite being free citizens, they are subject to larger forces and have less agency and control over their own fate.

In her exploration of contemporary black experience, bell hooks takes against rap music for crystallizing the harmful impacts of anti-intellectualism and denying childhood experiences in the pursuit of a hedonistic lifestyle. She asserts that from the 1960s, an "ethos of greed began to permeate the psyches of black folks." According to hooks, black culture and radicals moved from "brilliant critiques of white supremacy and capitalism" into "striving to get money by any means (selling dope, creating fashion)" and became more fixated on "having money to waste" that came to matter more than being "self-sufficient." However, only Ziggy Sobotka imitates this stereotype. He burns a $100 note in the local bar. Despite being instructed not to draw attention to his illicitly acquired wealth, he spends $2,000 on a sheepskin leather jacket and vintage 1970s Camaro that he calls "princess." Flashing materialistic goods ensures that Ziggy stands out like a sore thumb on the streets of West Baltimore, leading Cheese to easily locate and savagely beat his debtor. It is significant that Ziggy is listening to the Flaming Sideburns in his 1970s-style car and coat when Cheese finds him. The music used to underscore white dockworker scenes consists mainly of 1960s country music or 1970s-style rock music, be it Steve Earl or the Stooges, to further emphasize how they are trapped in the past and are living in the shadow of their parents' tastes, perspective, and worldview. The lyrics from each song are about finding one's way in life and breaking free of previous generational expectations, which is ironic, as it is the music of their parents' generation and not theirs. They do not have contemporaneous music to elucidate their plight. Comparatively, Barksdale reclines in his prison cell reading a magazine as inmates are dying from his poisoned heroin supply. While this chaotic mayhem unfolds, Barksdale listens to the upbeat sampled flute instrumentals from Russ's "The Flute Song" that underscore his ensconced demeanor. A song that relishes being able to "do whatever I want, whenever I want. I love it" underlines Barksdale's disposition. hooks sees rap music reinscribing anti-intellectualism for the benefit of "white supremacist capitalist patriarchy albeit in black face."[20] *The Wire* reclaims hip-hop music as speaking to authentic black experiences and underscores the black characters having a greater degree of control over their environment.

Ultimately, black characters are psychologically unimpeded by generational expectation as they break from enduring anti-intellectual pressures and cultural stereotypes identified by bell hooks. D'Angelo acquires knowledge to better understand the world, become attuned to his feelings, and forge his own life path. While Bell has D'Angelo executed for trying to break free of the Barksdale family, hooks's model of intellectual development is presented as worth pursuing. Cutty and Bubbles achieve redemption along these lines in later seasons, and D'Angelo could have broken free had Bell not acted secretly without Avon's approval. There is also a logic to Bell and Barksdale's running of their drug-dealing organization that challenges hooks's sociological observations regarding how power is maintained in black subculture. While both bosses are keen to instill deference in their staff through anti-intellectualism, they are not simply propagating the pursuit of wealth as a narcissistic soulless pursuit. They are seeking to gain a degree of control over their environment and circumstances as articulated by the rap music they listen to. In comparison, white characters are imperiled to varying degrees by their surroundings imbued by histories of eighteenth-century revolutionary privateering, nineteenth-century industrial innovation, and twentieth-century modernization, all amidst twenty-first-century gentrification. Frank Sobotka desperately tries to stall technological updates, begging Coxson for another year as treasurer. Coxson retorts that "it's our turn" in reference to his ethnicity. Frank tries to deter Coxson by imploring, "Black, white, what's the difference Nat? Until we get that canal dredged we're all n——s," to which Coxson instantly snaps backs, "Or Polaks." The white dockworkers are now at the bottom rung of the social pecking order for the first time and are desperately unequipped to deal with the hardships black people have endured for four centuries. Correspondingly, real-life dockworkers took exception to the way their vocation had been portrayed by the show, protesting that they had been depicted as "nothing but a bunch of thugs and dummies." However, Benewicz (the real-life inspiration for Frank Sobotka) managed to quash any outspoken rallies against the show, reminding his International Longshoremen's Association that the HBO production was bringing a lot of revenue—and union jobs—to the state of Maryland.[21] Despite any reservations that dockworkers had with how they were presented, the viewing figures of season 2 were the highest that the entire five seasons would achieve. Perhaps Simon and Burns had tapped into an enduring unconscious racial bias. Simon noticed, "We introduced a bunch of white characters and the numbers started going up." Nevertheless, a sustained comparative analysis between white and black characters through the course of this chapter reveals that season 2 confronts enduring anti-intellectual black stereotypes when juxtaposed against the social realist plight of white dockworkers. While this uptick in ratings meant that "everyone thought we had a plan to grow the show," the focus of the following season had not yet been decided.[22] Former schoolteacher Ed Burns was keen to focus on education, but given the racial politics at play in season 2 both on-screen and in terms of its viewing figures, Simon felt strongly that season 3 ought to examine Baltimore's political class, as "you just can't understand the streets without understanding politics."[23]

SEASON 3

The War on Drugs

Revolving season 3 around a fictional councilman confounded the writers' room. George Pelecanos found politics "fucking boring."[1] Burns felt that "every moment we saw of politics was one less moment we conceived a character that I liked." But Simon stood firm: "You can't get into education without establishing what oversees it."[2] Deferring their season on education for another year meant that *The Wire* would enter City Hall. To make their politics enrapturing, Pelecanos and Simon cornered novelist Richard Price at a Washington bookstore signing. After mulling the offer, Price met with Simon, Burns, and Pelecanos to outline political story arcs. But they soon struggled with authenticity. Political journalist Bill Zorzi was immediately hired. Having spent two decades chronicling politics for *The Baltimore Sun*, Zorzi was the man to populate Tommy Carcetti's story with realistic jargon, procedures, and stories. Even then, laying bare the ills of local politics proved to be their biggest challenge yet. But as the writers spitballed ideas, they heard of policy developments emerging in Switzerland, Holland, and Portugal treating heroin addiction as a health problem. Quickly, they sketched out ways they could dramatize attempts to legalize drugs in the United States.

With a lukewarm HBO taking much longer to green-light another season, tragedy struck. Executive producer Bob Colesberry died during heart surgery. Colesberry's ashes were scattered, and the funeral of his character, Ray Cole, was written into the series. Colesberry's final act had been casting Aiden Gillen six months before he passed. Arriving on set looking like a punk rocker, Gillen recalls Simon accosting him: "You were Bob Coles-berry's casting call, so whether we really wanted you or not, we had to give you the job." Promptly, Gillen was given a haircut and change of clothes. Zorzi took the Irishman, unfamiliar with the inner workings of local government, on a crash course into U.S. politics. It's no secret that Simon's old adversary Mayor O' Malley was chief inspiration for Gillen's character. Tommy Carcetti is a white councilman who splits the black vote to become mayor and later governor. In riposte, O'Malley likened the producers to drug dealers. For him, both are "the only people who benefit from the perpetuation of the city's past record of drugs and violence." O'Malley "would say that," Zorzi bit back. Carcetti's familiar tough-on-drugs rhetoric does "not lend itself to the life-and-death questions that the street world and police work often deal with." The purpose of season 3, then, is to demonstrate how "politics has everything to do with the war on drugs."[3] Correspondingly, this chapter tells the history of the War on Drugs, examines its impact on Baltimore, and uncovers how the season speaks to criminological studies into the allure of drug taking and dealing. It then considers why the decriminalization of drugs fails according to political science.

THE WAR ON DRUGS

The "War on Drugs" is shorthand for a federal escalation of drugs laws. At a 1971 press conference, President Richard Nixon declared drug abuse as "public enemy number one" when waging his new, all-out offensive. Holding individuals accountable for drug use, the 1970 Comprehensive Drug Abuse Prevention and Control Act shifted responsibility for drug enforcement from the Department of the Treasury to the Department of Justice. Given a proliferation of heroin addiction, two-thirds of the antidrug budget was allotted for drug treatment. Initially, methadone maintenance programs weaned addicts off the illicit substance. Shortly after Nixon's 1972 election, however, funding for treatment was redirected toward punishing drug users. New York governor Nelson Rockefeller's mandatory minimum sentencing laws meant that within his state lines, offenders were being sentenced solely for the amount of drugs in their possession. With two-thirds of New Yorkers supporting this change, Nixon followed suit. In 1973, the Drug Enforcement Administration was formed to implement the controlled substance laws. Meanwhile, a handful of kingpins with syndicates continued to control narcotics distribution in Baltimore. But as new federal laws were imprisoning adult dealers for lengthier terms, juveniles were brought in. Like Al Capone's Prohibition era, mobsters maintained community tolerance through donations, loans, and gifts. Among the most sophisticated was heroin dealer Maurice "Peanut" King, who carried "the threat of violence like a cloak," not shooting someone unless absolutely necessary.[4]

To break powerful individuals' stranglehold of drug distribution, President Ronald Reagan oversaw the biggest escalation of the drug war in modern history. The 1986 Anti-Drug Abuse Act earmarked $200 million for drug education, $241 million for treatment, but $1.2 billion for enforcement. To trigger a new mandatory minimum sentence, an assailant needed to possess either 500 grams of powdered cocaine or only five grams of crack cocaine. Given its cheaper production costs, crack was more prevalent in low-income minority neighborhoods. Therefore, 90 percent of defendants for crack cocaine charges were black despite usage rates between blacks and whites being roughly even.[5] From 1988, the Anti-Drug Abuse Act then targeted individuals. Running drug-dealing enterprises was an automatic life sentence. Drug users also faced asset forfeiture and had their access to federal benefits and student loans revoked. However, Reagan's biggest impact was the impetus on the mass incarceration of drug offenders and the growth of building prisons. Social programs were ceremoniously slashed, as deterrence was seen as the key to eradicating drug use. Analogously, Baltimore law enforcement waged all-out war against kingpins Ancel Holland, Peanut King, Melvin Stanford, Clarence Meredith, and Melvin Williams. Police Commissioner Frank Battaglia boasted that the million dollars spent annually was paying off, as his police department apprehended 41 high-ranking suppliers, a million dollars in cash, a million dollars more in property, 99 automobiles, and 1,110 guns.[6] But these takedowns did not dent Baltimore's $900 million annual heroin market. Peanut King's territory in East Baltimore descended into chaos as New York City dealers with discounted products pounced on the drug distribution void that had emerged. Criminal empires made way for cocaine cowboys like Tommy Lee Canty, a criminal boss in his early twenties who, lacking an organized crime apprenticeship, turned violence into an act of "impulse and emotion."[7] The accidental shooting of bystanders, a rare event in the kingpin era, became common. Homicide rates climbed sharply given extreme poverty, an unwieldy drug market, teenage immaturity, and abundant handguns. The harsher prison sentences that were dished out were regarded with vague indifference, as dealers were now conditioned to carry it like it means nothing.

During Bill Clinton's second campaign for president, Republicans attacked his relaxed approach to drug enforcement. So the president dramatically increased federal drug control spending from $1.5 billion in 1989 to $18.5 billion in 2000. By the time George W. Bush entered office, interdiction costs had risen 1,200 percent, punishment for drug offenses was often greater than for murder, and the prison population had skyrocketed from 300,000 in 1972 to 2.3 million. Tripling the rate of arrests from 580,900 in 1980 to 1,846,400 in 2005 had not decreased the demand for illegal substances. For Baltimore, a perpetual escalation of enforcement on drug users had disproportionately impacted black residents. In Maryland between 1996 and 2001, 81 percent of individuals sentenced for drug offenses were African American.[8] At this time, Baltimore became a key East Coast distribution point for Colombian heroin. Substantially more potent than its East Asian and Mexican counterparts, its higher strength, increased availability, and reduced price saw Baltimore crowned heroin capital of the United States in 2001. As *The Wire* first entered production, research by the Drug Enforcement Administration revealed that the city had the highest per-capita heroin addiction rate in the country at 10 percent. With drug-related crimes producing a homicide rate above the national average, Baltimore became known as "Bulletmore."

SEASON 3

Against this political context, season 3 begins with the demolition of Franklin Terrace towers, the Barksdale crew's most prized territory, pushing their dealers back out onto the streets. Avon Barksdale is released from prison early for his role in unveiling the cause of inmate deaths and takes against Stringer Bell's efforts to legitimize B&B Enterprises that now siphons its drug dealing income into property development. The show's writers were also aware that the new generation of drug dealers were decidedly detached from their ascendants, no longer playing the game with a sense of morality, decorum, and unbreakable rules. So a ruthless, borderline psychopathic rival for the Barksdale organization reflected this transformation. Against Bell's wishes, Avon decides to take his new rival Marlo Stanfield's (Jamie Hector) territories by force. Both gangs become embroiled in a bitter turf war with multiple deaths. With dwindling enforcer numbers including Dennis "Cutty" Wise (Chad L. Coleman), who retires to teach boxing; Omar robbing stash houses; Senator Clay Davis (Isiah Whitlock Jr.) defrauding B&B Enterprises; and Cedric Daniels's now-permanent Major Crimes Unit monitoring Barksdale's crew, Avon Barksdale's monopoly on Baltimore's drug trade enters its final days.

CURRIE'S FOUR MODELS OF DRUG USE

As drug-related harms were ravaging through North America, criminologists attempted to understand why overwhelming concentrations of youthful heroin addiction had become a new urban reality despite stricter enforcement. In mapping the commonalities between studies of drug abuse, Elliott Currie proposes four explanations for persistent illicit drug activity. His first is the status model. Here dealing is a draw for young Americans in deprived areas, not just for the monetary reward. Overseen by "fierce and all-pervading emphasis on acceptance by one's youthful peers," a short, violent life is preferred over the "ordinary world (of low wages, low status, and ceaseless, petty frustrations)." The "narrow legitimate employment options for poor youth" affront a person's self-esteem and dignity. Young adults interviewed across comprehensive studies had undergone several negative experiences in the low-wage labor market, regularly experiencing abusive, exploitative, and racist supervisors. They were drawn to dealing because self-employment in the illicit economy provided a "more dignified workplace" with the possibility to sustain a "sense of autonomy." Therefore, once young people have been thoroughly immersed in a lifestyle centered on the "excitement of violence, risk taking, and illicit acquisition" and the status this provides it is "much harder to interest them in accepting constraints of steady work."[9]

From the bottom of Barksdale's operation to the very top, all crew members value Currie's "status." In the first episode, we experience the excitement of violence and risk-taking that the hoppers are immersed in. Herc and Carver conduct a botched street arrest in a scene that was purposefully constructed as an homage to *Apocalypse Now* (1979), where an entire tree line is napalmed and a village attacked to take the surfing point away from the Vietcong. The simple plan of cutting off a block to seize drugs escalates out of hand as the officers fall victim to a well-rehearsed decoy counteroperation. Failing to capture a young boy running with what appears to be the stash through alleyways results in a fleet of marked police cars and a helicopter being called within seconds. The sequence concludes with a frustrated Carver jumping on the roof of his car, declaring that if the boy does not present himself and "you make us come back here tomorrow . . . I swear to fucking Christ we will beat you long and harder than you beat your own dick cos you do not get to win shitbird, we do." His increasingly maddened threats are punctuated by long shots that frame Carver as a lone, isolated figure, emphasizing his increasingly frenzied body language as his arms flail at each side and he beats his chest. The corner boys are not dealing drugs just for financial gain but also to enjoy the thrill of the chase.

There is a marked contrast between the boy openly smiling while running in a carefree childlike manner as if playing a game of hide-and-seek compared to the stressed, determined, and regimented Carver, who swings his arms backward and forward as he scowls, running after the boy. The young hoppers' ability to autonomously dictate events and control their environment in a way that outsmarts and publicly humiliates an entire police unit and its reinforcements is reward enough. It is a sense of achievement and pride that legitimate employment cannot provide. The children have outmaneuvered the police (essentially an "occupying army") and its far-superior resources.

Even experienced high-level enforcer Cutty struggles working as a landscaper. In episode 4, "Amsterdam," Cutty's boss explains that the extreme working conditions are consistent: "it's hot every day," he'll be in "the hard truck bouncing around every day," and his "back's going to be yelling . . . every day." The boss points out that "compared to pretty gold convertibles . . . there ain't a reward to leaving street . . . this is it." Reminded that he has been employed not for his skills but solely as cheap labor, Cutty returns to Barksdale. Here Cutty receives rewards in abundance that are not solely materialistic as his former landscaping boss implied. Cutty is respected by his peers for the skills that he has attained for enforcing the corners. Sitting in Slim Charles's (Anwan Glover) car, Cutty teaches young soldiers Sapper (Brandan T. Tate) and Gerard (Mayo Best) how to determine whether a dealer is stealing from Barksdale through surveillance. Cutty instructs Charles and his staff to pay attention to what jewelry the accused's girlfriend is wearing, as this will reveal whether the suspected dealer is stealing. Compared to being kept in the back of a truck like an expendable tool in his landscaping job, here Cutty sits in the back of a car with his own driver and team as he bestows valued knowledge from the back seat. Impressed with his knowledge and as further recognition of this newfound status, Charles gives Cutty a SIG silent handgun that holds more bullets and emits less sound than the enforcer is used to using. Following Cutty's failed attempts to start a lawnmower, which prompted the decisive chat with his then landscaping employer, Cutty is now treated with dignity. Here he is rewarded with autonomy to problem solve, his own respectful trainees, and a specialized handgun that he is unfamiliar with using regularly but is entrusted to operate given his skill. All these rewards amount to status compared to the lack of incentive that legal employment provides.

Pursing status also causes Bell and Barksdale to meet their demise. Their conflicting quests to derive respect from different peer groups result in Barksdale ordering Bell's execution after Bell leaks Barksdale's safe house location to the police. Bell is committed to turning their drug money into legitimate income, and he courts Senator Clay Davis to renovate residential properties in West Baltimore. Bell informs Barksdale that he seeks the approval of businessmen because he wants to avoid paying for consistent profits with "bodies" and prison time when it can be achieved through investing and diplomacy. Bell feels that he has graduated from the risk-taking from which Currie found young dealers deriving excitement. But Bell's legitimizing of B&B Enterprises is still driven by the fierce peer approval that Currie identified is required by dealers. After Bell's property developer consultant, Andy Krawczyk (Michael Willis), longingly gazes at Chunky Coates, who now owns a wealth of properties thanks to Clay Davis, Bell marches into Davis's office demanding that the senator fast-track B&B's property investments in an attempt to achieve the same levels of respect he commands from his street dealers. Comparatively, Barksdale continues to cultivate their street status. As Bell spends more time lunching with politicians and the drug dealers' cooperative in expensive suits, Barksdale continues to reside in their industrial safe house unit dressed in military regalia, surrounded by weaponry, including grenades and semiautomatic weapons, to plot with his trusted enforcer Slim Charles how they will "take corners" from Stanfield by force. Here Barksdale clutches his handgun for reassurance when arguing with Bell and derives strength from it when strategizing, often pointing it at his soldiers when issuing orders. Whenever Bell tries to convince Barksdale to invest in property or share business with Prop Joe's cooperative, Barksdale appears distracted instead, admiring his handgun or pressing it against his face for comfort. As they part ways, Bell infantizes Barksdale's obsession with street "rep[utation]," attributing it to their younger selves when they dreamed of a time that "our names could ring out on ghetto street corners." Now Bell feels that his newfound political peers have provided "the world at our feet." But after discovering that Davis and Krawczyk have been pocketing their money and making a fool of Bell all along, it becomes apparent that the reputations their names carry on street corners are all they ever had. There is logic to Barksdale's obsession with weaponry, militarized campaigns, and "playing soldier." He may be on the losing side of a turf war, but at least he still retains the autonomy, dignity, and status that Currie identified within his decreasing circles of influence, something that Bell can never derive from exploitative businessmen when he is doomed to be dragged down by his drug-dealing past.

Currie's second theory for persistent drug abuse despite increased federal enforcement is the coping model.[10] For many users, drugs help moderate the stress and insecurity of life within deprived communities. In inner-city areas, it can be harder to make ends meet given family crises, abusive relationships, lack of transportation, limited health care, no child care provision, housing problems, and stressful, insecure, low-paid work. Surrounded by triggers of endemic stress, drugs can become a way of medicating against emotional anguish, anxiety, and pain, a "functional" means of achieving some "mastery over specific life stresses." Edward Preble discovered high drug use levels among Puerto Rican youth in New York because, as an addict put it, "when you use drugs you substitute one big problem—which you can concentrate on—for a whole lot of different little problems."[11] Studies agree that addicts do not regard as their most pressing problem their drug use but rather their response to a litany of much worse predicaments, including the lack of access to basic food, shelter, and clothing.

Bubbles also takes drugs to cope with the competing stresses of his life. In episode 1 of season 3, he begins his day by accidentally damaging Cheese's car when transporting stolen radiators for scrap. Threatened with being shot, Bubbles's and Weeks's lives are spared by Marlo because Bubbles promises to use their scrap money to fix the car, and both give their trousers as a deposit. Instead, both addicts keep the money to buy new trousers and try to get high by sharing the one vial they can afford with their remaining money. Despite it being a bright afternoon, both addicts sit shrouded in darkness. Bubbles is annoyed at how it has all been "a long way to go for half a shot." Weeks tries to reassure him that "it'll be better tomorrow" as he starts entering a semicomatose state. Bubbles retorts, "Today I hunted down all that metal, I lugged it around like a dog. And nearly get killed over a scratch of metal so I had to beg for my life. Lost my trousers . . . . And then I'm beggin' again for half a shot" and "I'm not even high." Within the opening 10 minutes of the season, viewers have witnessed, as Preble identified, Bubbles substituting the problem of securing drugs for a series of three smaller problems: making ends meet, pleading for his life, and securing clothing. As the drugs start to kick in and medicate Bubbles from the mental anguish and physical pain he has experienced through the day, both characters jump out of their seats in shock as they hear shots outside. Within this deliberately darkened space, Bubbles and Weeks shelter themselves in a sleep-like stupor away from the ruthless lawlessness occurring right outside the window. Compared to the fast-paced cutting and tracking movements accompanying the thrill-seeking children evading Carver's arrest in the scene immediately before, this scene is filmed by a single long, drawn-out shot. Here Bubbles discusses the physically exhausting, traumatic, and humiliating experiences that one day has had on his well-being. This one long take moving steadily across the room and into Bubbles's face evokes the calming stillness that drugs provide the protagonist. Heroin momentarily permits him to master his immediate environment from a host of problems, including the chaos erupting outside.

The third principal reason for criminologists discovering that drug use was rife in deprived communities Currie defines as the structure model.[12] This is where people feel that their lives have been denied purpose and meaning compared to those living in more affluent areas who attach their worth to work and family. In this context, drug use can provide a sense of structure and purpose to those denied stable, meaningful work. Analogously, studies identified that the most important determinants of addicts relapsing following treatment are the degree of stability and structure available in their life, whether there is access to steady work, and if there is any prospect of caring for others.

Cutty manages to cut all ties with Barksdale once he finds structure, purpose, and meaning in teaching children boxing, something he cannot find in legitimate or illegitimate employment alone. It is the local Deacon (Melvin Williams) who, after a series of conversations, has the idea to channel Cutty's need to find meaningful fulfillment into opening a community gym. Initially, Cutty complains that the hoppers are too "wild," having thrown gym equipment around and undercut his instructions with homophobic slurs during their first training session. However, once advised to be more patient, Cutty perseveres and hosts a tournament with a Philadelphia boxing club in the penultimate episode, "Middle Ground." During the tournament, a handheld camera maneuvers right up against, between, underneath, and around the boxing children. The handheld camera intensifies this freneticism by cutting between a series of angles in close proximity to both fighters that heighten the impact of the heavy blows that Cutty's student Justin (Justin Burley) receives from a more experienced albeit younger opponent. Here Cutty instructs Justin to block, move, get some water, spit, and breathe. These instructions not only enable Justin to maintain two-minute rounds with the more experienced boxer but also permit the camera to rest on a visibly gratified Cutty tempering the scene. Says Pelecanos, "All we wanted to do was show that staying in the ring is a triumph."[13] From outside the ropes, a contemplative still camera observes Cutty overlooking the fight, smiling, nodding, and looking over his boxing prodigy proudly in close-ups. This is a marked contrast from the relationship that Cutty maintains with Barksdale apprentices Gerard and Sapper. In episode 4, "Amsterdam," when previously working for Barksdale, Gerard and Sapper capture the dealer stealing from their boss at night and proceed to beat him to death. Cutty watches from the shadows with a forlorn expression as the two men collectively beat and stamp the man to the ground. Cutty attempts to intervene, instructing both young men to stop "going like that," otherwise there "ain't going to be nothing left of him." In acknowledgment, Sapper stands over the man, unveils a metal bat, and hits the dealer on the head before he and Gerard rifle through the unconscious man's pockets and bicker over his possessions. Having initially found status and dignity in training younger Barksdale enforcers, Cutty finds their excessive bloodied beatings too much to face, literally, as he disappears into the shadows before the two men are finished. When the later boxing match concludes, however, Justin walks to the corner of the ring as the audience applauds, looks up to his coach, and asks, "How'd I do?" Cutty takes off Justin's headgear, looks his student in the eye, and affirms, "You did good," exchanging a fist pump. Throughout the scene, a noticeably proud Cutty, backlit by white light, is visibly gratified by the progress his boxing pupil is making. He now finds caring for others a more satisfying pursuit that imbues his life with structure compared to the status that Barksdale's apprentices ascribed to him, where he was expected to find callous violence as maliciously gratifying as his thrill-seeking enforcers. Focusing on and caring for his boxing apprentices enables Cutty to kick his recreational drug use.

The fourth and final explanation for drugs being so widespread in American inner cities despite stricter enforcement, among leading criminological fieldwork, is what Currie terms the saturation model.[14] Here, when everybody around a person is taking drugs, the decision to use drugs is hardly a decision at all. Studies of U.S. and U.K. cities with high unemployment found it to be a passive drift into a surrounding situation that everyone is doing rather than a conscious choice. Correspondingly, recreational drug abuse is so ingrained within every level of the Barksdale organization that drug taking is not an overtly conscious decision but rather an instinctual habit. As Barksdale starts losing his turf war, heroin paraphernalia begins to regularly surround his person. Cutty's redemptive journey into teaching children to box is all the more powerful because it is entwined with his coming off drugs. When operating surveillance into the dealer believed to be thieving profits from Barksdale, the rest of Cutty's team snort cocaine. When offered some, Cutty initially refuses because he has to provide a clean urine sample for his parole meeting the following day. However, when informed that the dealers around him are also due a parole meeting and can show him how to cheat the urine test, Cutty begins using cocaine with his peers. Similarly, annoyed after his first meeting with the Deacon, who has not instantly provided him with meaningful employment, Cutty attends a party where drugs and women are dispensed as easily as tap water. His initial shock at seeing people openly having sex and doing drugs in public areas is soon replaced with a glazed look of indifference after Slim Charles and Bodie take him into a bathroom and blow back a joint into his face, leaving him little option but to customarily ingest the substance alongside his beers as the others do. It is also this saturation of heroin at street level that leads Major Howard Bunny Colvin's (Robert Wisdom) attempts to legalize drugs. When wracking his brains to devise a solution to increasing crime rates, Colvin drives in his police car at night. Stopping at a red light, Justin attempts to sell Colvin drugs. Despite people in the street yelling "Narcos" as a warning and the rest of his team taking a step back from the car, Justin approaches the police car window and offers Colvin Spider Bags. In response, Colvin deliberately turns up his police car radio louder, but this action does not even register with Justin, as he simply asks, "You up or not?" It is only when Bunny puts his police hat on and looks Justin in the eye that the hopper steps back in fear and all the other corner boys laugh. Being so focused on selling heroin, Justin has not acknowledged the police regalia. He has become so conditioned to sell to whoever rolls by that he is not making a conscious decision when selling; it has just become a habitual routine. Whether characters interact with drugs for status, coping, structure, or saturation, season 3 agrees with Currie that drug abuse is an endemic "social phenomenon" for meeting "human needs that are systematically thwarted by social and

Figure 5.1. Cutty's path to redemption through the Deacon is not straightforward. HBO/ Photofest © HBO.

economic structures."[15] Illicit drugs are not simply a question of "individual" or "biochemical" need as was believed by War on Drugs policy, an issue that Colvin seeks to redress by decriminalizing drugs.

DECRIMINALIZING DRUGS AND POLITICAL SCIENCE

With drug dealing spreading more throughout the city, soon-to-retire Major Howard "Bunny" Colvin, commander of the Western District, sets up free zones, or "Hamsterdams," where drug dealing goes unpunished. Colvin uses this clandestine strategy to satisfy the recently promoted Chief Commissioner Burrell and Deputy Ops Rawls. Both are being pressured into meeting impossible crime reduction targets by the ambitious chair of the Public Safety Committee, Tommy Carcetti. The councilman sees a tougher approach to law and order as a platform for launching his mayoral campaign. But when Colvin's strategy becomes public knowledge, he is ordered to terminate his Hamsterdam directive. The former commander shoulders all the blame for the ensuing media frenzy and reluctantly accepts a demotion that ensures that he retires from the police department on a lower-grade pension.

Political figures receiving public backlash for attempting to legalize drugs is not a completely fictional tale for Baltimore City. During Reagan's drug war expansion in 1988, then Baltimore mayor Kurt Schmoke testified before the House Select Committee on Narcotics Abuse and Control, declaring that "we can guarantee that if we continue doing what we're doing, we will fail." Schmoke proposed, "If we're going to have a new war on drugs, let it be led by the surgeon general, not the attorney general," before suggesting "a measured and carefully implemented program of drug decriminalization." Committee chairman Charles B. Rangel immediately labeled Schmoke "the most dangerous man in America." The nickname stuck, and the politician once touted to become a future Democratic Party leader had left his political future in tatters. When Schmoke decided not to run for a fourth mayoral term in 1999, he believed that he did not have anything new to offer the city's escalating rate of deadly violence, producing more than 300 murders per year. By then, crack cocaine and new gangs had blown apart the city's older and comparatively stable heroin and marijuana operations in East and West Baltimore. He felt that "we were still making progress in some areas, but Baltimore was still a tale of two cities."[16]

Schmoke was ahead of his time, as his public stance on drug enforcement predated a new school of thought emerging during season 3's production called critical criminology. Unlike traditional criminology and its sole interest in street-level crime as recorded and defined by criminal law, critical criminology is interested in how widening inequalities—particularly how increasingly powerful, unaccountable corporations amass wealth—cause indirect harms for people living in concentrated areas of unemployment. Therefore, through season 3, juxtapositions occur between Baltimore's political leaders and the conversations they have at fancy restaurants and those whose lives are impacted by such decision-making. In this spirit, political scientists Kirkpatrick, Lester, and Peterson created a framework called police termination theory for better understanding why political policies combating inequality become terminated.[17] Applying this model to Colvin's policy of decriminalizing drugs enables us to better understand its failure.

HAMSTERDAM'S POLICY CHARACTERISTICS

Kirkpatrick, Lester, and Peterson believe that the first characteristic of a policy is its "reason for being." They argue that the mission of the policy must be relevant and that its purposes must not appear outdated or illegitimate in order for it to survive. From the get-go, Colvin struggles to articulate the purpose of his decriminalizing drugs to his Western District officers. In episode 2, "All Due Respect," Colvin announces the immediate suspension of undercover operations in the Western District following Officer Dozerman's critical condition after an undercover operation went awry. Standing at his briefing podium, Colvin unveils a brown paper bag. He explains that following the public consumption of alcohol becoming illegal, the first person to conceal a pint of elderberry through a brown paper bag created a "civic compromise" that "allowed corner boys to drink in peace and gave us permission to do the kind of police work that is actually worth taking a bullet for." Allegorically, Bunny reminds his officers that Dozerman was shot trying to buy three vials as he slowly drops one small vial at a time into the brown paper bag in close-up. He takes a moment before concluding, "There has never been a paper bag for drugs, until now." His poignantly symbolic approach to contextualizing the War on Drugs proves to be an indecipherable way of announcing a new decriminalizing policy. The scene immediately cuts to Herc and Carver sitting in their unmarked police car watching dealers selling drugs and frustrated that they can no longer intervene. Herc ruminates in frustration, "If we ain't doing hand to hands, then what the fuck?" and "That shit with the bag, what the fuck is that?" He is puzzled by Colvin's symbolic methods of launching the new free zones. When Colvin speaks at the podium, he has plaques of fallen officers mounted on the wall behind him. It is a conscious decision to deliberately juggle a "small wrinkled-ass paper bag" in one hand and even smaller and lighter vials in another against the memorials of fallen officers. Drawing a link between the fragility of officer lives and illicit substances is lost on both officers, as they still see their street-level arrests as police work worth dying for. The mission and purpose of Colvin's policy is not clearly stated enough to win over his officers, so much so that in episode 7, "Back Burners," McNulty, Greggs, and Sydnor stumble across Bodie pleading immunity when transporting drugs to a free zone. They ask Carver what is going on. Colvin spontaneously laughs. Because the reasoning behind Hamsterdam has not been properly outlined to Western District officers, it feels absurd attempting to explain it out loud. To regular police officers, comparing 1920s Prohibition with drug policing feels irrelevant, outdated, and illegitimate.

Second, in terms of policy characteristics, Kirkpatrick, Lester, and Peterson feel that the longevity of a policy mitigates against termination. Colvin's Hamsterdam policy is doomed to fail, as he regularly justifies it as a temporary measure when trying to convert the uninformed. Arriving at Bodie's arrest, Colvin asks Greggs, McNulty, and Sydnor not to inform headquarters because once things settle, he "will make a big show of locking everybody up and shut it down." As an afterthought, he adds, "The longer I have before having to brief the bosses, the more of a case I might have to prove how it works." This final point is a new development that was never factored into the policy's conception. As late as episode 9, "Slapstick," when revealing that the Hamsterdams exist to the local Deacon, Colvin shirks responsibility of his initiative's future survival on to his superiors. He explains, "They wanna keep my little experiment going that's on them" given his "plan to retire." It is only here, when the Deacon asks, "What happens when you turn the district over and there's nobody to defend it?" that Colvin first begins to think about its longevity. Not until later, when Johns Hopkins public health academics and charities install needle exchanges, condom distribution, on-site blood testing, food packages, and drug treatments, do the health benefits become apparent. This proves too little too late. Colvin only manages to convince McNulty and the Major Crimes Unit staff from informing their superiors about the free zones when McNulty interrupts Colvin's ill-thought through policy longevity. Here McNulty takes Colvin to one side to seek clarification that their bosses do not know. Colvin affirms, "Fuck the bosses," to which McNulty smiles in agreement. True to his character, McNulty convinces his team to keep quiet, as he derives pleasure from seeing Rawls and Burrell humiliated. Outsmarting their superiors means more to McNulty than the longer-term benefits of legalizing drugs, something that was not built into Colvin's policy from the start.

Interestingly, Kirkpatrick, Lester, and Peterson's third policy characteristic that prevents a program's termination is invisibility. Public exposure leads to termination, as organizations that are concealed from the public avoid regular scrutiny. Operating covertly enables Colvin's Hamsterdam policy to come into existence. He locates three free zone sites simply by scouting areas with his deputy, Dennis Mello (Jay Landsman), in secret. At Armistead Gardens, in episode 3, "Dead Soldiers," Mello asks Colvin whether it is a good idea not to tell anyone. Colvin confirms that "ignorance is bliss, Lieutenant," as if conferring with Kirkpatrick, Lester, and Peterson. Colvin issues this Chaucerian quote as the camera cuts to a long shot of both men through the inside of one of the vacant properties scheduled for demolition with barred windows and broken glass framing their tiny figures. Directly associating broken glass with ignorance is a pointed comment at the failure of broken windows theory, which has guided policing the War on Drugs. This punishing of all minor infractions with the maximum possible penalties to prevent the spread of crime has not lessened rates of homicide or drug taking in Baltimore. Maintaining secrecy is what protects both men, their superiors, and their subordinate officers from prosecution. When Colvin achieves a 12 percent cumulative crime reduction, he does not reveal his methods. Rawls remains suspicious but is satisfied with the results and so does not probe further. Colvin initially convinces a *Sun* reporter (tipped off by Herc) not to cover the story for another week, as it will jeopardize the alleged bigger cases. Colvin pretends he is in the process of securing a high profile arrest having pushed trafficking into designated areas. This extended invisibility is what then enables Colvin to make sufficient headway in improving the conditions of the Hamsterdams with academics and charities. However, what forces Mayor Royce's initial willingness to maintain Colvin's methods ceases when Carcetti informs news reporters that Royce's office is complicit in the harms of drug addiction. Like policy termination theory, visibility directly leads to its termination.

In accordance with Kirkpatrick, Lester, and Peterson's study, the policy fails because it is not complex enough to survive. Hamsterdams are sourced by two men without the support of any superiors, political actors, specialists, or their Western District staff. In episode 6, "Homecoming," Colvin discovers an elderly lady still living in what he thought was an empty block in the Broadway area. He manages to convince his superiors to approve her for social housing as an "essential state's witness." Then Colvin finds it increasingly difficult to maintain order in the Hamsterdams, as certain dealers begin robbing one another and a hopper is shot. To preserve the Hamsterdams, in episode 9, "Slapstick," the body is illegally moved off the block so that Homicide investigators will not be drawn to Colvin's experiment. He then negotiates with the drug dealers, asking them to bring him the murderer so that he can protect the operation to which they comply. Kirkpatrick, Lester, and Peterson feel that a complex policy dealing with complex issues appears to be more resilient against termination pressures. This ad hoc policy, however, enacted and prolonged by the efforts of one commander, is increasingly vulnerable.

Kirkpatrick, Lester, and Peterson's fifth and final policy characteristic, crucial for initiatives enduring termination, is a policy's distribution of benefits. Simon himself believes that a cost-benefit analysis of Colvin's Hamsterdams would reveal "how a utopian idea" can become a "dystopian nightmare no matter how good the intentions."[18] Once the Western District cops convince the mid-level dealers to operate from the free zones, the benefits to Colvin's Western district are stark and immediate. Episode 6, "Homecoming," opens with a montage of idyllic corners, shot with a warm orange hue, with elderly residents hanging out washing and watering plants outside their front doors while the young sell lemonade, play basketball, and ride scooters. The benefit of moving drug dealers to designated areas produces utopic scenes of the young and old enjoying their locality without fear.

In the next episode, "Back Burners," however, Bubbles stumbles on the Hamsterdams and finds a nightmarish space. For the Western District corners to benefit, the cost is a scenario too unbearable for a seasoned addict to stomach. Academics Busfield, Owens and Twomey liken Bubbles entering Hamsterdam to Dante Alighieri's *Inferno*, the first volume of a three-part poem, *The Divine Comedy*, that recounts a journey from hell (Inferno) to purgatory (Purgatorio) and then to heaven (Paradiso). Reversing this formula, having already experienced the paradise that Colvin has created, Bubbles now enters a contemporary equivalent to Dante's nine circles of hell and the sins they represent.

Bubbles enters the designated Hamsterdam area at night as "darkness [also] shadow'd o'er the place." A viewer occupies Bubbles's POV interspersed with tight close-ups of his scared, disbelieving reactions to individuals overindulging in consumables—Dante's gluttony—in the form of alcohol and drugs to the point of vomiting. In among the streets filled with "shadowy smoke," where "tormented souls" wander aimlessly, Bubbles first sees adolescents fighting, emulating Dante's circle of wrath, where inhabitants fight for all eternity. Bubbles is then confronted by a young man who aggressively attempts to sell his radio. This represents the circle of "greed" populated by souls who spent their lives squandering possessions. When Bubbles politely declines the offer, the seller is irked, leans into Bubbles's face, and yells "fuck you" twice before kicking Bubbles's trolley. The greed morphs into an act typical of Dante's circle of "violence," where those who have disfigured people and property are imprisoned. Bubbles then comes across a man who wishes to buy candles and toilet paper. The man addresses Bubbles as "sellerman," mimicking the name "Soloman," and projects his deep, booming voice and open arm gesturing from his doorstep as if preaching. While besmirching a religious figure, the man's wild-eyed face and unkempt hair are illuminated orange from the open fires burning outside and inside his property, thus embodying one of Dante's "arch-heretics." Belonging to the circle of "heresy," the dealer is similarly entombed with all his drug-using followers in "degrees of heat," unable to leave the house in case his stash is stolen.[19] Bubbles agrees to return with the household amenities the dealer needs but is tempted by Dante's "treachery" as Bubbles's terrified body language suggests that breaking the trust struck with the drug dealer would be preferable to his own safety. Bubbles is then confronted by Dante's "Lust" as he sees a woman fellating a drug dealer on a chair out in the open. Averting his gaze, Bubbles finds Johnny Weeks in a doorway. Bubbles tries to persuade his friend to leave the property, but Weeks declines eerily, whispering, "Look around you, it's a soldiers' paradise man." This is Dante's "limbo," an inferior form of heaven within a boarded-up dwelling where sinners spend eternity. Distracted by the sight of another wrathful fight breaking out, Bubbles turns back around and finds that Weeks has disappeared back into the property, where his body will later be found.

When Colvin attempts to convince Carcetti of the Hamsterdams' benefits, he again reverses the ordering of Dante's *Divine Comedy*. In episode 11, "Middle Ground," the commander takes the councilman first to the now quiet idyllic corner where Dozerman was shot, the Western District police station where police now have the resource to detain a criminal responsible for 14 church burglaries, and a community center where the public praises the police's newfound ability to know all the residents by name. After showing Carcetti "the good," Colvin braces him for "the ugly." As Carcetti walks down the street, his journey is filmed in the same manner as Bubbles's discovery of the Hamsterdams. Pelecanos instructed that a hellish atmosphere be evoked by the actors' eyes. So director Joe Chapelle filmed the close-ups at 24 frames per second using a superlong lens to tighten in on Bubbles's and Carcetti's faces as they register the "dysfunctionality" of the free zones. Both scenes are deliberately overlaid with "so much sound" that you "can't isolate" individual sounds other than touts shouting "redtops" to sell heroin.[20]

In the utopian areas, camera movements are dictated by citizens riding bikes or scooters and running with basketballs. This is at odds with the free zones where the camera clings to the face of anyone who enters, slowing down time, accompanied by a cacophony of sounds to evoke the shock they experience. As Simon reflects, "Hamsterdam is no glorious liberal easy solution. We wanted to make it as ugly as it might be. At the same time the rest of the district did become livable. That trade-off is an honest one and is one that ought to be considered."[21] In line with Kirkpatrick, Lester, and Peterson's policy termination theory, Colvin's Hamsterdams fail because they meet only one of the political scientists' characteristics that can guard against policy termination: invisibility from public scrutiny. Despite Colvin's unclear mission and purpose, lack of longevity, and complexity, this unequal distribution of policy benefits is the final nail in the coffin for a policy surrounded by the all-encompassing federal War on Drugs doctrine.

THE WIDER POLITICAL ENVIRONMENT

It is this political environment surrounding Colvin that also ensures that his Hamsterdam policy fails. Kirkpatrick, Lester, and Peterson explain that the first variable of the political environment affecting termination is a system's prevailing political ideology. At the city level, this fictional Baltimore's political sphere is ridden with people clamoring only to increase their power, wealth, and influence. As Simon envisaged, "Everybody is passing a buck, everybody is inconsistent, everybody is willing to manipulate facts to their own personal advantage."[22] Councilman Carcetti wants to become mayor, so he uses his subcommittee to apply pressure on Royce, Burrell, and Rawl's leadership of the BPD. This personal career ambition is what results in all three men committing to dropping felonies by 4 to 5 percent and keeping murders below 250 for the year. When Colvin's Hamsterdams emerge from these targets, Mayor Royce attempts to pin the blame on Burrell, but Burrell suggests that, in exchange for seeing through the rest of his term as police commissioner, they blame Colvin alone. Otherwise, Burrell will tell the press how each district was purposefully pressured into manipulating statistics. Congruently, the Hamsterdams are blamed squarely on Colvin, the "solitary police commander who under great pressure proved to be amoral, incompetent, and unfit for command," as Rawls states at the committee hearing in the final episode. Then at the state and federal levels, Royce agrees with federal government representatives from Washington, D.C., that Colvin's actions were an aberration and in no way reflect the policies of his administration.

Royce makes this commitment to the U.S. attorney and deputy drug czar so that his city will not lose $292 million for law enforcement, their operating budget, capital expenditures, and up to half a billion tax dollars distributed from state capital Annapolis annually. Royce is forced to continue deterring drug use via enforcement by the economic doctrine of more powerful federal institutions willing to bankrupt the entire city. The power that these higher offices retain is also a draw for the ambitious city politicians who are legally and economically tied to the prevailing political ideology of the War on Drugs if they want to secure promotion.

Working against an overriding ideology proves insurmountable for Kirkpatrick, Lester, and Peterson's second feature of a political environment seeking termination: the size, strength, and determination of anti-termination coalitions. Coalitions within Colvin's Western District are not strong enough or unified enough to push back against city, state, and federal institutions ceasing the free zone policy. The agreement that Colvin strikes between his police staff and drug dealers is fragile at best. The only way that Colvin manages to convince his officers to buy in to the idea of the free zones is through the promise of unleashing violence against drug dealers. Colvin unveils his new strategic plan for the district in episode 3, "Dead Soldiers," after his deliberately poetic paper bag speech. When Colvin clarifies that drug dealers will "go about their business without any interference from us" in designated areas, his staff are riled that they will be unable to "look them in the eye." To win over the room of Western District officers, Colvin hints that the payoff for them will be doing "real police work." Colvin allegorically and rhetorically asks, "Would you rather shoot a fish in the ocean, or would you rather gather them up, carry in a few small barrels?" But what clinches their commitment is Mello cutting in, reassuring them that "you still get to kick the shit out of the mopes who don't move off our corners," instantly ushering in laughter, applause, and cheering from the officers. Colvin has more difficulty winning the trust of the dealers, who suspect that it is a police trick to round them up and apprehend all of them. To first obtain trust from mid-level dealers, Colvin gathers all of them up and promises to unleash "biblical" violence on those "bucking the new system" compared to "the smart ones," who will be "making money hand over fist." This promise of making more money and avoiding severe beatings is not quite enough. To make the Hamsterdams operational, Colvin instructs his officers to bang noncompliant dealers senseless as long as "it can walk itself out the emergency room." We then see a montage of arrests in episode 6, "Homecoming," where dealers' shoes are thrown down the drain and their cars seized. They are then slammed against police vans, pepper sprayed, and disposed of in the woods, where they are instructed to follow the North Star to get home with their hands still tied. This is a coalition forged in violence. The officers who are dispensing physical injuries on drug dealers experience great catharsis whilst those on the receiving end of such brutality are prevented from selling heroin from their favored location given the intensity and regularity of such violence. Thus, meting out physical injuries proves to be the clinching factor for both parties. Neither officer nor drug dealer are ideologically unified as they are still guided by prejudices instilled by the war on drugs.

According to Kirkpatrick, Lester, and Peterson, the penultimate factor within a political environment that can mitigate against policy termination are the possibilities for compromise. Unfortunately, within the police force, there is no willingness to compromise immediately above Colvin. The CompStat meetings chaired by Rawls and Burrell are effectively show trials where all commanders must account for their district's crime statistics. If majors cannot deliver on the 4 percent drop in crime, they are humiliated in front of their peers. CompStat was a method of policing developed by the New York Police Department where regular performance meetings compared crime statistics to hold police leaders accountable for their delivery of crime reduction strategies. While established to provide a degree of responsibility, coordination, and debate among police commanders, Simon uses these scenes to reveal CompStat's capacity to become authoritarian. Visually, the blinds in the CompStat room operate metaphorically. When "brutality is set to occur," the blinds are shut. It is within a darkened CompStat room in episode 3, "Dead Soldiers," where Major Marvin Taylor (Barnett Lloyd), commander of the Eastern District, is relieved of his duties when he cannot account for the increased number of church burglaries, a mystery that Colvin's team solves once his Hamsterdams are operational and more officers are freed up. Similarly, in a later scene, the commander of the BPD's Quick Response Team is berated for a rise in nighttime car theft and is forced to accept that "prevention is the way to go, and we will immediately change our hours to reflect the data." In both scenes, the camera is positioned below Rawls's desk, providing him with an imposing aura through its low angle. Here the camera roves slowly from side to side as Rawls scolds the majors. Its movements are stirred by the commanders' humiliated reactions, which in turn are framed by tight static close-ups focusing on their panic-stricken sweating faces when defending their statistics. In contrast, whenever Colvin tries to shed "a little light and truth" into this room, the blinds are open.[23] In his first CompStat meeting, in the same episode, Colvin proudly reveals that crime has risen 2 percent in his district. Rawls is taken aback by Colvin's gumption and refusal to downgrade felonies into misdemeanors. Power is momentarily reversed, as Colvin occupies a low angle in revealing some honesty in the cold, hard light of day and the camera no longer moves as Rawls speaks. Instead, the camera is affixed on Deputy Ops Rawls from a high angle to signify how he is being put in his place. Colvin wants to use the CompStat meeting room to debate more effective drug enforcement policies. Accordingly, in episode 10, "Reformation," Colvin unveils how his decriminalizing drugs strategy has worked to bring down his district's crime rates to a sun-soaked CompStat room. With the blinds fully open, Colvin stands in a low-angle shot while the camera gradually pushes through into his face and the corresponding reaction shots of Rawls and Burrell remain at eye level. Colvin is trying to get the police department's chain of command to acknowledge some inalienable truths. However, following these attempts to utilize CompStat as a forum for compromise, the regular cinematography of these meetings resumes. Rawls and Burrell later dethrone Colvin behind closed blinds as Rawls smugly informs Colvin and his fellow majors from a low camera angle that Colvin has been "disgracing himself and his command." The major then retorts, "Get on with it motherfucker," the exact same dialogue spoken by Stringer Bell before he is murdered by Avon Barksdale's hired henchmen Omar and Brother Mouzone (Michael Potts). Colvin's firing is likened to an execution. He has tried to turn CompStat into an arena of compromise as advised by Kirkpatrick, Lester, and Peterson but cannot engage the political environment into altering its overriding view on the War on Drugs.

It turns out that Mayor Royce's office provides Colvin's ideas a fairer hearing, and the Hamsterdam policy momentarily obtains a powerful ally and willingness to compromise. In his initial attempt to save his own skin, Burrell passes a collection of letters from community associations, businesses, and citizens and Colvin's statistical reports denoting a 14 percent drop in Western District crime to Mayor Royce. After taking the time to read the information, Royce invests days trying to find a legal loophole that could make Colvin's decriminalizing drug use policy work. Over the final two episodes, the mayor hosts meetings in his office with a public health academic and Baltimore's health commissioner (played by former mayor Kurt Schmoke), who advocate continuing the policy for the "harm reduction" achieved. The mayor simultaneously hosts state delegate Odell Watkins (Frederick Strother) and his chief of staff, Coleman Parker (Cleo Reginald Pizana), who reaffirm that the state-level governor and legislature, alongside the federal Department of Justice, will use this opportunity "to piss on the city from a great height." Through the week, Royce mediates discussions between both parties, seeing if he can't find a "middle ground" to "keep this going without calling it what it really is." His attempts to find a solution end when Carcetti tips off the press and then, watching news reports of the Hamsterdams from his office, snaps Royce out of his efforts to decriminalize drug dealing. Confronted by the scenes of people openly buying and selling drugs, the camera focuses on the mayor's horrified expression in close-up, as was used to frame Bubbles's and Carcetti's reactions to visiting the free zones in person. Royce swiftly throws out all the staff from his office apart from Parker, to whom he confers, "What the fuck was I thinking?" Compromising proves fruitless within a political environment so legally and economically invested in the War on Drugs. As Simon states, "You need to be . . . tough on drugs" when "running for office in America."[24] The fact that Royce spent a week trying to reach a compromise gives Burrell and Carcetti more ammunition against him. This is the final aspect of Kirkpatrick, Lester, and Peterson's political environment: "the speed of the termination process." In line with the three academics' policy termination theory, Royce has spent too long trying to establish a narrative to counter the termination of the Hamsterdam program. Burrell is now able to blackmail the mayor by threatening to tell the press that his police department could have closed the Hamsterdams earlier had the mayor not brought in his "liberalized do-gooders to seriously consider this horseshit." Ultimately, the prevailing political ideology, the weakness of anti-termination coalitions, and the lack of time and ability to reach compromise across city, state, and federal government institutions means that the political environment cannot accommodate decriminalizing drugs in the Western District.

As season 3 concludes, Carcetti is offered a rare moment to introduce meaningful social policy that could break the cycle of deprivation drugs cause throughout Baltimore's Western District communities. Chairing the Health and Safety Subcommittee hearing into Colvin's drug decriminalization, Carcetti initially elevates the debate beyond "who knew what when . . . to make a political point or two." He decides to "forgive major Colvin out of his frustration and despair" and castigate politicians for surrendering West Baltimore's "prized communities . . . to the horrors of the drug trade." The scene concludes with a camera shot looking up to Carcetti sitting at the front bench with the camera itself placed behind the heads of Rawls and Burrell sitting in front of him. The camera does a very slow push through the gap between the shoulders of the two policemen right up to Carcetti's face, slowly omitting councilors Eunetta Perkins and Anthony Gray (Anthony Mann), sitting on either side of Carcetti, from view. Starting from a position of relative distance, Carcetti's abilities as a communicator enigmatically draw the public and camera into his declaration:

Enough to the despair which makes policemen think about surrender. Enough to the fact that these neighborhoods are beyond saving. Enough that this administration's indecisiveness and lethargy to the garbage which goes uncollected, the lots and row houses which stay vacant, the addicts who go untreated, the working men and women who every day are denied a chance at economic freedom.

At this point, Carcetti's speech appears to be in ideological alignment with the thrust of season 3. In agreement with Currie's four models, he infers that drug abusers (whether due to status, coping, structure, or saturation) are victims of deep socioeconomic inequalities, as uncovered by critical criminologists, that deny impoverished workers rightful treatment and economic freedom. In accordance with political science, Carcetti has referenced policemen and politicians being complicit in allowing addicts and working men to suffer. The councilman appears to be on the cusp of suggesting that the political environment ought to compromise on its prevailing ideology and introduce radical social reforms impervious to policy termination. However, Carcetti concludes,

If we don't have the courage and the conviction to fight this war the way it should and needs to be fought, using every weapon that we can possibly muster, if that doesn't happen, well then we're staring at defeat, and that defeat should not and cannot and will not be forgiven.

Carcetti's closing comments are met with rapturous applause echoing through the city chamber. While an eloquent and politically impassioned speech, the substance of Carcetti's final sentence, according to Simon, "is the same crap that's been foisted on people for the past 30 years." Carcetti's final sentence is arguing that if the war on drugs is fought "a little more aggressively" through punitive law enforcement, it can be won. Simon believes that the sincerity of Carcetti's speech and the camera correspondingly being drawn closer to him "imply truth." Occupying the optics of political campaigning means that the telegenic Carcetti appears to be a viable mayoral candidate. He is framed as "the great white hope" without addressing "the substance of the issues."[25] Initial reactions to season 3 proved this. It went by without so much as a high-profile figure or newspaper op-ed entertaining a cost-benefit analysis of legalizing drugs. The United States was so entrenched in the drug war that there was little commentary beyond viewers who saw season 3 and discussed it. *The Wire* needed time and subsequent seasons to penetrate political discourse.

SEASON 4

Education

The Wire had been canceled for good. There was no coming back. The cast and crew were accustomed to waiting four months until a fresh order for more episodes arrived. But this time, a renewal did not come. The website Savethewire.com emerged, inviting viewers to send letters to HBO's CEO, Chris Albrecht. "I have received a telegram from every viewer of *The Wire*—all 250 of them," he publicly quipped. The CEO was content with season 3's reviews and its conclusion to Avon Barksdale's story. He tried to appease Simon, suggesting, "Let's just call it a day, and you can write something else for us. Something that might be a hit." But the president of HBO Entertainment, Carolyn Strauss, conceded to Simon's persistence. He and Bill Zorzi had already written two episodes of *The Hall*, a spin-off focused on Carcetti's character that was 75 percent politics and 25 percent set within *The Wire*'s universe. Strauss held a meeting between herself, Simon, and Albrecht to hear Simon out one last time. Simon pitched how season 4 would have centered on children in Baltimore's school system, and then a final season could finish with a focus on the media culture. After 35 minutes of laying out character arcs and plotlines, in his usual brazen manner, Simon closed his speech, prophesying,

> Look Chris, years from now you're going to be trying to explain your life to somebody. Maybe a friendly stranger who sits across from you. He's leaning over while you try to make sense of life. You don't know what else to say, and you're going to say, "I'm the guy who renewed *The Wire* for five years." That man's going to look at you very sympathetically. He's

going to say, "That's great sir, but it's 2 a.m., and you need to finish that drink and get out of here."[1]

"All right," relented Albrecht, "we'll do it." Simon shook Albrecht's hand, declaring, "You won't regret it." "I'm already regretting it," the CEO grunted back. As Simon left, Strauss was staring at the writer in astonishment as if he had been brought back from the dead. His work had been resurrected. "I can't believe you talked yourself back into a show," Strauss stammered in complete disbelief, "you were canceled." But by this point, Albrecht was thinking, "Let's just do it. We don't want to hear from this guy anymore."[2]

Two days later, HBO confirmed that *The Wire* had a fourth season under the condition that Simon brought back the actors. "I'll get them all," he promised. Luckily, this proved straightforward. Released from his contract, Andre Royo had returned to Los Angeles when Simon called the Bubbles actor. "I can't make you," Simon appealed, "but if you want to come back, we'd love to have you." Royo looked over at his family thinking about the rigmarole that had come with relocating all of them to the West Coast. After a careful pause, he exalted, "Let's finish what we started man. This is *The Wire* baby!" Says Simon, "I went and got the actors back. Give them credit. No agent came to us and said, 'Okay he's coming back. He wants double.'" A principal reason that *The Wire* survived perpetual cancellations was its comparatively low budget of $50 million per season, a number that was never exceeded, one-quarter of what the final season of *The Sopranos* cost due to rising actor wages. Dominic West, however, proved more difficult to manage. Missing his daughter back in the United Kingdom and keen to work in films, he was given a paltry three weeks of filming in season 4 under the condition that he would return to his leading role in the final season. Even then, midway through season 4, Noble remembers West's accent lapsing before the actor began forgetting his lines. Sonja Sohn gathered all the actors to stage an intervention. "Don't waste this opportunity," she instructed West, "this is important for so many people." Pierce recounts that this motivational speech brought his on-screen buddy cop "back from the brink." However, West remembers the episode somewhat differently. He had been partying for three days straight with his friends, "not aware any of my fellow cast members were trying to take me in hand." "They did that a lot . . . being supportive" without you necessarily realizing.[3]

West's covert dressing down was particularly crucial for season 4, as more parts were being played by untrained actors. This type of casting, attributed to social realism, dates back to British drama/documentary films of the 1930s and 1940s. Here untrained locals could highlight "the hitherto unheard voices of the marginalised, against the previously unseen backdrop of their habitat," more so than trained performers.[4] In keeping with this tradition, cocreator and former teacher Ed Burns wanted actors with "the stamp of childhood on their faces."[5] Pushed for time, casting director Alexa Fogel found two kids from Chicago, one from New York, and one from Baltimore: Jermaine Crawford. Crawford found his scenes in actual classrooms with real inner-city schoolchildren to be a challenge. Assistant directors likened directing classroom scenes to "herding pigeons."[6] But this aided Crawford, as the children around him were "undergoing the circumstance I was able to go in and out of once they said action and cut." It "just grounded me to make it realistic as possible."[7] Similarly, Tootsie Duvall was persuaded to leave her job as an attendance monitor at Reservoir High School to play Assistant Principal Marcia Donnelly. Felicia "Snoop" Pearson, who plays an eponymous member of Marlo Stanfield's crew, was also an inspired casting choice. Snoop was arrested at age 14 for fatally shooting another girl, she claims in self-defense. On her release, a chance encounter with Michael K. Williams in a nightclub led to an invitation to visit *The Wire*'s set. Impressed with her presence and her ability to deliver Baltimorean street vernacular, Snoop was invited to play Marlo's enforcer. But Snoop missed her first day, as she was being arrested for carrying a pocketknife in a stolen car. Then during her first scene, script supervisor Claire Cowperthwaite was unsure of Snoop's delivery: "Is this show subtitled?" she asked, "because I have no idea what she's saying."[8] Nevertheless, the gamble paid off, as Snoop was soon hailed "the most terrifying female villain on television."[9]

PLOT

Although he loved the experience, Richard Price had already left *The Wire*'s writing team. Replicating the "identical tone" of a showrunner whom he considered to be a "socialist, pinko, Red" proved to be too frustrating for a novelist accustomed to penning his own novels.[10] So accomplished novelist Dennis Lehane was brought in to bring Ed Burns's real teaching experiences to life. Four new characters enter Edward J. Tilghman Middle School's eighth grade. Namond Brice (Julito McCullum), son of imprisoned Barksdale soldier Roland "Wee-Bey" Brice, is forced by his mother to deal drugs for Marlo's crew as their Barksdale protection money runs dry. Randy Wagstaff (Maestro Harrell) is conflicted between either cutting class to sell sweets or avoiding suspensions that could compromise his foster care.

Michael Lee (Tristan Wilds) is taken under the wing of Marlo's enforcers Snoop and Chris Partlow (Gbenga Akinnagbe), who protect him from his abusive father. Duquan "Dukie" Weems (Jermaine Crawford) is stigmatized for his heroin-addicted parents. Former police officer Roland Pryzbylewski teaches all four boys in his new job as an eighth-grade math teacher. Initially, Prez struggles to maintain order. His journey evokes Burns's experiences of teaching geography at Hamilton Middle School and finding "a little sliver of a moment to teach" when educational ability ranged from first grade to sixth grade within a single class. Meanwhile, former commander of the Western District Howard "Bunny" Colvin now works for a Johns Hopkins study attempting to deter children from criminality. Namond moving to Colvin's class is also based on Burns's experiences of separating "corner kids" from "stoop kids" to get "kids into special programs."[11] Writer and Black Lives Matter activist Mekeisha Madden Toby praises season 4's revealing "the school to prison pipeline long before it . . . had a recognizable name." So to unpick what Madden Toby mentions in passing as schooling's "racial inequities," this chapter begins with a history of the unique racial dynamics underpinning Baltimore's school system.[12] It then adopts critical race theory to determine how Prez's and Colvin's classes help inner-city students given Baltimore's education sector's historical challenges. Then the chapter explores how the four boys come of age compared to the protagonists of African American novels. Overall, the chapter determines how race, in season 4, informs a person's educational development inside and outside the classroom within the wider context of African American writing.

BALTIMORE COUNTY PUBLIC SCHOOLS

The Baltimore County Public Schools (BCPS) have always shared an uneasy relationship with state and federal legislatures, resulting in low levels of funding and academic attainment. The U.S. Supreme Court's 1954 case *Brown v. Board of Education* ruled that racial segregation in schools was now unconstitutional. However, by 1975, the Office for Civil Rights cut $23 million in federal aid from Baltimore's schools, as almost half were still failing to comply with a minimum 50 percent African American enrollment. The inner city had become majority black as white families moved to suburbia, manufacturing jobs were replaced by corporate/service sector jobs, and depleted white working-class neighborhoods held antibusing protests to prevent interschool transport. Education scholars Kasarda, Bluestone and Harrison, and Carnoy agree that urban blacks lacked the education to participate in the new growth sectors of the urban economy and so were disproportionately impacted by deindustrialization.[13] Given these challenges, the Morris Gold-seker Foundation produced *Baltimore 2000*, a study that found the BCPS to be "ineffective, undisciplined, and dangerous," training children merely for "menial" employment.[14] In response, Mayor Schmoke sued the State of Maryland for the funds that Baltimore pupils needed for a comprehensive education stipulated by the state constitution. The resulting agreement gave Baltimore more money from the state, but the mayor had to surrender his authority over the school budget and school board. African American leaders were critical of Schmoke's deal for rowing back on hard-fought victories won against the state's larger racial antipathies, a political system where Montgomery County officials openly criticized black inner-city Baltimoreans to gain white suburban votes. However, the racial antipathy goes both ways. BCPS staff are 80 percent black and are historically reluctant to work with business, as the overring concern remains that "is whitey trying to take over our school?"[15] Due to these impasses, by 1999, the education aid provided by Maryland for disadvantaged black students in Baltimore was below the national average and eight times lower than Mississippi and South Carolina—equivalent states that are majority white with concentrated pockets of black deprivation. By 2022, Baltimore City *and* Baltimore County occupy the Maryland School Report Card's lowest rankings in terms of test results, graduation rates, and attendance levels. Baltimore County had 14 percent of its schools scoring below average in 2019 and 24 percent in 2022, the city 53 percent and 75 percent. Since 1954, Baltimore pupils have been condemned to an inadequate education due to the uniquely tense relations between the city's black educators and the state's white politicians and businesses.

PREZ'S AND COLVIN'S CLASSROOMS

Given this racial division underpinning the BCPS, critical race theory will help investigate how Prez's and Colvin's classes address and overcome racial politics at classroom level. Critical race theory emerged in the 1970s as lawyers, activists, and academics uncovered that the advances of the civil rights era were being eroded through emerging subtler forms of racism within the everyday experiences of most people of color. Critical race theorists examining schools therefore provide a framework for finding how racial inequality has been embedded in school discourses, curricula, management structures, and classes. In particular, the three-stage analysis led by Zamudio of classroom organization and management enables us to consider how racism manifests in *The Wire* and can be overturned at the classroom level.

1. What Posters, Messages, and Slogans are Displayed in the Classroom?

Looking to the posters displayed in Prez's and Colvin's classrooms dem-onstrates what dominant ideologies about meritocracy, individuality, and cultural assimilation are being advanced racially. Having inherited blank noticeboards, Prez begins his first-ever class in episode 3, "Home Rooms," with black civil rights leaders prominently displayed across the right-hand wall. In the top left-hand corner is an illustration of Baltimore-born Thur-good Marshall, an American civil rights lawyer who successfully argued for the 1954 *Brown v. Board of Education* ruling, later serving as the Supreme Court's first African American justice. Directly beneath Marshall is an image of Rosa Parks, a civil rights activist best known for coordinating a boycott of the Montgomery buses in Alabama for more than a year, resulting in a 1956 Supreme Court decision that bus segregation was unconstitutional. In the top right corner of the display is a portrait of Frederick Douglass, a literary author who campaigned for abolitionism, having been a slave in the Baltimore docks. Directly beneath Douglass is a portrait of Harriet Tubman, another abolitionist who, after also escaping slavery, oversaw 13 missions to rescue 70 enslaved people from Maryland to Philadelphia using a network of safe houses known as the Underground Railroad. Prez's display is a means of inspiring his students to work hard and obtain meaningful change.

However, these achievements in legally challenging segregation or escaping slavery mean little to the students. The display does not last beyond Prez's first day. As Prez's first students enter his classroom, he instructs them to check his "seating chart." Despite putting together this elaborate "home room seating plan" with name placards on each individual desk, all ignore him. At this point, the viewer cannot see the civil rights leaders displayed as the camera moves quickly to capture the hubbub of students eagerly running past the wall to hug and catch up with one another following the summer break. Prez then nervously introduces himself as "your home room teacher" in a separate medium shot alongside his chart and name written in block cap-itals on the blackboard behind him. Meanwhile, the students sit at their desks beside the civil rights activists in a separate shot as if segregated into two sections of the classroom. Before Prez can "find out who you are," Principal Donnelly ceases the lesson through the intercom, explaining that a problem with the bell means that there will be a room change in one minute. With limited time, Prez tries to hand out bus passes to certain students but strug-gles, as they are not sitting in their assigned seats and he cannot be heard above their loud socializing. Walking through the classroom, Prez drops the passes and trips over a desk, bringing the civil rights display into focus for the first time. Prez's understanding of black culture grounds his movements through the classroom. Prez discovers that he has issued all the bus passes to the wrong students when Sharlene demands to know, "Where my passes at?" Prez explains that "Crystal is not on the list" as denoted by her desk plaque. Sharlene shouts back, "Crystal! I look like Crystal to you? I'm Sharlene" as Harriet Tubman and another image of Malcolm X are prominent on either side of her head albeit out of focus. To check whether the correct students have received their passes, Prez asks the pupil in Ronald Parker's seat his name. Kareem scoffs, "Kareem Williams, Ronald over there" as Parks is visible behind Kareem's head. Then as the bell rings and all the students leave, Prez is pushed around, trying to redistribute the bus passes to the correct students. Concurrently, Randy stands up from his desk, with Marshall and Parks visible behind him, to steal hall passes so that he can sneak out and sell sweets. The posters are meant to inspire the students to improve social justice though inventive yet legally reputable means but have been juxtaposed with their misbehavior.

These civil rights leaders represent Prez's expectations and understanding of black culture as he brings the posters into focus when gathering his bearings on the pupils' side of the classroom. Viewers quickly learn students are more concerned about making money, their name, their reputation, and standing up for themselves. The posters are blurry when framing the actions of Randy, Kareem, and Sharlene because hard-fought civil rights achievements of the past mean little to their current circumstances. In a later math class, Kareem discusses his love for the Philadelphia 76ers with Tubman's picture behind him. Another pupil, Laetitia, moves from her desk, with Parks's image behind her, to instigate a fight with Chiquan for repeatedly reflecting the sun's light into her face through a wristwatch. Despite past bus boycotts, Supreme Court rulings, and the abolition of slavery, this is still a racially segregated classroom overseen by white middle-class arbiters of knowledge trying to control the actions of black students. These historical leaders carry meaning only for Prez, who cannot connect with students beyond his appropriating of black culture. By the end of Prez's first working day, he tidies his classroom standing by the civil rights display that has now been defaced. In cold, hard focus, a bolt has been drawn through Marshall's neck and a scar on his forehead has repurposed him as a Frankenstein figure. Douglass has been given an eye patch, and Tubman has had a penis drawn on her head. Civil rights achievements of the past remain abstract to the black schoolchildren of West Baltimore. The pupils have less socioeconomic capital than their forefathers because Baltimore's public school

Figure 6.1. Prez is initially isolated from his black pupils surrounded by noticeboards displaying information that is more familiar to him. HBO/Photofest © HBO.

system's prolonged fallout with federal lawmakers and state politicians following desegregation has, alongside deindustrialization, helped worsen the students' circumstances.

With the civil rights display defaced and Laetitia slicing open Chiquan's face with a box cutter as revenge for humiliating her, Prez has posters saying that "choices have consequences" and "math rules," first affixed to either side of the classroom door in episode 4, "Refugees." This is an attempt to deter students from acting rashly and deferring their passions to his subject. In the lesson following Laetitia's attack, Prez attempts to console his pupils, but all are disinterested. Instead, on hearing that Prez was a cop, they playfully mimic scenes with one another of police brutality, to which they are accustomed. As Prez tries to maintain order, Randy uses the distraction to leave the classroom and sell sweets again, walking past both posters on either side of him as he exits. Initially, these new posters are taken as a challenge to question Prez's authority more fervently. When Prez issues Namond with detention for avoiding his classwork in episode 5, "Alliances," Namond scrunches up his detention slip, standing in profile with the "choices have consequences" poster, and goads the former policeman to "beat me, you know you want to." By episode 7, "Unto Others," however, the posters come to be a pointed indictment of teachers' ineffectiveness. Principal Donnelly informs Prez before his math class starts that Randy's suspension has been lifted. Having previously been accused of being an accomplice to rape (when he was guarding the toilet door for a mutually consensual act), Tiffany has since dropped the claim. Standing by the "choices have consequences" poster, Donnelly informs Prez that "it's out of my hands." The same poster is also prominent in episode 11, "A New Day," when Prez learns that Randy's life is in danger for his actions. Earlier, Randy revealed details of Lex's murder to Donnelly to avoid a harsher punishment for the rape accusation. Prez gave the information to officers he trusts, but Herc accidentally revealed to his suspect Little Kev that Randy gave them the information. In both instances, the "choices have consequences" poster is a chilling reminder that Randy's fate has been in the hands of white middle-class Donnelly, Prez, and Herc, who could now be responsible for Randy's imminent death. With the "choices have consequences" poster in sight, Prez now instructs Randy to not tell the authorities anything from now on. When Bunk and Freamon later visit Prez at work and press him for more information on Lex's murder, Prez defiantly tells them both, "I'm siding with my kids" with the poster in full view behind both officers, fully aware that if he hands Randy to the police again, he will have effectively sealed his pupil's death sentence. The posters aimed at disruptive black children are now a chilling reminder of the unequal power that the white school staff have over their children's lives beyond the classroom, as any lapse of judgment could carry fatal consequences. Overall, Prez's posters initially reinforce white middle-class assumptions of what would inspire and motivate students of color. However, as time passes, the meaning of "choices have consequences" evolves into being a reminder of the unequal power dynamic that the white teachers have over their pupils.

The posters used in Colvin's corner kids' classroom are decidedly different. Each prompts students to talk about, process, and regulate their emotions. In their first class, in episode 7, "Unto Others," Namond's teacher, Ms. Duquette (Stacie Davis), stands in front of the prominently displayed "class rules" poster as she asks the children why they come to school not wearing their uniform. The rules stipulate that students are "responsible for their own behavior in the group," "accountable for the contribution to the assigned task," and "expected to help any group member who asks for help," that they will "ask the teacher for help," and "not put down other students." But these instructions are not instantly adhered to. When Namond is asked to leave for singing in class, he is initially buoyant, exclaiming, "See you motherfuckers in three days." But as it dawns on him that he will have to sit in detention and cannot be suspended, he proceeds to throw a chair and cuss at his teachers, pleading them to suspend him because "school gotta have rules." As Namond continues to protest, another poster comes into focus behind him revealing the "C's of decision making," which are "clarify," "consider," and "choose." At this moment, Namond is unable to follow any of this guidance. Instead, he is made to sit in the adjacent office. In this office, directly in Namond's eyeline, is a poster displaying "core skills," which are to "share ideas," "compliment," "offer help," "recommend," and "exercise self-control." Instead, Namond shouts, "Fuck you" whenever Colvin tries to inquire about his feelings.

Nevertheless, over time, these instructions start cutting through. Colvin devises a group project whereby all the children who are still too disruptive to participate in regular classrooms articulate what they feel constitutes "courage on the corner." Episode 11, "A New Day," reveals the results displayed in the center of the classroom. The flip chart specifies that outside of school on the corner, all the children are required to be brave enough to withstand "staring down a stickup boy" and "being sent overnight to Cheltenham" (a youth detention center). They must also "not back down from larger kids," "stand up to police," and "stand with your boys." Then the teachers translate this task into an exercise that instills trust, as students are requested to stand on a stool blindfolded and fall backward to be caught by their classmates.

As Duquette produces the stool, she stands by the class rules that preach the values of teamwork and courtesy. A compromise has been reached between the class rules and the corner kids' own values as Namond executes the task successfully. Whereas Colvin in earlier lessons has been standing free from class posters, opting to observe Duquette's class, here he convinces Namond to do the task while standing in front of a poster that lists "skills for dealing with feelings," which are "knowing your feelings," "expressing your feelings," and "expressing concern for one another." Another notice on the left side of Colvin's head while he convinces Namond reads, "You can control your anger tell yourself that you can." Then, when Colvin asks Albert to have a go, the boy declares, "Fuck you stupid bitches" and storms out. In the next scene, he and Colvin sit in the adjacent office, again displaying core skills of the class that espouse helping classmates and to "exercise self-control." Sitting by these instructions, Colvin calmly and sensitively suggests to Albert, "Maybe we can help." Initially, a tearful Albert refutes Colvin's request. But then, when Colvin praises Albert for "doing really well in class" and to "just give it a try," Albert confesses that his mother was found dead of a drug overdose that morning. Essentially, over time, these posters and their messaging have worked. Compared to Prez's use of historical figures, math rules, and the reminder that choices have consequences, more sensitively worded instructions that are less abstract in nature and aimed at encouraging students to understand their emotions have an effect. They underpin lessons invested in the lived experiences of pupils as advocated by critical race theory. Similarly, the three teachers running the class are not white, so encouraging students to open up and express themselves to teachers with a similar understanding feels safer. Prez, as a white former police officer, is somebody pupils have been conditioned to remain guarded against, something that black school leaders have felt toward white politicians and white business leaders throughout the history of Baltimore's education system.

2. Student/Teacher Interactions

Prez's initial classroom posters culturally appropriate the aspirations of his black eighth graders as they present the civil rights achievements as something they should aspire to. On experiencing a clear disconnect between accomplishments of the past and experiences of his own pupils, Prez then reflects on his own practice through the "choices have consequences" mantra placed beside his classroom door overlooking his desk. Similarly, Colvin aligns himself with posters that help students process their emotions. Both teachers make these breakthroughs once they begin listening, understanding, and responding to the day-to-day experiences of their students. Such developments, however, prove possible only by radically altering the nature of the traditional student/teacher interaction. Usually, the teacher's desk, being at the front and center of the class, infers that "the teacher is the font of all knowledge" and that "the inherent knowledge of students . . . is not valued."[16] By subverting this dynamic, Prez and Colvin invite the lived experience of their students to inform their teaching methods.

Prez appears isolated when initially adopting the traditional method of conversing with his students. Initially, a divide is established between Prez, who is rooted to his desk, where he is framed exclusively by medium and long shots. In comparison, the children are filmed in separate close-ups as they react to his instructions. When Prez crosses the threshold into the children's side of the classroom, the camera becomes handheld as he physically ceases altercations. Changing this traditional dynamic comes during a lunch break in episode 7, "Unto Others," where Prez approaches Michael and Kareem playing poker. Again, Prez leaves the comfort of his desk to discipline his pupils. Having been reassured that no money is involved, Prez instead engages in conversation about their culture and games in their patois. Michael reveals that he has a flush and isn't sure whether it beats Kareem's three nines. Kareem confirms, "It do." Michael looks to Prez, asking, "It do?" to which their teacher replies, "It do." Prez then teaches his students how to count diamonds in a deck. For the first time, Prez is framed in this side of the classroom by a steady close-up. Michael then asks Prez to teach them the odds of dice, as that is what they play on the street corners. From this moment, Prez begins to alter the teacher/student dynamic in a constructive manner whereby students can understand the logic of math and apply it to their own real-world experiences. Randy proceeds to make more money by betting on street games and using his winnings to buy cheaper sweets in bulk online and sell them at school for a higher price.

Later in the same episode, Prez upturns all the desks. His pupils kneel on the floor in groups using the tops of the desks to roll dice against. The camera now roves across the floor with all classroom posters moved off-screen. Prez walks through the class and crouches down to interact with each group on the same level as they make bets with Monopoly money. On seeing Randy lose a bet, Prez kneels next to him, pulls up his sleeves, and shares a mid-shot, where it is revealed that he is no longer wearing his teacher name tag, explaining why Randy "should have bet against the roll." Prez then puts the dice back into Randy's hand firmly before stating, "Good to have you back Mr. Wagstaff" and issues a gentle shoulder punch as acknowledgment of Randy's achievement. Interacting with his students on their level, casually conversing as they would on street corners, with elements of his formal teaching attire lessened, causes Prez to miss the head of eighth grade entering the classroom to observe. He confides in her, "Trick them into thinking they aren't learning, and they do." The traditional barrier between teacher and pupil has been quelled as Prez roams the classroom with the camera freely and confidently no longer needing help to restrain his students from fighting.

Essentially, in terms of education theory, Prez has identified his students as kinesthetic learners. Neil Fleming and David Baume's VARK model defines *visual* learners as those who use images and graphics to understand, process, and retain information. *Auditory* learners understand when listening and speaking in classroom discussions. *Reading* and writing learners process information most effectively when taking notes. *Kinesthetic* pupils, however, are hands-on learners who understand information best through tactile simulations of real-world scenarios. In discarding tables and chairs, Prez emulates his pupils' familiar street environment within the classroom. Prez's initial teaching does not resonate, as it is visual when he draws diagrams on the board to help elucidate math puzzles, aural when he repeats the same math problem many times over, and reading when he has students read passages from Greek mythology aloud as the language tests draw nearer. However, this kinesthetic learning is what engages his students and enables them to retain information. As the series develops, Prez then begins to introduce more props that facilitate his children's learning and further break down traditional teacher/student interactions. By episode 9, "Know Your Place," the classroom of his first lesson is barely recognizable. Desks are now bunched together in groups of four so that students can face each other in a more socially engaging environment, replicating their lunchtime seating arrangements. Prez walks through the classroom observing groups of children counting cards, using calculators, tape measuring each other, and researching subjects on Prez's desk computer. Sections of the classroom are no longer demarcated between pupils and teacher, as children are learning at their own discretion in accordance with their own interests.

In comparison, Colvin's research project goes a step further, handing more autonomy to their corner students to better understand their pupils' perspectives, worldviews, and values. The breakthrough here comes when Duquette has a conversation with the children about their career goals in episode 8, "Corner Boys." Initially, their classwork task is to explain where they see themselves in 10 years professionally. Colvin interjects and changes the assignment to "What makes a good corner boy?" Having previously struggled to get the students to open up, all of them now enthusiastically offer their thoughts, speaking over one another in the process. Later in the lesson, having focused the topic on the children's lived experiences, Colvin is able to host a discussion around how each would deal with a member of their crew who they suspect is stealing from them. While Namond and Zenobia agree that they would simply "fuck him up," Darnell challenges the group consensus, explaining that he would take the stolen money from his worker's wage and give him the benefit of the doubt, as all agree that they would not want to lose a good worker. Then all agree that if their worker still continues to steal, he would need to be beaten up. Now there is little discernible divide between Colvin, who stands in the semicircle of desks, pitching them questions. This new method of interacting further draws out the logic underpinning the children's thought processes, prompting them to solve problems, engage in ethical debate, and reach a consensus involving everyone's different perspective. In the final scene of this "what makes a good corner boy" lesson, the teaching staff give Namond the floor, while the three teaching staff stand by their desk, sandwiched in between the class rules poster detailing the appropriate behavior that children must exhibit in class and the three C's of decision making. Namond walks around the classroom guiding the camera's movements as Colvin did previously. Here Namond accuses the adults of hypocrisy, as classroom rules such as "don't lie," "don't cheat," or "don't steal" are regularly broken by institutions, governments, and corporations. A clear reversal of roles, removing teachers from the comfort of their classroom posters and their freedom to move around the room, permits Namond to interrogate the adults' values. Namond now volunteers this information. Previously, when Duquette formally asked Namond how he felt and noted all his responses with her pen and clipboard while standing in front of the class rules poster, he refused to comply. Now with the formal student/teacher dynamic reversed, Namond feels comfortable enough to explain, "We do same as y'all, but when we do it, we are treated like animals." Having gotten to the root of Namond's frustrations, Colvin then sets the next class assignment to write for the teachers the rules of the street.

Ultimately, Prez and Colvin have independently developed models of learning that defy traditional modes of student/teacher interaction. They design lessons based on the lived experiences of students of color. In line with critical race theorists' studies of classrooms, designing lessons in this manner permits "dominant social and cultural assumptions regarding culture, intelligence, and meritocracy" to be challenged.[17] Both lessons teach the curriculum in a manner that respects the children's intelligence by having them solve problems within replications of their cultural environment

Figure 6.2. Namond begins to disrupt the pupil teacher dynamic in his corner kids class. HBO/Photofest © HBO.

autonomously, guided by their interests. Colvin advances critical race theory further than Prez, as he draws his pupils to their oppressive ideological orientations. Here Namond can articulate how he feels subordinated by institutions, corporations, and socioeconomic inequalities. The difficulty comes when applying pupils' knowledge to what Colvin feels "they don't know": the final stage of Yosso's and Zamudio's models of critical race theory, advancing social justice and managing student frustrations when it is not achieved.

3. Managing Student Resistance

Critical race theorists subscribe to the view that pupil resistance is a form of feedback. Within the American education system, research shows that more assertive approaches to discipline are used with students of color, while permissive approaches to discipline are reserved for white students. In permissive classrooms, shouting out answers is tolerated, ignored, or gently corrected. When that same behavior is enacted in assertively disciplined classrooms, pupils are placed on the fringe of the class. This leads to more acting out and harsher punishments. While the more assertive approaches are intended to curb student misbehavior, they disproportionately target students of color for school suspensions/expulsions and school detentions. Finding a balance between permissive and assertive discipline puzzles Prez. His preliminary inability to effectively deal with interjections or recognize signs of escalating dissension could be blamed for the escalating feud between Laetitia and Chiquan that leads to Chiquan's hospitalization.

Having struggled to maintain order and prevent Chiquan from moving seats to goad Laetitia, episode 5, "Alliances," opens with Prez introducing a new assertive discipline system. He has a small grid pinned to the noticeboard beside the blackboard with the title "monthly achievements," whereby students are incentivized to be more compliant. Here each student will earn a sticker for completing their classwork, doing homework, and behaving in class. At the end of each week, the four students with the most stickers get a prize and are eligible for a grand draw at the end of the month. In comparison to this relatively small, indecipherable handwritten table is a much larger table drawn on the blackboard with five columns. At the top of each column is the name of each math class that Prez teaches. For those who misbehave, "your name goes here," explains Prez as he writes down Namond's name for interrupting him. Those who have their names written in the table attend "detention for a full hour after school with no exceptions." As Prez writes Namond's name, a series of names from the two classes that Prez has already taught that day are clearly visible and will be displayed to all the classes that he will teach throughout the day. The priority of this new approach is clear: his class is now driven by a zero-tolerance form of discipline whereby those who interject and interrupt the class are humiliated. Prez's discipline system, however, does not last beyond episode 5, as he soon discovers that it does not deter students from misbehaving, as they still seek peer approval by challenging his authority.

Prez manages to balance assertive with permissive approaches by discreetly dropping this detention system. Instead of clamping down on Michael's and Kareem's gambling as soon as he sees it happening, he talks to his students and learns that he can incorporate the math curriculum into street corner games. Previously, Michael was held back in detention, as he did not feel incentivized to do his classwork despite being capable. Now, following this lunchtime conversation, Michael proudly displays all his correct homework answers for Prez. Threatening punishment does not work. Rather, students are motivated by lesson plans that speak to their experiences and interests. Instead of punishing and humiliating students for all minor infractions, Prez keeps them onside by utilizing their humor. For example, instead of sending Calvin to detention for copying Kwanese's homework in episode 7, "Unto Others," he simply makes light of the fact, to the whole class, that he need not copy her name at the top of the worksheet. By episode 8, "Corner Boys," Prez docs not instantly discipline Calvin with detention for gossiping while he pitches a math problem. Instead, Prez exerts control of the situation by inviting Calvin to show the class how he solved the problem. By episode 12, "That's Got His Own," when Prez designs a math problem around a married couple settling a bill, Prez promises to deal with their interfering questions about marital intimacy once they solve the math problem. Instead of punitively issuing detentions and suspensions for any form of dissent, as typically experienced by black schoolchildren, Prez develops discretion. Student misbehavior is stopped by inviting the pupil in question to contribute to the task or by deferring the classroom's questions about wider issues to additional lessons. As the season progresses and Prez gets to understand his students and their home situations, needs, and academic abilities, he presides over an orderly classroom.

The clinching factor that enables Prez to maintain control of his classroom constructively rather than punitively is that his most disruptive students—Albert, Zenobia, Darnell, and Namond—are moved to Colvin's corner kids' class. Initially, Colvin asserts discipline, confirming Namond's interjection that their new class "is prison," specifically, "solitary." Leaning over Namond using his towering frame to intimidate and stun the class into silence, Colvin claims that "this is the hole up in here." However, this police style of discipline stifles assimilating corner kids into regular classrooms. Instead, helping students process their emotions (as propagated by classroom posters) and applying the worldviews and skills of their pupils to lesson plans (by radically altering the teacher/student dynamic) is what makes progress. This new approach is successful only because the children are not suspended, excluded, or given detention for disrupting class. A lack of assertive punishment gives the teaching team more time to develop an understanding of their pupils' needs and produce bespoke learning. Unfortunately, the state superintendent deems Colvin's lessons too focused on socializing the students rather than teaching them the curriculum. From a resource standpoint, the corner kids' program is canceled because only three of the 12 students have a chance of returning to regular classrooms. Mayor Carcetti's chief of staff, Michael Steintorf (Neal Huff), personally informs Colvin that his research project findings cannot be rolled out across Baltimore's schools, as he is effectively "segregating" the children, a problem that has historically prevented Baltimore children from receiving adequate state funding. The program is particularly untenable, as Mayor Carcetti is cutting Baltimore's school budget. Existing staffing, programs, resources, and entire schools are already compromised, never mind additional expensive programs. Fixated on becoming governor, Carcetti is unwilling to beg the current governor for money that would relinquish his control of Baltimore's school system. Refusing fiscal assistance means that Carcetti's career ambitions of becoming governor will not be hindered, as he will not have to explain to middle-class suburban voters in Washington, D.C., that their taxes bailed out Baltimore's schools, much like Mayor-turned-Governor Martin O'Malley who also did not include Baltimore's school system in his strategic priorities. The racial optics of ending Colvin's program cannot be ignored. Carcetti's white chief of staff, Steintorf, acting as gatekeeper, will not take the study manned by nonwhite researchers to the white mayor for consideration, especially when satisfying white suburban voters is their priority. Instead, it is easier to continue to oversee a system that manipulates test scores to mask deeper infrastructural problems. Despite Prez's students not passing their tests, 38 percent are deemed proficient at math because his eighth graders can do math two grades below their level as was happening at the time.[18] Like the real BCPS, a stalemate between white politicians and black teachers continues to stifle meaningful reform.

Applying critical race theory to classroom scenes demonstrates a capacity for change. Prez oversees advances by radically altering the organization of his classroom. The messages of his posters begin to question teacher bias. His student/teacher interactions replicate street environments to produce kinesthetic comprehension of the curriculum. This is complemented by a balanced and receptive approach to discipline, resulting in a less violent and chaotic classroom. As Prez welcomes the corner kids back in season 4's final episode, "Final Grades," Albert quips that Prez's "worst nightmare [is] right on you." However, Albert's remark does not prompt laughter from his peers, as his statement is met with awkward silence. Albert swiftly retracts the statement, claiming, "Nah, I'm just playing." Kareem then answers Prez's math problem and happily accepts his teacher's invitation to cross the classroom floor, take Prez's chalk, and demonstrate how he solved the problem on the board. However, the scale of achievement reached in the classroom would not be as emotionally powerful or moving without access to the private lives of Namond, Dukie, Randy, and Michael.

COMING OF AGE AND THE
AFRICAN AMERICAN NOVEL

While season 4 was being broadcast, literary academic Claudine Raynaud identified the six stages that a young black protagonist entering adulthood

Figure 6.3. Left to right: viewers of season 4 are introduced to the new schoolboy characters Dukie, Randy, Michael, and Namond. HBO/Photofest © HBO.

negotiates within African American–authored literature over the past 150 years, a schema that proves useful for measuring how each of *The Wire*'s four central schoolboy protagonists come of age differently in contemporary Baltimore. Despite Randy revealing knowledge of Lex's murder to placate Assistant Principal Donnelly from compromising his foster care, the laws of the street condemn him as a snitch. Randy's house is therefore firebombed by school bullies, his foster mother is hospitalized, and he is returned to a violent group home. Michael's Stanfield enforcer training protects his brother from their abusive father, gains him independence, and provides a home for his friend Dukie, who has become homeless because of his parents' heroin addiction. Namond, pressured by his mother to sell drugs, is adopted by Colvin, knowing that the boy is not hardened enough to survive the streets.

1. Discovering Racism

According to Raynaud, the discovery of America's racism is the catalyst of a black protagonist's development. Coming of age involves "inscribing that fictional moment against the tradition of slavery." Therefore, a "recognition of belonging takes place" within the narrower circles of the family and black community, where "society is often viewed as a threat, if not as the enemy." Coming of age for Raynaud, then, signals "emancipation" from the "childhood" servitude to paternalism and its traces as ascribed by master to slave.[19] This moment of discovery occurs for Namond in episode 6, "Margin of Error," when he experiences the Barksdales cutting off his mother from their protection money. From this instant, Namond's circles of belonging narrow further, excluding him from his community and then family. The only way that Namond can emancipate himself from servitude to the Barksdales and alleviate himself from his mother's abusive control is to meet her demands and sell drugs. Leaving their home to meet Brianna Barksdale, Namond's mother, De'Londa Brice (Sandi McCree), instills her son with confidence, reminding Namond that he is "representing your daddy . . . a soldier." Both leave the house dressed in their Sunday best while others in their community attend church. This is significant because it demonstrates the extent of the Brices' loyalty to the Barksdales to the point of religious fervor. However, the Brices' world comes crashing down in the next scene, where Brianna Barksdale informs both Brices in her front room that "there's no more money coming in." Namond's mother takes the news badly, threatening that Wee-Bey could inform on Avon to increase his former employer's prison sentence. Brianna then leans forward, declaring, "I wanted you to both hear it from me so there ain't no lies from here on in . . . you should have enough money going forward son. Your father has not been disrespected here." While Brianna dispenses this dialogue, the camera closes in on Namond from mid-shot to close-up as he slouches forward with a glazed expression, too embarrassed to look Brianna in the eye. The camera moves to Namond because Brianna Barksdale does not want him seeking retribution as an adult. The camera closing in on Namond's uncomfortable disposition, signifying his isolation. Discovering that they are now alone as a family, cut off from the previous hierarchy of the black community, compels De'Londa to force her son into selling drugs and finding independence as a dealer.

In comparison, Randy first encounters racism through Principal Donnelly in the same episode, "Margin of Error." Summoned to her office, Donnelly informs Randy that Tiffany is accusing Paul and Monell of rape, and his part in being a lookout means that there "will be an investigation, you'll be suspended" and could "be expelled" or "face criminal charges." Pleading with Donnelly not to call his foster mother, Randy persuades Donnelly to hang up the phone by revealing that he knows about Lex's murder. The unequal power relationship is visually evoked as Donnelly calls Randy from the waiting area into her office by opening the door and beckoning him in slowly with her index finger in silence. Donnelly is then shot at a low angle, ensuring that she sits above Randy at her desk while Randy is shot from a high angle that looks down on him, pleading for his future and placing his head in his hands. In the foreground of Randy's high-angle shot are framed pictures of Donnelly's family and children. This highlights the racial divide between the white middle-class professional supporting her family compared to Randy, who has no family and must plead to retain what little stability he currently has. There are echoes of slavery, as Randy is effectively pleading for his life while formally referring to his superior as "Mrs. Donnelly" as slaves would refer to masters. Again, as with Namond, Randy has been forced into a corner and is effectively begging for his future. Donnelly gives the information about the killings to Prez, who passes the information through the chain of command to Herc. When questioning Little Kev, Herc accidentally reveals where he got the information. Randy's fate is determined by white authority figures, so he learns never to reveal information again, as they are an untrustworthy threat to him. As young West Baltimoreans, both Randy and Namond learn how they are at the behest of more powerful figures. Their meager social capital stands for little in relation to those who have benefited from the racial inequality of the city founded in segregation, be they ruthless black kingpins who have come to fleetingly dominate the drug trade or white suburban teachers born into comparative privilege. The boys' circumstances change in an instant through others who preside over their fate.

2. Subversion/Negation of the American Dream

On discovering racism, protagonists in an African American bildungsroman must then subvert or negate the American dream. Black protagonists coming of age soon realize that this correlation between hard work and fiscal reward is not applicable to them. Instead, they must learn to better understand the workings of their oppression to reach adulthood. This realization comes to Randy in episode 6, "Margin of Error." On election day, a Carcetti campaigner offers the boy $40 to hand out leaflets. Randy splits this money with Dukie, Kernard, and Donut. Michael refuses, as he has already decided to negate the American dream model by working for Marlo. The three other boys subvert the American dream by downing tools before the job is complete. Randy accidentally reveals that he has already been paid, to which Donut retorts, "The man got nobody to blame but himself. It's his fault for paying up front." Following this swift lesson, Randy learns to befriend those who have power over him and subvert their stake in the American dream to his own ends. In episode 9, "Know Your Place," Randy discovers that he can buy sweets cheaper online to make larger profits. Not being old enough to own a bank card, Randy asks Prez to buy him the sweets. To get the quantity of sweets he needs, Randy bets on men playing dice in the street using his newfound classroom knowledge of probabilities. Prez agrees to buy the candy because Randy didn't personally throw any dice. Likewise, Dukie works out how to get to level 40 on Prez's classroom computer game by activating the cheat mode. He essentially works out how to avoid the hard work of undergoing all the levels to achieve instantaneous reward. Finally, Namond is initially the richest of the children given the computer consoles, jerseys, and jewelry lavished on him by his mother. However, this comparatively opulent lifestyle is eviscerated when the Barksdale money runs dry. Overall, the boys learn that the money they have does not equate to how hard they or their families have worked. They must think creatively to manipulate capital.

3. Choosing between Rebellion/Submissiveness

Choosing between rebellion and submissiveness is crucial for an African American literary protagonist. The goal when coming of age is to mature so as to face the outside world. Therefore, according to Reynaud, the African American novel can either propose "a solution to the formation of the black subject in America or depict the impossibility of such a solution."[20] The same is true of *The Wire*. Namond rebels by becoming adopted by his teacher and former commander of the Western District, Colvin. Namond is repeatedly disciplined by his mother for preparing vials at home while playing video games, coming home short on profits, not getting his Afro cut to avoid police targeting him, and not personally ensuring that Kernard "feel some pain" for stealing Bodie's stash. Each time Namond is disciplined, De'Londa threatens to tell Namond's father, Wee-Bey, as punishment for shaming the family name. In return, Namond turns to his boxing teacher, Cutty, and Carver, telling them in episode 12, "That's Got His Own," "I can't go home" because "she expect me to be my father but I ain't him," setting in motion a series of events where Wee-Bey agrees to Colvin's guardianship, as his son is not "made for the corners like we were." In comparison, Randy and Dukie have no option but to embrace submissiveness. With his house firebombed and foster mum hospitalized, Randy submits to the group home, where he is beaten up and his money is stolen. Similarly, with his junkie parents evicted from their home, Dukie moves in with Michael, whose apartment is paid for by Marlo. Permanently infantilized, Dukie floats through life needing parental figures to care for him. Instead of maturing, he does not attend high school and lives as if he's Michael's surrogate son.

4. Killing the Father

Only Michael undergoes the fourth stage of the coming-of-age journey. When Michael's father returns, Prez offers Michael a pass to see the school counselor for suddenly appearing detached in class. Michael's boxing teacher, Cutty, also notices a change and puts his hand on Michael's shoulder, to which the boy recoils, misreading the adult's offer of help as a predatory advance. Given the options available, Michael decides to be taken under the wing of Marlo Stanfield's enforcers Snoop and Partlow because they can instantly turn his abusive predicament around. Michael's mother relapses into heroin addiction, pawning their food to feed her habit, and demands access to her Division of Social Services welfare payments that Michael controls. When Michael's father demands that his eldest son hand over the money, he hugs Michael's younger brother Bug and caresses his shoulders, effectively threatening to abuse Michael's brother as he did Michael if the money is not handed over. Partlow and Snoop promise to fix any problem Michael has, so he joins them in pledging allegiance to his new Stanfield "family." Then, when Partlow beats Michael's father to death in episode 10, "Misgivings," the scene is followed by Michael drinking milk, smiling at his mother, and standing tall beside the kitchen countertop, as he is again the patriarch of his biological family. Michael rebels against the wishes of his mother and his friends, who suggest that Prez or Cutty can help, because Marlo's protection can swiftly and most efficiently rectify his circumstances by immediately killing his father.

5. Crossing Class Lines

As to whether class lines must also be crossed for *The Wire*'s African American protagonists, it is a long and gradual process with mixed results. In episode 9, "Know Your Place," when Colvin takes Namond, Darnell, and Zenobia to Ruth's Chris Steak House as a reward for their classwork, the children's inability to use the restaurant is a humiliating experience. Namond is reluctant to give their white hostess his coat. As they walk to their table, the camera occupies each child's POV looking at all the smartly dressed white people talking over their food before stopping to look up at the passing schoolchildren in silence. The camera then cuts back to a close-up of the embarrassed child's face in reaction. There is clearly a clash between the fashions of the diners in formal attire and the black West Baltimore schoolchildren in casual sports jackets. When the waiter pulls out a chair, nobody sits on it, as they assume that it is her own seat. They are not used to being offered help from a smartly dressed and well-spoken white person. When ordering, they need to be informed that the "specials" do not refer to discounted supermarket food. The children struggle with placing their napkins and try not to laugh too loud so that people do not look at them. Then as the waitress details the specials, the camera cuts to close-ups at the table of each child, who clearly do not understand what the foods, methods of cooking, and sauces are. The extent to which the children are unable to assimilate with the white middle-class surroundings even surprises Colvin, who tells his teaching colleagues that he "knew they'd be at a loss but didn't realize [the] extent of it." Nevertheless, over time, Colvin's wife is impressed with Namond's manners when they host the boy over a weekend, leading to their adoption of him. Class lines can be crossed once Colvin's corner kid lessons begin making progress over time.

6. Concluding through Deferral

As the season concludes, it aligns with the sixth and final stage of an African American novel, a moment of deferral. Reynaud explains that the final chapter is a "postponement of what can never be in this time or in this world."[21] The hero never fully completes their progress into coming of age, as most novels end on a note of ambivalence. The very final shot is of Namond breakfasting and completing homework on the Colvins' front porch in an idyllic suburban neighborhood. As Namond's new foster parents go inside, his friend Donut pulls up in front of the house in a stolen car. Donut produces a West Side hand gesture with three fingers to which a grinning Namond nods at in recognition. The camera then pans to Donut's car, observing his driving from the front porch where Namond sits, as Donut drives it down the street through a stop sign, causing other cars to brake. The camera cuts back to Namond's grinning face in appreciation and then cuts back to the crossroads at the end of his block to the calming sounds of wind chimes and birdsong. The season is ending on a moment of deferral. Namond's looking over the crossroads infers that the only student who has successfully crossed class lines will forever be tempted back into his former life. This chapter has demonstrated that the four boys sit within an overarching racial division between schools and politicians that manifests in curricular structures, processes, and discourses right down to the classroom. Utilizing critical race theory enables Prez and Colvin to momentarily push back against these forces to transform classrooms into spaces where teachers and pupils can reassess their oppressive ideological orientations and equip them for dealing with and perhaps overcoming their socially maligned circumstances. However, for the four boys themselves, just like their literary ancestors, coming of age remains nearly impossible with potentially life-ending consequences. For this reason, season 4 achieved the greatest critical reception yet with critics hailing how child actors with little professional experience could portray children "on the cusp . . . with heart-breaking clarity all the factors that could make or break them."[22] Season 4 was the only season to achieve a 100 percent rating on *Rotten Tomatoes*. Having set the bar so high, concluding *The Wire* through a fifth and final season would prove to be Simon and Burns's most insurmountable challenge yet.

CHAPTER 7

SEASON 5

Populism

Albrecht needed to make savings—fast. The CEO had overstretched HBO's budget green-lighting too many new productions: Simon's adaptation of Evan Wright's *Generation Kill* for one. Blissfully unaware, Simon was scouting locations in Mozambique to double up as sites for the 2003 Iraq invasion when his mobile rang. It was Strauss. *The Wire* was canceled—again. But like a *Generation Kill*, marine Simon would not go down without a fight. He immediately flew back to the United States and ordered Albrecht not to "leave the bodies in the vacants." Albrecht put it to Simon, "I'm giving you seven hours for *Generation Kill*. Can you finish *The Wire* in 10 episodes?" Trimming back story lines was not ideal, but it was better than nothing, so Simon took the offer, although something started to feel different about this production. During the last two months of filming in the summer of 2007, viewers began finding the show. The production team had to hide from mobs of people keen to observe Omar's fate. Simon also had journalists from *The New Yorker* and the *New York Times* shadowing him to write curtain raisers for the final season. Simon made it clear to them season 5 is about "perception versus reality," particularly "what kind of reality newspapers capture."[1] Simon's former employer, *The Baltimore Sun*, allowed its name to be used under the condition that the drama not be filmed in its offices or feature current employees. Simon circumnavigated this problem by re-creating the *Sun*'s office on a soundstage and populating it with former *Sun* colleagues. After production wrapped, Simon got a congratulatory e-mail from Albrecht: "That was really great. The only thing that could make it better would be two extra hours." Simon's two-word reply simply read, "You motherfucker."[2]

Season 5 begins with Mayor Carcetti cutting the police budget to redress the education deficit. The Major Crimes Unit's investigation of Marlo Stanfield's drug dealing operation is redirected to prosecuting Senator Clay Davis for corruption. However, McNulty soon diverts resources back to the Marlo investigation by faking evidence of a serial killer preying on homeless men. Meanwhile, as *The Baltimore Sun* faces budget cuts, fresh-faced reporter Scott Templeton gleefully publishes fake news stories, claiming to have even been contacted directly by McNulty's fake serial killer. As Templeton's story gains traction, Carcetti spins the narrative into pledging to help the homeless for his imminent campaign for governor. When Daniels gets wind of McNulty's fabrications, he informs Carcetti, who orders a cover-up, as the issue is central to his campaign. Meanwhile, Freamon gathers enough evidence to arrest Marlo and his top lieutenants. But as the case was secured on an illegal wiretap, attorney Maurice Levy (Michael Kostroff) secures Marlo's release on the condition that he permanently retire. Repeatedly at the *Sun*, city editor Gus Haynes (Clark Johnson) attempts to expose Templeton's fake stories but is demoted for repeatedly criticizing their star reporter. Omar is shot dead by Kernard in a corner store following Marlo's raised price on the outlaw's head. This seismic event is missed by the news because the likes of Templeton, Carcetti, and Davis are concerned more with perpetuating falsehoods to further their own careers.

The outlandish thrust of season 5 continues to divide fans, critics, and writers of *The Wire* alike. Richard Price thought that "David had a little too much of an ax to grind." Pelecanos concurs that "it's the most didactic of the seasons," and cowriter Burns has still "never seen season 5."[3] The *Washington City Paper* felt that anger had gotten the better of the showrunners Simon and Zorzi, claiming that Simon "couldn't make his point any clearer if he bought a full-page ad in the *Sun* with just the words financial cutbacks destroy the moral integrity of newsrooms."[4] *The Atlantic* accused Simon of having "embraced evil full-bore." Compared to the "complex bureaucratic fuckups" of previous seasons, both fictional editors happily run the paper into the ground simply for being "unvarnished assholes" and "straight psychopaths."[5] *Entertainment Weekly* went further, suggesting that Templeton is the "only truly irredeemable character" the show ever conjured up, his villainy so telegraphed that the actor went on to direct the Oscar-winning *Spotlight*, about the *Boston Globe*'s uncovering of the Catholic Church's widespread child sexual abuse, as penance.[6] Over the pond, U.K. critics took more issue with the serial killer narrative. *The Guardian* felt that "a scintillating exploration of Baltimore's cops and criminals turned into The Jimmy McNulty Show" and so compromised the "observational realism the previous four seasons were built on."[7] But the most venom came from *The Baltimore Sun*'s David Zurawick. After glowing reviews of previous seasons, the critic likened season 5 to "a cancer that grew deeper and deeper into other parts of the drama as the season wore on."[8] It is safe to say that he was not a fan. To test these criticisms, this final chapter considers how season 5 predicted the rise of populism across world politics given the election of Turkey's Recep Tayyip Erdoğan, Argentina's Javier Milei, Brazil's Jair Bolsonaro, Hungary's Viktor Orbán, U.K. prime minister Boris Johnson, and U.S. president Donald Trump. It uncovers how different definitions of populism begin taking hold over Baltimore's newspaper, police force, and politics in contravention of their founding principles. The chapter then concludes by employing popular criminology to determine why McNulty's fabricated serial killer is the only news story that can gain traction toward enacting some meaningful change across the city's institutions.

THE BALTIMORE SUN, 1837–

Simon has claimed that the final season "was not the work of people angry at *The Sun*." Rather, it was "written by ex-journalists who love the craft and who fear for its future. Following *The Sun*'s third buyout, it was never going to be the paper I wanted it to be."[9] So what kind of paper had it been?

Founded in 1837, Arunah S. Abell's *Baltimore Sun* was late to a crowded marketplace, battling seven dailies, seven weeklies, five semi-weeklies, and two monthlies with loyal readerships dating back 46 years. Abell introduced the first sustained and extensive systems of swift cooperative news gathering involving complicated combinations of four horse coaches, special locomotives, chartered ships, and even carrier pigeons to outrun the slowly expanding lines of the magnetic telegraph. Reporting the news faster than its competitors meant that it could sell copies of its content to exchange papers in Maryland, Ohio, and Kentucky. It's here in the aftermath of the Civil War that the *Sun*'s human interest stories, which Simon values so highly, began to uncover what life was like for everyday folk. From 1919 to 1981, the *Sun* was managed by family dynasties. In the era of John and Hamilton Owens from 1927 to 1956, accompanying human interest stories were long editorials and feature articles occupying the "grace, tone and length of essays" written from an "intellectual point of view . . . grounded in extensive reading" to espouse abstract theories of government over practical applications.[10] But by the 1960s, the *Sun* took a more liberal path on civil rights and assisting the needy. When 77-year-old William Schmick Sr. retired in March 1960, his son William Schmick Jr. and a new generation of younger reporters were dissatisfied with the paper's 30 years of entrenched conservatism and questioned with increasing intensity American involvement in the Vietnam War. Schmick Jr.'s editorials and philosophy on reporting were to enlighten or persuade the modern reader, who welcomes guidance but resists a shove. Interestingly, the paper supported Richard Nixon for president in 1960 given the paper's doubts over John F. Kennedy's domestic policies. But by 1964, its editorial pages strongly supported the Civil Rights Act and enthusiastically endorsed Lyndon B. Johnson as a president of "extraordinary force, wisdom, and vision."[11] This is the *Sun*'s heritage that Simon idolizes, a liberal championing of the oppressed while being unafraid to devote to long, sprawling column inches to theories of governance.

Shortly before Simon joined the *Sun* full time in 1981, 47-year-old John Reginald Murphy was the first editor hired outside of its offices. To keep up with the *Boston Globe*, the *Philadelphia Inquirer*, and the *Miami Herald*, Murphy expanded the *Sun*'s network into foreign bureaus. Now the *Sun* prided itself on taking a strong stand on human rights as a liberal newspaper underpinned by traditional center-right approach to international policy. In 1984, Murphy's *Sun* endorsed Regan's presidential campaign for his unapologetic readiness to have the United States play the role as the world's leading superpower. However, chasing writing awards simultaneously became the paper's priority. Alice Steinbach's 1985 Pulitzer Prize–winning story on the experiences of a blind 10-year-old was the paper's first in 36 years. A year later, the Abell company was bought by the Times Mirror Company. On May 17, 1987, the 150th-anniversary edition boasted the biggest-ever issue circulation, reaching an all-time high of 596,694 copies. This turned out to be the paper's nadir. Perpetually declining circulation decreased its value by two-thirds when it was sold again to Chicago's Tribune Company in 2000. Eight years later, while *The Wire*'s final season was being filmed, the paper declared bankruptcy. By the summer of 2009, 60 editorial employees, fully one-quarter of an already decimated staff, were laid off in a single day, a much larger scale than season 5 had predicted. Simon's depiction of the *Sun* is at a crossroads, with many of its staff keen to maintain its legacy of in-depth reporting while being pressured to chase awards and fight for survival among diminishing resources. Such conditions prove ripe for populism to poison the integrity of the news cycle.

POPULISM AS IDEOLOGY

Populism refers to divisive political leaders who secure power by capital-izing on the electorate's increasing feelings of marginalization due to eco-nomic and cultural globalization, increasing levels of immigration, and the decline of ideological class politics. In so doing, the claims of populist lead-ers can prove to be contradictory, unproven, outrageous, and even conspira-torial. European political scientist Cas Mudde set the agenda first defining populism as "a thin-centred ideology" that considers society to be ultimately separated into two homogeneous and antagonistic groups: "the pure people" and "the corrupt elite," where the populist argues that politics should be an expression of the *volonté générale* (general will) of the people.[12] For Mudde, populism does not exist in any pure form or coherent ideological tradition. Political scientists who subscribe to this model may focus on the ways popu-lists are invested in "the suppression of diversity" through a homogeniz-ing of society into two camps.[13] Nevertheless, all belonging to this tradition argue that populism is not a deliberate communication strategy that can be employed by anyone. A populist's actions are always guided by their inher-ent belief in a thin but divisive ideology between the corrupt elite and the pure everyman.

This general worldview that society comprises of morally upstanding people forever victim to a corrupt, out-of-touch elite can be attributed to Simon's depiction of *The Baltimore Sun*. Throughout season 5, the news-room is consistently separated into two homogeneous and antagonistic groups: executive editor James Whiting (Sam Freed) and his ally, manag-ing editor Thomas Klebanow (David Costabile), are regularly at odds with the reporting staff. When first introduced to the *Sun* offices, city desk editor Haynes smokes cigarettes with reporters outside the back of the newspa-per offices where the printed papers are loaded onto delivery trucks. This frank discussion informs our perception of the editors. Talking about the threat of possible layoffs, veteran police reporter Roger Twigg points out that Klebanow has a taste for hiring "sweet young . . . models with straight hair and big traffic light eyes." Political reporter Bill Zorzi, playing himself, then chips in, affirming that the young women Klebanow hires "can't write a lick," to which Haynes confirms, "Our esteemed managing editor certainly does favor a certain type." All men infer that Klebanow is morally cor-rupt exploiting cost-saving layoffs to leer at young women, simultaneously eradicating the diversity of the newsroom. Haynes then ascends the stairs to instruct Metro reporter Mike Fletcher (Brandon Young) to start writing, City Hall reporter Jeffrey Price to find news on the upcoming city council meeting, two journalists idling in the boardroom to start investigating a fire, and overnight copy editor Jay Spry to research cutbacks on city bus lines. Director Joe Chappelle felt that the dialogue-free scenes here are unusually long but give audiences "an idea of where they [the journalists] are in relation to one another."[14] Haynes converses and reasons with print workers, deliverymen, editors, journalists, and photographers from all departments across all genders, ages, and races. The duration of camera shots that follow Haynes up the stairs and through the offices, giving the impression of one smooth, elongated take, signifies that Haynes is a unifying everyman. He shares the general will of his fellow staff from the basement to the boardroom, committed to uncovering news buried under the bureaucracy of city council meetings and Johns Hopkins press conferences. Actor Clark Johnson likens his Haynes character to Robin Hood, a "good man" protecting what "news gathering really means."[15] He holds together the extensive systems of news gathering that Abell first founded in 1837 within a depleted modern context.

In line with *populism as ideology*, the only people standing in the way of Haynes's harmonious common will are his editors. Introduced later in the first episode, managing editor Klebanow hosts a meeting where section editors pitch him stories. Throughout the meeting, there is a clear divide between Klebanow and the rest of the team. While all the editors sit around a table, the managing editor sits behind his own desk, where he is exclusively framed by a long shot, isolated from his team, all of whom are framed by close-ups. Klebanow is keen for his reporters to produce a story on the cutbacks to the Maryland Transit Administration's routes and the impact it will have on commuters, the snag being that Klebanow has forgotten that he axed their transport reporter in their last round of buyouts. Then, as James Whiting walks in midway through the meeting, metro editor Steven Luxenberg mocks him, referring to him as "your eminence" for "slumming it at the metro meeting today," as if royalty anointed to his position because of his name rather than his capabilities. Engaging in a meeting beneath his station, Whiting grins in acknowledgment. As Whiting enters, he reclines directly in front of Klebanow's desk, silently looking through the printouts of news stories in a shared long shot with Klebanow sitting behind him. This dynamic between the senior editors and their staff is disrupted when regional affairs editor Rebecca Corbett mentions a 15-inch column they have received from the College Park stringer on the University of Maryland not meeting its desegregation targets. Whiting immediately interrupts, framed by a long shot at a great distance from Corbett, stating, "I've been told, numbers aside, that the campus has become much more hospitable to minorities."

When Luxemberg asks, "Really?" Whiting qualifies his point by explaining that he had lunch with their dean of journalism. Corbett tries to interject in a close-up, stating, "Nevertheless they haven't," to which Whiting continues to simply talk over her, declaring that the dean told him "how the last few years have really transformed the school's reputation with black faculty and students." Haynes challenges this view wryly, pointing out that "he's a white guy right?" to which Whiting informs them that "he is an excellent journalist and reliable source; I think race is beside the point." Haynes then confides in Corbett and Luxenberg as they return to their communal desks that the newsroom should be a place where people of all walks of life can argue. Here the drama occupies a criticism of the newsroom that could be construed as sharing an affinity with a populist ideology, as the general will of the newspaper staff is unified and morally righteous compared to the out-of-touch management more interested in satisfying themselves and their equally privileged friends.

Repeatedly, the cinematography separates the high-ranking editors and their newspaper staff into two homogeneous and antagonistic groups, pitting the "the pure people" against "the corrupt elite." In episode 2, "Unconfirmed Reports," Whiting launches a story series on Baltimore's schools,

Figure 7.1. There is a clear division between journalists and their most senior of editors. HBO/Photofest © HBO, Photographed by Paul Schiraldi.

asserting that he wants pieces that "concisely and clearly explain how the school system has failed inner city children," shutting down Haynes's view that they need to consider a wider lack of parenting, drug culture, and economic contexts. Whiting dismisses this as "getting bogged down in details," instead issuing instructions to "limit the scope" of the story while turning his back to the communal table of his reporters. Whiting villainously swivels his reclined chair away from his reporters, rolling his eyes and adjusting his tie as if he has heard these concerns before. Despite Haynes's challenge, Whiting emphatically asserts, "I don't want some amorphous series detailing society's ills," akin to the paper's proud tradition of writing editorials through the 1920s to 1960s grounded in extensive theories of government.

This division between an out-of-touch, corrupt elite and their honorable reporters still invested in the paper's traditions of holding power to account is furthered in episode 3, "Not for Attribution." Here both editors announce the latest series of cutbacks to staffing. Whiting's suit, braces, and bright red tie clash against the open-top checkered shirts of his reporters. Standing on a table with a puffed-out chest, Whiting looks out into the distance as if readying troops for battle, informing his reporters, "Chicago has given us some specific budgetary targets." In direct response, a collection of close-ups reveal Haynes exhaling in disbelief, junior reporters Templeton and Alma Gutierrez (Michelle Paress) looking to the floor as if in physical pain, and both Corbett and Twigg sharing a glazed expression, looking ahead into the distance mournfully. Fletch rolls his eyes knowingly, and Price scowls at Whiting through the corners of his eyes. Whether young, old, black, white, Asian, male, or female, all are unified through their lack of respect for their immediate superior, who relishes this spotlight before handing over to his second-in-command, Klebanow, for the specifics. Both Whiting and Klebanow repeatedly defer decision-making to an amorphous "Chicago" office, permitting them to wipe their hands clean of the devastating impact that cutbacks have on their staff. In comparison, even the most reprehensible police leaders do not mindlessly accept their orders. Despite being ruthless careerists, Deputy Ops Rawls and Commissioner Burrell still share kinship with their men, referring to them as "our people" when pushing back against the mayor's budget in episode 1. In Carcetti's office, the police leadership convinces the mayor to remove a cap on secondary employment to improve morale among their workforce. In contrast, Whiting and Klebanow are aligned with the *Tribune* cutting back staff even further despite the paper still being profitable. Both editors relish calling each worker into their office one at a time at the opposite end of the office. As if conducting a show trial, they inform each reporter of their fate. When called over, Haynes is informed that both men are "counting on" him "to transition the new team." He is effectively being kept to mentor cheaper reporters who will eventually replace him. With Haynes left voicing skepticism of this approach, Whiting tells him that "we are just going to have to do more with less," a cowardly deferral to the *Tribune*'s economic strategy of pursuing larger profits without regard for the welfare of the disenfranchised journalists who still hold investigative reporting in high regard.

The newspaper offices emulate a populism-as-ideology power structure, as both groups are antagonistically at odds with one another. The morally pure reporters are unified against their elite employers, who are complicitly corrupt in continuously pulling resource away from the paper and concentrating its wealth for its Chicago-based shareholders, who have little interest in the affairs of Baltimore, an economic model derivative of international corporations growing ever larger due to laxer global economic regulations. While Simon and Zorzi's drama is not deliberately or outwardly populist, the newspaper office scenes reveal the resentment and economic anxiety many American workers were feeling at that time. Working environments like this with such a disparity between morally corrupt management figures and their staff is what populist ideology exploits. Trump was able to win six swing states in 2016, which had previously voted Obama twice, by taking advantage of the increasing marginalization Americans were experiencing.

POPULISM AS A STRATEGY

Many political experts are less interested in populism's ideology, as they see populism as a deliberate communications strategy employed by an enigmatic leader to seize and sustain power through a loyal following. Here a populist can afford to be inconsistent with their positioning on issues when it is politically expedient to do so because they are sustained by a loyal fan base that is invested in the personality of their leader over his or her ideological consistency. To understand populism as a strategy is to examine how populist leaders mobilize, communicate with, and maintain loyalty from their unorganized followers through a bypassing of regular intermediaries, such as political party mechanisms and traditional media outlets.

In *The Wire*'s final season, Mayor Carcetti exploits the charismatic public persona that his team has cultivated to strategically secure the governorship. Having never expressed an interest in homelessness, Carcetti swiftly turns the public outcry toward homeless victims of a serial murderer into an opportunity to make grand policy commitments to tackle rising levels of homelessness and criticize the sitting Republican governor for allowing homelessness to increase. In so doing, Carcetti emulates the *populism-as-strategy* approach, as he bypasses traditional Democratic Party mechanisms to secure and mobilize a loyal following by communicating in a manner markedly different from traditional methods of political communication. The season begins with Carcetti stuck between a rock and a hard place. Having publicly promised the Fraternal Order of Police union in season 4 an end to the "department's obsession with stats" and an increase in pay, pensions, and equipment, season 5 begins with police morale at an all-time low. Sergeant Ellis Carver struggles to get through Western District briefings without officers protesting about their unpaid overtime and openly brawling in the parking lot over the state of their squad cars. Handheld camera shots connote the police on the verge of anarchy. In the very next scene, Carcetti explains privately to Rawls and Burrell that he needs a double-digit reduction in crime alongside the cuts that he has issued the police budget to fund the schools deficit. His ambitions to become governor appear to be in tatters, as shorting the police department to fund the schools leaves Carcetti as "a weak ass mayor of a broke ass city," as summarized by his adviser, Norman Wilson (Reg E. Cathey). Carcetti no longer has a strong mayoral platform to campaign on, as the $54 million he has diverted into the schools from the police budget has improved the test scores of third graders up 15 points, but in his first two years as mayor, crime has risen 8 percent each year from where he started. Analogously, Carcetti is unable to garner press interest or public enthusiasm for his continued mission to revitalize the Port of Baltimore. In episode 6, "The Dickensian Aspect," Carcetti opens the new Westport development, proudly asserting to the handful in attendance that he is building on the legacy of mayors "D'Alesandro," William Donald Schaefer, Schmoke, O'Malley," as it is now "my administration's turn" to continue regenerating the port. The ribbon-cutting ceremony is so lowly attended that former dockworker Nick Sobdotka of season 2 single-handedly sabotages the event, protesting that the mayor has torn down the port and sold it to "some yuppie assholes from Washington." Carcetti's well-trodden campaign strategy issued by the Democratic National Committee (DNC) to secure the governorship is not working.

Carcetti comes to embrace the populism-as-strategy approach during a subsequent press conference at the BPD on the homeless killings. Before going onstage, Carcetti privately complains with his adviser and chief of staff down a side corridor that this negative news story will bump his Westport story down the news agenda. To reassure Carcetti that the campaign plan is working, both have the mayor repeat the DNC's instructions to "build something downtown and stick your name on it," "get crime to go down," "stay away from schools," and "keep my boyish good looks," as if to reinscribe his faith in the national party's approved model of traditional political campaigning. Irked that the room is bursting with reporters compared to his

Westport opening, Carcetti instantaneously goes off script, complaining that "you guys aren't around when we're making real progress." As Carcetti then bumbles through a typical "tough on crime" statement from the podium, a camera frames him in a low-angle long shot from the front and an over-the-shoulder shot to reveal the gaggle of press at his feet. However, Carcetti quickly repositions his stance on addressing the killings as the camera cuts to frame him in a close-up and he puts himself forward as a champion of "those who have fallen through the cracks of our society." Now characterizing food banks and shelters as tokenistic, he tells the media, "I believe there is a different way of governing," and as the camera pushes through closer and closer into his face, he explains, "I believe that in the end we will be judged not by the efforts we make on behalf of those who vote for us, contribute to our campaign or those who provide for our tax base. I believe that we will be judged by what we provide the weakest and most vulnerable. That is the test, that is my test." This new approach is populism as strategy because Carcetti now isolates himself visually and verbally from previously traditional means of political campaigning and communication. Visually, the repositioned camera isolates Carcetti from the press and police, signifying how he is beginning to utilize unmediated quasi-direct speech to the public. Verbally, Carcetti bypasses regular intermediaries by criticizing campaign contributors, taxpayers, and voters to create and speak to further loyalist supporters as well as mobilize the marginalized homeless.

As Wilson points out before the speech, Carcetti's "boyish good looks" are all that the mayor has left from the DNC-approved four-point election campaign plan. Carcetti's charisma is the only political capital he has left, and he utilizes it to pivot his policy commitments away from the traditional terrain of schools, crime, and port redevelopment at a time that is politically expedient to do so. As the national media are in attendance, Carcetti opportunistically feigns a personal care for the homeless while articulating an anti-elite rhetoric toward traditional political party mechanisms. In a subsequent debrief, Steintorf commends the "passion" and "spirit" that Carcetti summoned in the police press conference, while his adviser Wilson praises Carcetti by emphatically yelling, "Praise be." Here religious language connotes how Carcetti is now looking to summon belief and faith in his image from his supporters despite, as he confesses, not really caring about the homeless cause. He made the point only because the whole case has "pissed me off." The scene concludes with Carcetti smiling and uttering the term "homelessness" with an upward inflection, signifying surprise that this is an issue he is now going to campaign on, before exclaiming, "I'll be damned." This is clearly populism as strategy, as he is no longer campaigning on an

Figure 7.2. Carcetti improvises during a police press conference to launch his governor election campaign. HBO/Photofest © HBO, Photographed by Paul Schiraldi.

issue he believes in. Carcetti chooses to campaign on what is expedient for his political career in a way that draws people into his charm.

In episode 8, "Clarifications," Carcetti ramps up his campaign by attending a Healthcare for the Homeless charity candlelight vigil on the City Hall steps for the serial killer's alleged victims. Here Carcetti has fully embraced populism as strategy to become governor as he delivers an even more zealous speech to an increasing number of unorganized followers gathering around the cult of his personality. Carcetti manipulates the vigil as a means of bypassing traditional media outlets and institutions to directly communicate with his followers. The speech begins with a camera panning down from the City Hall roof to Carcetti speaking at his podium as he announces that "these people I share the stage with tonight are representatives of the hundreds no the thousands of the citizens without shelter or protection in this city." This camera movement emphasizes that Carcetti is seeking to separate himself from those who hold the corridors of power in City Hall. As the camera pans down to Carcetti, he is framed in a long shot from the back of the crowd demonstrating the extent to which people have come to see him speak in direct contrast to his Westport opening. Then the camera tracks along a line of homeless people sitting on chairs to the side of the podium as, in close-up, Carcetti heatedly asks the crowd, "Why does this have to be?" as if to make visible the maligned homeless in the same breath as denouncing the political establishment not providing "the same levels of federal commitment to American cities" for the past seven years. Then, in a low-angle shot of him at his podium, Carcetti shouts, "These people with whom I share the stage with cannot be invisible." With each new line of the speech, the camera cuts between shots of adoring faces in the crowd looking up toward their savior and shots that are increasingly closer to Carcetti's face as his speech reaches a messianic crescendo, the crowd applauds, and he shakes hands with each homeless person sitting beside him. This is populism as strategy because Carcetti has managed to attract unmediated support from large numbers of mostly unorganized followers, mobilized the homeless into becoming publicly visible, and attacked those in power. Carcetti's rhetoric presents himself a man of the people, while the camera angles slightly undercut this narrative, suggesting that his followers view him as some sort of savior. This is clearly a populist strategy rather than a populist ideology because when Carcetti learns that the serial killer was invented by McNulty, he conceals the public from the truth so not as to impact his campaign image. As Wilson summarizes, the police "manufactured an issue to get paid," and "we manufactured an issue to get you elected governor," so "everyone [is] getting what they need behind some make-believe." The key difference between Trump and Carcetti is that Carcetti has not knowingly lied from the start of his campaign. Lying is something that Carcetti chooses to maintain once he discovers the truth. This is why Simon claims, "I did not anticipate the political collapse of the country in terms of [Donald] Trump. [Tommy Carcetti] is a professional politician. Donald Trump is sui generis."[16] That said, the felonious dealings of Senator Clay Davis are actually a more fitting comparison with Trump's rise to power, as both display a certain style of performance to repeatedly lie their way out of trouble.

POPULISM AS PERFORMANCE

The final school of thought for understanding populism focuses on the performances of populist figures whereby they first appeal to "the people" utilizing slang, outlandish gesturing, and eccentric clothing to separate themselves from "politics as usual." Clay Davis encompasses the *populism-as-performance* strategy. In season 5, Davis becomes a target for the newly elected State Attorney Rupert Bond. Bond redirects the Major Crimes Unit's Freamon and Sydnor into forensically investigating Davis's financial records uncovering that the senator has been withdrawing money from his nonprofit charitable initiatives and depositing the exact same sums into his own personal bank account. Facing several counts of stealing from his own charities with the possibility of a 10-year sentence for each count, Davis is called to testify at a grand jury deposition before the trial. Leaving the deposition, Davis looks to be a broken man. Sydnor and Freamon observe Davis occupying a thousand-yard stare and steadying himself against a bench before leaving the courthouse visibly shaken and terrified, having seen the cast-iron evidence firsthand. However, when Davis is confronted by the media outside, he looks to the floor, gathers himself, and lifts up his head, now displaying a beaming smile. Davis openly denies that he is the target of an investigation of theft and fraud, exclaiming, "No partner, nooo [laughs], some people are confused about some things." By inhabiting a performance, Davis brushes off the serious allegations as a "misunderstanding." Here Davis excoriates himself from politics as usual by referring to the reporters by their first names and immediately portraying himself as an avuncular figure helping a dysfunctional system iron out its problems by simply issuing clarifications.

In comparison, State Attorney Rupert Bond is very much representative of traditional politics. His opening speech to the press on the city court steps as the trial commences in episode 5, "React Quotes," exudes traditional virtues of the political establishment. Bond is equally serious, earnest, and intelligent in explaining the reasoning for the case. As an expert and professional in his field, Bond's statement to the press is couched in legal nuance explaining that "this indictment is the result of an 18-month investigation by the state attorney's office and the Baltimore Police Department." Bond puts himself forward as a representative of the complex machinery of government working across institutions over a protracted series of consultations, reviews, reports, and lengthy iterative cross-referencing of evidence. With this grounding, he informs the press in attendance, "It shines a light on a cornerstone issue for any representative government." While Bond explains the details of the case, the camera watches Pearlman's movements in the crowd as she whispers information to the journalists, helping to color how they report the case. The whole scene is representative of conventionally slow politics as Bond clearly reads from his prewritten script in an authoritative yet decidedly monotone way with little to no gesturing or inflections in his words. With plans to run for senator, he paints himself as a serious, calculated, unemotional operator quoting laws to signal that he can be trusted with high office. So convinced by Bond's composed display, Carcetti is convinced that Davis "ain't getting up from this."

To turn around his fortunes and win what appears to be an open-and-shut case, Davis summons each stage of Moffitt's three-point populism

Figure 7.3. Senator Clay Davis appears to be a broken man when he first learns of the criminal charges he is facing. HBO/Photofest © HBO.

as performance. First, Davis inhabits the first stage of populism as performance: *appealing to the people*. Here the populist performer claims to "really know" what people are thinking and in certain instances denies expert knowledge and champions "common sense" against bureaucrats and government representatives.[17] He undercuts the narrative that Bond has established on the courtroom steps by appearing on East Baltimore community radio station WOLB 1010 AM to align himself with his fellow black Americans. His radio interview begins with his informing his interviewer how difficult it is being a black person in high office before then focusing on "the people know—*now I'm talking about the people now*—the people know what I've done for West Baltimore and this city as a whole—they know the battles I've been fighting in Annapolis every day, they know these charges ain't nothing but BS." Here Davis asserts that he is talking to the people three times in quick succession and that he is appealing to their interests, affirming that he knows what they are really thinking. Here the banner for the WOLB station comes into view behind him, prominently displaying that the grassroots community station is "your news talk network where information is power!" Davis concludes the interview, promising, "I have committed no crime, and I am going to keep on doing the people's work without breaking stride" before the host reminds listeners of the gathering at the courthouse to "lift every voice." Davis legitimizes his felonies by appealing to the people.

Cut to the next scene, and on the courthouse steps, Davis's followers witness former Mayor Royce delivering a speech, using Moffitt's second stage of populism as performance: convincing Davis's loyal voters that society is undergoing *crisis, breakdown, threat*. This second stage provides populists with an impetus to act decisively and immediately bypass complex governmental machinery in favor of short-term and swift action over the "slow politics" of policy negotiation. The scene opens with a long shot of a cheering crowd holding placards surrounding the steps right up to Royce's level. There is a marked contrast from Bond's carefully curated scene where the state attorney is framed by a commanding low-angle shot and reporters maintain a respectful distance at the bottom of the steps. Comparatively, Royce is filmed at eye level as he informs the people in attendance that the legal representatives of Baltimore want them to believe that "their so-called facts cannot be denied" before encouraging the crowd to agree that "we have some facts of our own, don't we?" This time, from Royce's approximate point of view, from an over-the-shoulder shot, the crowd of ordinary voters are directly in eyeline, looking straight at Royce and passionately repeating the lines expected of them. Comparatively, Bond was talking down to a group of reporters as they made careful notes at his feet, clearly knowing their place in the legal hierarchy. Royce then goes on to hysterically shout, "We don't want them picking our leaders for us, do we?" and "We will not stand idly by as they single out our leaders and selectively . . . persecute them just because they have the courage and fortitude to stand up for us" to rounds of applause. This scene is eerily similar to the 2021 "insurrection," where Trump told his followers on January 6 in full view of the Capitol building at his Save America March that "we will stop the steal" of the 2021 election as "we fight like hell . . . down Pennsylvania Avenue." Likewise, Royce, a former political leader with a loyal fan base, whips the crowd into a frenzy of applause so as to "let them hear you loud and clear . . . we're going to keep him [Davis] and damn anyone who says otherwise." Both Trump and Davis use a speech to mobilize their supporters against those who legitimately hold political office by characterizing them as belonging to an elitist conspiracy. It is made clear that Royce's speech on the courthouse steps is a performance designed to question and undermine the legitimacy of the legal process, as the scene concludes with Royce whispering to Davis out of earshot from the crowd that "you better" win. The passion underlying Royce's and Davis's performance does not extend to their own personal beliefs. Both men conceal this vocalizing of their concerns that Davis may not win behind smiles to their followers while Royce holds Davis's hand up.

Then, when taking the stand, Davis heightens the regularity of the third and final stage of Moffitt's populism as performance. *Bad manners* is where populist generate public appeal by regularly harnessing swearing, political incorrectness, and being "colorful" to oppose the traditionally appropriate rigidness and technocratic language of established politicians. By episode 7, "Took," Davis becomes unapologetically defiant about his lawbreaking. When pressed by his own lawyer to account for the four separate $11,000 payments that were withdrawn from his charities into his own personal bank account, Davis simply responds that he has no records because last winter, "half my district was gonna have the heat turned off." He then uses this prompt to inform the jury, "Let me tell you something man . . . my neck of the woods it's a jungle out there. . . . Hell, that TV show *Survivor*, man they want good contestants they need to come around West Side . . . hell and fear factor aww shit don't even get me started," prompting laughter from the jury and the public gallery. Davis then elaborates, "Let me tell you something brother, I don't know how they do it out in Roland Park [an upper-class streetcar suburb from the 1890s to 1920s that he accuses Bond of coming from], but my world is strictly cash and carry." He continues, "Let me tell you brother, step out the door hit the corner of Mosher and Pennsylvania, you better believe my pockets are bulging, but by the time I get to Robert Street . . ." Davis then proceeds to stand up and turn his pockets inside out to demonstrate to the jury that they are empty while pouting his lips and blowing raspberries in a clownlike manner, prompting the jury to laugh and the gallery, filled with his supporters from outside the courtroom, to applaud. Davis then vows to the court that if found innocent, he will keep acting as before "until they got me laid out in Marches Funeral Home," to which the public gallery reaches such an ardent applause with whooping and hollering that the judge struggles to maintain order in the courtroom. Davis is given the space to paint himself as a martyr giving the powerless, ripped-off, and voiceless members of his community direct access to cash to pay their medical and heating bills by coloring this narrative with bad manners. The accused senator oversteps the appropriate codes of acting in the courtroom by cussing, referring to his lawyer as "my brother," and making assumptions about the prosecutor's background in an overly slapstick manner, from pulling faces for comedic effect to supposedly coming close to tears when he defiantly pledges that he will continue to look after his constituents in the same way should he be found innocent. Editor Kate Sanford explains that they deliberately shot the long courtroom sequence beginning with wide shots,

the middle of the proceedings with medium shots, and then the final seg-
ment with close-ups. This deliberately "reels the viewers in" to the cruder
and more eccentric elements of this "emotional performance."[18] As Davis
then leaves the trial a free man, Bond asks Pearlman, "What the fuck just
happened?" to which she replies, "Whatever it was, they don't teach it in law
school." Some 20 years later, it is obvious that Davis was employing each
stage of Moffitt's populism as performance.

MCNULTY'S SERIAL KILLING

Within this emerging milieu of populism, the only news story that can gar-
ner public interest toward fixing homelessness, questioning the BPD's conduct, addressing the existing governor's shortcomings, and putting a stop to
Marlo's widespread homicides is a fabricated serial killer story. McNulty's
faked serial killer abides by Steve Chibnall's eight-step formula of crime
reporting that popular criminologists are continuously utilizing to better
understand the public's enduring fascination with murder. McNulty employing each stage of newsworthiness is what eventually mobilizes the press, the
police department, politicians, and the public into caring about the homeless
and providing him with the resources he needs to charge Marlo.

1. Dramatization

According to Chibnall, the news is compelled to emphasize the action and
drama of the unfolding situation at the expense of "underlying patterns of
motivation."[19] McNulty realizes early on that there must be a degree of
drama to the manner in which victims are murdered to capture the newspaper's attention. In episode 2, "Unconfirmed Reports," he and Bunk are
called to a homeless cadaver overdosed on alcohol in a vacant row house.
McNulty, without warning, upturns the chair that the body fell from before
shoulder barging exposed plasterboard until it cracks, sprinkling its dust over
the back pocket of the dead body. McNulty then turns over the dead body
and rips open the collar of its shirt before strangling it to give the deceased
bruise marks on his neck. After each moment, there is a dramatic pause as if
McNulty considers stopping before escalating his degree of tampering with
the crime scene and defiling the body. Watching on, a baffled Bunk protests
in disgust, "You sick fuck" as McNulty behaves erratically and dramatically.
After ripping the man's clothes, he tells Bunk as if narrating his actions,

"There's a serial killer in Baltimore, and he preys on the weakest among us; he needs to be caught." Then as Bunk leaves in disgust, McNulty turns the body over onto its front and pulls it up from its waist so that the dead man lies with his head on the floor and rear end in the air as if in makeshift downward dog position. McNulty firmly rubs down the body's back toward the neck so that blood rushes to the head to make it appear as if the strangulation happened when the man was alive. Adding evidence of a dramatic struggle to the dead homeless man is needed to pique some press interest.

2. Personalization

However, according to Chibnall, events are understood primarily through the personalities of characters involved over any larger societal issues. In episode 3, "Not for Attribution," McNulty soon learns that linking three murders, however dramatically, is not enough to attract sustained press interest. McNulty reaches out to junior reporter Gutierrez, whom he informs that the murders are linked because the killer has tied a red ribbon to the wrists, something that McNulty himself has retroactively added to reports and to corpses. This ensures that the killings are given a few lines in the Metro section of the paper and prompts sergeant Landsman to assign McNulty for two days on the allegedly linked murders before putting him back on the rotation. McNulty has added personalization, giving the serial killer an identifiable behavioral characteristic: a modus operandi. He also ascribes a personality to the invented victims, in this instance, vulnerable homeless people at the mercy of a killer with a superiority complex. Adding personality to the dramatic killings is enough to attract some interest from the newspaper and the Homicide Department, but it is not seismic enough for McNulty to secure enough resources and manpower that can be surreptitiously diverted to investigating Marlo.

3. Titillation

According to Chibnall, news thrives on catering for "the voyeuristic predilections of its readers" given a commercial imperative to titillate readers over studious reporting of "politics and social problems."[20] Freamon understands that sex sells and, when McNulty asks him for help at the end of episode 3, advises that they need to "sensationalize" the murders by giving the killer "some fucked-up fantasy something bad, real bad" to "grip the hearts and minds" and "give the people what they want from a serial killer." With the department seemingly uninterested in three murder cases linked by a red ribbon, Freamon and McNulty proceed to imprint a set of dentures on a fourth body in episode 4, "Transitions," to infer that the killer has bitten his victims. During an informal meeting in episode 5, "React Quotes," Templeton asks McNulty for more information beyond the killer simply being a "sexual compulsive." To make the story "come alive" and make the front page, the use of a red ribbon may be "kinky," but it is "not enough." McNulty then divulges that the killer started biting his victims, which satisfies Templeton as being newsworthy enough for a leading story, and rushes off with Guttierez to make the second edition. McNulty is then pleased to find the following morning that *The Baltimore Sun*'s front-page headline reads, "Sexual motive season in killings of homeless," the strapline elaborating, "Bite marks tied to serial slayer." Having added a degree of titillation enables McNulty to make the front page and attract some attention from Landsman, Daniels (recently promoted to deputy ops), and Carcetti, who are willing to provide McNulty with two extra detectives to work the case with additional overtime hours. This is not quite yet the amount of additional manpower that can be used to surreptitiously secure charges to Marlo, but it is a significant start.

4. Structured Access

Biting also grounds the story in structured access to authoritative pronouncements of experts in the field. Both reporters accept McNulty's word as a credible expert that the serial killer has started biting because the killer is "maturing." McNulty informs both reporters that "maturing" is a technical term: "when a serial killer starts becoming obsessive, he starts to develop an intricate pattern in what he does with the bodies." Despite simply recycling the words of his colleague Freamon, both reporters defer to McNulty given his authority as a homicide detective. The biting information coming from McNulty confirms for them that the story warrants front-page treatment.

5. Immediacy

The most crucial of Chibnall's imperatives that finally gives McNulty the level of public interest he needs to secure the amount of resources needed for the Marlo investigation is immediacy. As Freamon comes to realize that Marlo is using cell phone photographs to communicate with his crew, he needs McNulty to secure the correct wiretapping technology to capture the photos as well as the staff needed to decipher the code within them. By episode 6, "The Dickensian Aspect," McNulty's efforts have provided Freamon with bugs, cameras, and a wiretap following the fabricated killer's biting hitting the headlines. To upscale the investigation into securing Freamon with the resources he needs, McNulty heightens the immediacy of the killings by sending photos of a homeless man to Templeton. Episode 7, "Took," begins with McNulty and Freamon significantly raising the immediacy of the situation by ringing Templeton with a voice modulator, posing as the serial killer threatening to kill again. The episode's opening emulates the cinematography of an action thriller, adding a heightened tension to the proceedings. As Templeton receives the call, a handheld camera emulates his shock as he hurriedly tries to grab the attention of his editors to note down what the serial killer is telling him. McNulty and Freamon have a limited time frame, space, and volume confined to the BPD's server room, where they work, hoping not to arouse suspicion as they use a phone masked as Marlo's cell phone. Simultaneously Homicide officers hurriedly attempt to locate the physical location of McNulty's phone. Freamon has already factored Homicide into his plan and so altered the phone company paperwork on the case to a cell phone that he has Sydnor plant in the harbor. Immediacy is the most important factor because turning the case into an active serial killer announcing who his victims are ensures that the story continues to make headline news, compels Judge Phelan to sign a new wiretap order, and leaves a furious Carcetti with little option other than to finally lift the ban on police overtime. Now McNulty becomes what Bunk refers to as "the queen of diamonds," as he is able to divert any equipment and overtime to his fellow under-resourced Homicide detectives.

6. Novelty, 7. Conventionalism, and 8. Oversimplification

While immediacy is the most imperative of Chibnall's criteria for crime newsworthiness, the criminologist's final three imperatives play a constant role. At each stage of bringing a story of serial killings to the press's attention, McNulty is providing a different "novelty" by adding a "fresh twist of interpretation" to sustain the reader's interest in unfolding events. As Templeton asks McNulty shortly before the detective divulges the biting revelation, the reporters need "something with a twist" to publish a fresh headline article on the existing story. Then, despite the public pressure and political will that McNulty and Freamon manage to divert from the homeless to taking Marlo off the streets, no meaningful large-scale change is produced. The *Sun* reverts to Chibnall's "conventionalism," thus alleviating the need for further investigation. As a copycat killer emerges emulating McNulty's faked techniques to kill a further victim, the man's arrest closes the case for all involved, particularly the newspaper. Finally, there is "oversimplification" that Chibnall claims is the glossing over of the subtle complexities of motivation and situation. In the final episode, Chibnall's final step comes to pass when Corbett reveals to Haynes that the *Sun* is crediting its own coverage of the homelessness issue for "changing the governor's mind" despite there being no proof. The paper has painted itself as the hero of the story crusading against the governor's neglect of the homeless when, in fact, as Haynes points out, the governor has restored funding because "Carcetti's been beating the shit out of him on the issue." The *Sun* has not consistently reported on the complex intertwined societal factors that produce homelessness, nor has it consistently campaigned to help the homeless as it would have traditionally. According to this final season, the paper now follows Chibnall's reductive eight-step model, which McNulty can exploit to pressure his BPD superiors into dispensing resources. The paper takes credit for the resulting political change only as an afterthought to lobby for a Pulitzer Prize as is the editorial priority of their Chicago shareholders.

While many critics feel that season 5 was too heavy-handed in communicating its criticism of newspapers, some years later, it is clearly a season that astutely uncovered the roots of what would become known as populism. *The Wire*'s last-ever episode concludes with the show's signature montage. McNulty takes a moment to look out over the city skyline before looking to the camera and displaying a wry smile. We then see Templeton receiving a Pulitzer Prize and Slim Charles assuming Marlo's role. Carcetti is made Maryland governor, declaring that it is "a great day for Baltimore." Haynes pridefully looks over his busy reporters. Valchek is made commissioner of the BPD, asserting that his new hat "fits like a glove." Meanwhile, Dukie shoots up heroin, Rhonda Pearlman ushers in her first case as a judge, Chris Partlow walks across the prison yard to Wee-Bey, and Rawls is promoted by Carcetti to Maryland State Police superintendent as a reward for keeping the faked serial killer story under wraps. Initially, the thrust of the montage is to highlight, as all the others have, how nothing changes and the drug war continues to roll on across both sides of the law. In this instance, however, our attention is specifically drawn to individuals who willingly and repeatedly propagate lies securing promotions while those who have exhibited some integrity and promise—McNulty, Haynes, and Dukie—find their circumstances still unchanged, even worsened. Simon felt that this final montage "tried to say something new about the characters" and "tried not to repeat ourselves."[21] Within this familiar closing montage, then, are also signs of hope. Lester Freamon embraces his girlfriend Shardene, D'Angelo's ex, proving that this romantic union has outlasted the first season, when they were last seen together. Bubbles finally walks up the stairs from his sister's basement to enjoy dinner with her and her child at the dining room table. Following a year of sobriety from heroin, Bubbles has made the ascent to redemption. A crucial part of his recovery has been spending time with *Sun* reporter Fletcher, who has written an honest piece of narrative journalism— in the style Simon used to write—to help society address its problems. This hints that there are still journalists fighting to preserve the paper's tradition of educating its public in complex theories of governance through the compelling stories of downtrodden Baltimore residents, all despite the *Sun*'s editors following Chibnall's eight-step tabloid model of sensationalizing and simplifying crime reporting to win awards. Therefore, season 5's biggest departure from previous seasons is the recognition that there is some capacity for progress, no matter how small, for certain individuals among the institutional power structures of the drug trade. A person's fate is not necessarily always predetermined as previous seasons would have us believe, even if institutions are becoming embroiled in populism.

CONCLUSION

The Lasting Impact of *The Wire*

ON UNIVERSITIES

Twenty years since *The Wire* first debuted on our television screens, the show continues to change the world. One of the biggest impacts it continues to have is on university campuses. "I actually went to a university to speak about the wire in Utah," says actor Seth Gilliam (Ellis Carver). "I talked to the kids who were excited to be discussing the subject matter. . . . I don't know a lot of cop shows that have this far-reaching impact almost a generation later."[1] For Idris Elba, this is what he values more than any award because any conversation that becomes curriculum eventually "becomes an instrument of change."[2] Confirms Clarke Peters (Lester Freamon), *The Wire* "promoted a conversation that is still ongoing. It has become a reference point in universities not only here but in England as well."[3] And the subject range is endless.

Sociologists feel that *The Wire* has something to teach their students about poverty, class, bureaucracy, and the social ramifications of economic change. Former president of the American Sociological Association William Julius Wilson was among the first to utilize *The Wire* for teaching because he found it "more poignant and compelling [than] that of any published study, including my own."[4] In terms of medical science, former president of the European College of Neuropsychopharmacology David John Nutt confirms that "what the drug does in the brain you actually see in *The Wire*."[5] Former Baltimore City health commissioner Peter L. Beilenson also uses the show in his public health studies course at Johns Hopkins to hook student interest in urban policy and public health issues affecting cities across the nation.

Furthermore, the show has inspired more scholarly interventions than any other American television program. Jonathan Havercroft and Shirin

Deylami have compiled studies in *The Politics of HBO's The Wire*. Arin Keeble and Ivan Stacy's *The Wire and America's Dark Corners* brings together critical essays that analyze the show's view of the War on Terror. David Bzdak, Joanna Crosby, and Seth Vannatta look into the show's philosophy in *The Wire and Philosophy*. Tiffany Potter's and C. W. Marshall's *The Wire: Urban Decay and American Television* and Stanley Corkin's *Connecting The Wire: Race, Space, and Postindustrial Baltimore* are grounded largely in urban geography. Jocelyn DeVance Taliaferro's and Tia Sherèe's *Teaching the Wire: Frameworks, Theories and Strategies for the Classroom* instructs teachers how to use *The Wire* to meet existing course objectives on leadership, gender expression, sexuality, education, and democratic policy. All the while, film and television scholars have endlessly identified how the show has uniquely combined issues of race, class, and genre, including Liam Kennedy's *Race, Class, and Genre*. Sherryl Vint's *The Wire* concludes that "real social change" happens only if audiences "recognize *The Wire* as more than compelling television."[6] Ten years later, has this social change come to pass?

ON BALTIMORE CITY

The Wire has instigated change directly through Baltimore community initiatives overseen by its cast and crew. David Simon and Ed Burns's Ella Thompson Fund is named after a real person whose life story features in *The Corner*. Following the rape and murder of her 12-year-old daughter, Thompson becomes increasingly determined to rekindle community spirit as a volunteer for the Martin Luther King Jr. Recreation Center. Thompson is depicted as a one-woman peacekeeper, commanding respect from corner crews and convincing them to deal drugs elsewhere.

Shortly after *The Corner* was published, Thompson died of a heart attack while distributing donated computer equipment when driving her car. Before her death, Simon and Burns had agreed to donate their speaker fees from *The Corner* book tour into a new fund to help Thompson program recreational activities across four different centers. At the time, both men were not making huge revenues from speaking. But following their subsequent collaborations with HBO, the Ella Thompson Fund now has $2 million in its bank account. Overseen by the Parks and People Foundation, the fund contributes to the charity's six-week SuperKids camp, which keeps local inner-city children fed and literate through the summer months for free with 31,000 graduates to date. Like Cutty's boxing gym, the fund also helps provide middle school pupils with travel, kits, equipment, coaching, and food to participate in team sport competitions. High school children are also offered paid internships to enter the jobs market. For the foundation's director of development, Carolyn Younce, *The Wire* "validated the need for organizations like ours." It also helped spur the Johns Hopkins Center for the Prevention of Youth Violence into informing decision-makers on the need for trauma-informed care across Baltimore.[7]

In a similar vein, actress Sonja Sohn (Kima Greggs) cofounded her own nonprofit, ReWired for Change, to deter children from crime. In 2008, Sohn toured the country with other *Wire* cast members to educate young Americans about voting rights. She soon discovered that they had influence. In North Carolina, people who had not voted in previous elections were now doing so. From 2010 to 2015, Sohn made it her personal mission to utilize her celebrity to empower and educate Baltimore's most at-risk 7- to 13-year-olds already implicated in crime. After-school classes took place at the Village House community home in East Baltimore. Here a weeklong program would begin with an episode of *The Wire* to start discussions about the characters, issues, and themes in relation to the pupils' own experiences. *The Wire* was central to Sohn's four-step program, enabling participants to (1) understand the importance of self-reflection, (2) positively affect their own family and community, (3) understand their relationship to public institutions, and (4) undertake civic engagement to enact the change that society needs. For CEO Sohn, season 4 spurred people into action. "When you're out there in activist circles you start to realize that the change agents out there trying to change policy to make society better were so influenced by this show."[8]

Curiously, Wendell Pierce (Bunk Moreland) has a different approach to improving Baltimore's social inequality, what he calls "gentrification without displacement."[9] Following ReWired for Change's operational years, in 2016, the actor announced his plans for a $20 million apartment complex. The Nelson Kohl building, of which Pierce is the largest investor, sits within the city's Station North neighborhood, an arts and entertainment district just north of downtown. Built on an empty lot, the all-rental units range from $1,400 to $2,100 per month, priced out of reach for an average resident of Baltimore, where the median income is $41,000 per year. Critics are quick to point out that apartments overlooking a train station that whisks workers to Washington, D.C., in less than an hour are not meeting the housing needs of a city undergoing an affordable accommodation crisis. But Pierce insists that he is creating mixed-income and mixed-use neighborhoods that will ultimately benefit low-income, minority ethnic residents. He feels that the prices of his apartments are raising the incomes and property values for all Baltimoreans. His strategy also involves reserving units at a cheaper rate for artists displaying work, providing a developer apprenticeship, and helping first-time buyers on the property ladder by restoring vacant row houses with Pierce's team acting as guarantor. Whatever the method, Simon, Burns, Sohn, and Pierce have clearly had direct involvement in changing the city, from schooling its children to investing in property, following their involvement on *The Wire*.

ON RIOTING

On April 12, 2015, 25-year-old Freddie Gray made his way through the Gilmor Homes housing project in West Baltimore. As bicycle patrol officers Garret Miller, Edward Nero, and Brian Rice turned a corner, Gray instinctively ran. He was pursued by all three lawmen before Miller forced Gray to the ground and restrained him. Searching Gray, the officers found a folding knife that appeared to violate an outdated local ordinance on switchblades. Gray's request for an asthma inhaler went ignored as he was handcuffed and placed in a prisoner transport van without being secured. The van drove off but stopped a block away, where flex cuffs were applied to Gray's wrists and his feet shackled before he was reloaded onto the prison van face down. The van made two additional stops where no medical assistance was provided despite Gray's pleas for help. The officers would later say that Gray had been out of control, kicking the inside of the van and requiring further restraint. But observers had recorded images of Gray being loaded back into the van motionless, his legs hanging lifelessly out the back. Those present were convinced that Gray was suffering from a spinal injury that had caused his legs to stop working. When the van arrived at the Western District station 45 minutes after the initial arrest, Gray was not breathing. He underwent surgery the next day for three broken vertebrae and an injured voice box. He remained in a weeklong coma and died on April 19 from his spinal injuries. His spinal cord was 80 percent severed.

Videos of Gray being dragged by police surfaced online alongside images of him clinging to life, hooked up to tubes and machines in the hospital. Civil unrest soon erupted. Within six days of Gray's arrest, hundreds of people demonstrated outside the Western District police station. After Gray died, protests continued to unfold outside BPD headquarters and City Hall. A week later, on April 25, a major protest in downtown Baltimore turned violent. Thousands of protestors assembled in the Western District to join a City Hall rally. Approximately 200 demonstrators clashed with Baltimore Orioles fans attending a game at Camden Yards stadium. Here a small group from each crowd started throwing smashed bottles at one another and brawling. The situation swelled into a hostile scuffle between black protestors, white suburban fans, and bar patrons. As demonstrators were then confronted with 50 police officers in patrol uniform, everyone involved channeled their attention into pelting the officers with rocks and bricks. Then, as the crowd began destroying parked police cars, additional police wearing riot gear swept down Howard Street, where 12 people were arrested, and the crowd was eventually dispersed.

Then, after Gray's funeral on April 27, civil disorder intensified. Amidst rumors that high school students were planning a "purge" from Mondawmin Hall to downtown on the day of Gray's funeral, police shut down the Mondawmin metro stop. Nearby streets were blockaded, leaving students from Frederick Douglass High School unable to leave the area via public transportation. Police accounts insist that school-aged students attacked police with bricks. However, teachers and parents contend that the incident was ignited when police in riot gear forced riders off buses and blocked roads. Allegedly, it was only after police left their children stranded that some vented their frustration by throwing rocks and water bottles. Nevertheless, the violence rapidly spread. Two patrol cars were destroyed, 15 officers were injured, and an under-construction senior housing project was razed to the ground. Rioting continued through to April 28. As businesses were looted and burned, Governor Larry Hogan declared a state of emergency, deploying the Maryland National Guard. As military vehicles descended on Baltimore, the remaining crowds were dispersed, and a curfew was established.

In the wake of this citywide disorder, *The Wire*'s production was also deployed to calm the rioting and help the city make sense of what had occurred. As violence ensued, David Simon, Wendell Pierce, and Andre Royo issued statements. When Novak's Grocery Store was burned down—the location where Omar is shot dead—Royo tweeted, "To my Beloved city Baltimore. I feel your pain. Stand up. Rise UP without breaking down! Discipline not Destruction.[10] Then, as a state of emergency was declared, David Simon released a statement on his website urging the rioters, "If you can't seek redress and demand reform without a brick in your hand, you risk losing this moment for all of us in Baltimore. Turn around. Go home. Please."[11] Perhaps this did have an indirect impact, as when the National Guard stood down on May 3, not a single civilian died, and far fewer people were injured than the 1968 riots.

Later that year on July 28, 2015, Sonja Sohn organized an event called "Wired Up!" where cast members performed monologues written by Penn

North residents who had been subjected to police brutality and subsequent rioting. To a crowd of 1,000 attendees at the Lyric Opera House, Sohn, Gilliam, Royo, Michael K. Williams, Larry Gilliard Jr., Felicia "Snoop" Pearson, Chad Coleman, Jamie Hector, Deirdre Lovejoy, and Anwan Glover each performed. Every monologue had been developed by Sohn's ReWired for Change workshops with members of the public. Dominic West, Wendell Pierce, and David Simon all had prerecorded messages projected. One particularly emotional monologue came from Robert Wisdom (Howard "Bunny" Colvin), who spoke from the perspective of a man who has seen more tragedy in his 25 years than many do in a lifetime. Overall, the event was designed to celebrate the unsung community heroes of Baltimore. Sohn told the audience, "We're actors, and what we can do is to build a platform to raise voices that need to be heard."[12] In between speeches, awards were given to community leaders, including the founders of Safe Streets, youth mentors, Lieutenant Colonel Melvin Russell of the BPD, and social justice activist Makayla Gilliam-Price. At apposite moments, *The Wire*'s cast and crew have given maligned voices a platform and brought a range of community leaders together in dialogue with victims of racial prejudice and police officers to help impoverished Baltimore communities rationalize civil disorder.

Following her Wired Up! event, Sonja Sohn utilized her community connections to direct *Baltimore Rising* (2017). Her debut documentary captures the protestors taking to the streets and the pretrial hearings of all six officers implicated in Freddie Gray's death. Although they are often on opposite sides of the conflict, the film compassionately follows local activists, police, and community leaders trying to make a positive difference. Her film's aim is to remind us that "when we are in conflict, we can communicate with one another in a respectful manner" to devise solutions and reach agreements so that the city can proactively forge a more peaceful future.[13] This is a positive impact that has emanated from *The Wire*'s legacy. When the killing of George Floyd erupted into national outrage, some Black Lives Matter protests snowballed into civic disorder. Minneapolis was burned and looted. Curfews were established in New York, Washington, Atlanta, and San Francisco. Baltimore was not one of them. Following the 2015 Freddie Gray riots, Sohn's Wired Up! event and 2017 film had helped the city become more predisposed than others to reflect on how to campaign for change. Grassroots community organizations were now in closer dialogue with each other, their constituents, and government institutions. Journalists now observed that "thousands took part in passionate peaceful protests and organized for future lobbying efforts. They vowed this time to create lasting change."[14]

ON BLACK LIVES MATTER (BLM)

When Baltimore state attorney Marilyn Mosby filed charges, including man-slaughter, assault, reckless endangerment, and misconduct, against the six officers involved in Freddie Gray's death, she stated in her May 1, 2015, press conference, "I heard your call for 'no justice, no peace.'" This state-ment was in direct recognition of the Black Lives Matter catchphrase that had been chanted through the streets of Baltimore before the 2015 Freddie Gray rioting. In fact, some attribute the Gray protests first turning violent because chants of "black lives matter" were met with a few Orioles baseball fans angrily retorting, "We don't care." The BLM movement emerged in the wake of George Zimmerman's acquittal of killing unarmed black teenager Trayvon Martin in Florida in 2012. The 17-year-old was shot dead in the chest returning home late from his local convenience store carrying only a pack of Skittles and a watermelon juice cocktail in a can. Zimmerman was able to claim self-defense, invoking Florida's Stand Your Ground law given how Martin was black. In response to the acquittal, Alicia Garza took to Facebook, writing, "Our lives are hanging in the balance; young black boys in this country are not safe. Black men in this country are not safe."[15] Patrice Cullors, seeing Garza's post, wrote "#blacklivesmatter," and within days, the hashtag began spreading online. The third and final founder of BLM, Opal Tometi, then took Cullors's hashtag and created Facebook, Tumblr, Twitter, and Instagram accounts. BLM was born. For the next year, Garza, Cullors, and Tometi used the #blacklivesmatter hashtag to share cases where they saw racially motivated killing to create a community focused on ending racially disproportionate police brutality.

When Darren Wilson shot Michael Brown dead in Ferguson, Mis-souri, on August 9, 2014, Brown's body lay in the blazing sun for four and a half hours. This horrifying yet prosaic image was captured and shared on social media with enough frequency that the very next day, thousands of people showed up in Ferguson to attend a peaceful vigil, chanting, "No jus-tice, no peace." Protests over Brown's death spread to more than 150 cities. If BLM began after the killing of Trayvon Martin with a hashtag, it was from Ferguson and the aftermath of Brown's killing that a new generation of young activists emerged. The demonstrations, outcry, and rioting that emerged in Baltimore in the wake of Freddie Gray's death the following year were equally significant moments for the growing BLM movement. It was after Brown's death that FBI Director James Comey realized that his agency did not know how many black civilians had been killed by police, as police departments were not required to submit such data. In response, the

Washington Post collated as much information as was publicly available to reveal in its "Black and Unarmed" article that blacks were seven times more likely to be shot and killed as whites. All three murders being captured so viscerally on social media and shared via the BLM group to reveal widespread patterns of injustice is what led "many black citizens to say 'enough is enough'" and "to stand up for their rights against oppression."[16]

BLM then peaked on June 6, 2020, when half a million people rallied in 550 locations across the nation on a single day in remembrance of George Floyd. On May 25, the 46-year-old black man had been murdered in Minneapolis by Derek Chauvin, a 44-year-old white police officer. Floyd had been arrested after a store clerk alleged that a purchase had been made using a counterfeit $20 bill. Chauvin knelt on Floyd's neck for more than nine minutes while Floyd was handcuffed and lying face down in the street. Floyd became more and more distressed, complaining, "I can't breathe" and calling out for his mother as Chauvin continued to apply pressure, crushing his windpipe. The recorded murder went so viral that experts have estimated that between 15 million and 26 million people participated in some type of BLM event throughout the spring that year from India to Syria, Australia to Nairobi, and Bangkok via Canada. The protests of 2020 were striking not only in their scale but also in their diversity, reflecting a shift in national consciousness that events in Baltimore had played a key part in. In 2015, when BLM demonstrators first took to the streets, only half of all Americans considered racial discrimination a big problem. But by June 2020, according to a Monmouth University poll, that number had jumped to 76 percent. According to a Civiqs poll, 27 percent of people had supported BLM in 2017, but by 2020, 52 percent of the population supported its cause. As American voters cast their ballots in the 2020 presidential election, the Associated Press found that 90 percent of voters felt that the 2020 protests over police violence affected how they cast their ballots, and for 75 percent, it was a major decision.

Where *The Wire* specifically sits within the BLM story is subject to intense debate. Looking back, *Hollywood Reporter* critic Inkoo Kang writes, "In the first season . . . *The Wire* . . . has the effect of normalizing police brutality as a part, even a perk, of the job."[17] In direct response, Pierce argued that *The Wire* predicated the BLM protests. The show "was the canary-in-the-mine that forecasts the institutional moral morass of politics and policing that lead us to the protests of today." For him, "art is where we come together as a community to confront who we are as a society, decide what our values are, and then act on them," which certainly can be attributed to Sohn's Wired Up! event and the *Baltimore Rising* documentary.[18] Following these polar-opposite arguments, Racha Penrice's *Cracking "The Wire" during Black Lives Matter* occupies a more measured and less polarizing view. For her, there was a widespread "denial of humanity" of black characters in American television. By "today's standards giving agency to the so-called villains doesn't appear so radical and that frankly is because *The Wire* succeeded."[19] For Penrice, *The Wire* was the first accurate televisual portrayal of the ways in which black lives are lived. While the show did not predict how police reform would come to be discussed, it did help instigate a cultural shift enabling such a debate to take place that would eventually inform people's voting habits.

ON DRUGS

Baltimore's BLM protests in 2020 may have resisted civic disorder following the Freddie Gray riots of 2015, but the number of fatal drug overdoses has more than doubled. Drug and alcohol intoxication deaths, which were falling during *The Wire*'s run, exploded from 152 in 2008 to more than 1,000 in 2021. This is well over double the number of homicides, giving Baltimore City the highest overdose fatality rate of any U.S. city. Such an escalation in deaths comes from the countrywide prescribed opioid epidemic. Despite heroin's long history of usage in Baltimore, synthetic fentanyl has proven to be much cheaper to produce and is 50 times stronger. Instead of waiting months for poppy fields to grow in Mexico, dealers can order precursor chemicals and make the fentanyl in clandestine labs, generating far more doses with far less labor. It is also worth noting that the overdoses themselves are racially disproportionate. From 2016 to 2017, the fatal overdose rate from fentanyl and other synthetic opioids increased by 61 percent among black Americans compared with a 45 percent increase for whites.

While fatal overdoses are rising, particularly for black citizens, arrests for drug possession and drug-related incarceration rates are falling. Arrests in Baltimore peaked at 114,071 in 2003 during *The Wire*'s run, but by 2020, arrests had declined by more than 100,000 to 14,022. In 2020, there were 1,348 drug offense arrests—half the rate of 2019's 3,770 arrests and far fewer than 2014's 46,231. Simon attributes this industrial-scale decline in arrests to State Attorney Mosby's charging the Freddie Gray officers for false arrest when negligence would have sufficed. Simon feels that this was translated by officers as "I can go to jail for making the wrong arrest, so I'm not getting out of my car to clear a corner."[20] But this explanation alone does not account for the sustained decline in drug arrests after 2019, especially when all six officers implicated in Gray's death were acquitted in 2016. In 2021, a change in approach to policing drug abuse was established. To curb the spread of coronavirus, through the city's prisons, Mosby announced that the city would no longer prosecute low-level drug possession. What surprised many people, including BPD Commissioner Michael Harrison, was that this triggered a decline in property crime by 36 percent, with 20 percent fewer individuals entering prison and 39 percent fewer entering the city's criminal justice system. There were also 13 fewer homicides that year. Harrison told the *Washington Post* that "there's a correlation between the fact that we stopped making these arrests and crime did not go up." After falling crime rates through 2020, Mosby implemented COVID criminal justice policies in April 2021, claiming that "the era of 'tough on crime' prosecutors" is over in Baltimore, vowing that police resources would now concentrate on drug trafficking, violent criminals, and working with nonprofits to address "people struggling with drug addiction, and homelessness."[21]

Taking over from Mosby in 2023, State Attorney Ivan J. Bates was then able to oversee a fall in homicides by 21.5 percent in 2023—Baltimore's fewest homicides since 2014, the last time there were fewer than 300. This is remarkable given that following the Freddie Gray riots, 2015 ended with 342 homicides, the second highest in the city's history and a per-capita record. Then, from 2015 to 2021, homicides never fell below 300 per year. Mayor Brandon Scott, research by Johns Hopkins, and local journalists credit the violence prevention work conducted by the Mayor's Office of Neighborhood Safety and Engagement for the seismic decline in murders. The office was established in April 2022, brought together existing community groups like Safer Streets, and is starting to pay dividends.

As 2023 ended, Baltimore's fatal overdoses were up, but drug-related violence and arrests were down. Season 3 may not have produced any immediate discussion about legalizing drugs, but now, whenever political initiatives are launched, comparisons with Colvin's Hamsterdams are immediately drawn. *The Independent* and the *Washington Post* likened Mosby's 2021 COVID criminal justice policies to *The Wire* plotlines. Also, when Brandon Scott was sworn in as mayor three years after the final episode was broadcast, he was quizzed about his relationship to the show. Instead of brushing it off like the previous mayor, Scott acknowledged the accuracy of its portrayal. But then Scott asserted, "How we handle ourselves, how we come together, how we celebrate and do things together. I think that's the thing that was missed in the TV show and that folks, like myself, have to show people."[22] And this has been *The Wire*'s impact on local politics ever since. Anybody holding political office in Baltimore feels compelled to recognize and acknowledge the accuracy of the show's portrayal of Baltimore before using it as a springboard to reduce crime rates.

Thanks to *The Wire*, former mayor Schmoke's call to decriminalize drugs no longer seems as impossible as it did in 1988. Baltimore's more liberal attitude to policing possession could be seen as deriving from the legalization of marijuana sweeping across the country. In 2012, Colorado became the first state to legalize marijuana for recreational use, with Washington, California, and Alaska following shortly after. *The Wire* was the first television show to realistically entertain how drug decriminalization could be rolled out and was the first to implant the idea in people's minds that drug addiction should be treated as a health problem and not as a crime. Since this depiction has become further ingrained in the cultural conscience, Baltimore politicians have dropped the zero-tolerance approach toward policing drugs. They now look the other way at small levels of possession so that police resources can be diverted to community-led Group Violence Reduction initiatives. This is similar in spirit to though not as absolute as BLM's calls to defund the police for more community initiatives. If anything, *The Wire* has given Simon's and Schmoke's unrelenting views of drug abuse as a health problem a platform and increasing credence over time for lawmakers, civilians, and activists. *The Wire* and all the creatives associated with it will forever be a reference point that needs to be contended with as drug policies are further altered and amended.

WE OWN THIS CITY

Twenty years since David Simon first instigated a debate about drug use, his most recent Baltimore-based drama, *We Own This City* (2022), has been even more critical of the BPD. Based on Justin Fenton's 2021 book of the same name, HBO's six-episode season chronicles the corruption of the BPD's Gun Trace Task Force. Unlike *The Wire*, the drama jumps backward and forward in time between the creation in 2007 of the specialist unit, designed to concentrate resources on repeat violent offenders likely to be toting illegal firearms, and eight members of the task force facing trial. Charges that the task force faces include searching people without justification, entering homes without warrants, pocketing money, and recirculating drugs through the community. In the end, ringleader Wayne Jenkins (Jon Bernthal) receives a 25-year sentence, and the seven officers working alongside him receive sentences of 7 to 18 years. Simon's drama captures a perfect storm whereby, in the aftermath of Freddie Gray, communities of color were demanding they had "had enough of being treated this way by our police department." Simultaneously, "the guys who were willing to get out of their cars and police, even if they were doing it corruptly and for their own advantage, were now even more valued than before." *We Own This City* is a much more pernicious depiction of how the BPD serves its black community compared to the handful of principled police detectives operating through *The Wire*. For Simon, if *The Wire* had a political message, it was "End the drug war." And if *We Own This City* has one fundamental message, it's "END. THE. DRUG. WAR."[23]

If anything, the enduring success of *The Wire* has enabled its key creatives to hold power to account. While Fenton was reporting on the Gun Trace Task Force trial in *The Baltimore Sun*, Simon instructed his book agent to publish Justin Fenton's incredible story. Then a year later, HBO executive Kary Antholis asked George Pelecanos to adapt it as a miniseries. The author swiftly agreed under the condition that he bring in David Simon, Nina Noble, Ed Burns, and Bill Zorzi. As Simon's team began producing *We Own This City*, Sohn was already directing her second film, *The Slow Hustle* (2021), a documentary about the unsolved murder of detective Sean Suiter, who was due to testify in court against the Gun Trace Task Force the day after his body was found. While Suiter's mysterious death is acknowledged in *We Own This City*, Antholis also asked Sohn to add her signature investigative documentary treatment to the incident given her access to community figures and penchant for compassionate storytelling. Her documentary follows Suiter's family working through the theories that he was executed by officers to silence his testimony right through to the accusation that he committed suicide, being faced with informing on his colleagues. In investigating the theories behind Suiter's death, something that Simon's drama avoids, Sohn's second feature adds some positivity to Simon's increasing negativity, suggesting that the Suiter family's pursuit of justice can be achieved as long as the community continues to demand it.

"IT'S ALL IN THE GAME"

The Wire's enduring strength lies in its ability to resonate with individuals and play a key part in formulating their understanding of the drug war and the mechanics of civic institutions to this day. Writer Pelecanos confirms that in his experience, people regularly "come up to me and say, 'I became a teacher because of *The Wire*' or 'I became a volunteer community activist.' I think that's the best you can hope for . . . pulling people through the keyhole occasionally to change their worldview and perspective."[24] *The Wire* is a television show that can still inspire people into changing the world no matter what their position in society, nay, the world. When Russian opposition leader Alexei Navalny was sentenced to indefinite jailtime in a Siberian prison, he declared, "Well, as the characters of my favorite TV series *The Wire* used to say: 'You only do two days. That's the day you go in and the day you come out.'"[25] Even more remarkably, the Hawaii Supreme Court quoted Slim Charles when ruling against the U.S. Supreme Court's 2022 expansion of the Second Amendment. The State of Hawaii decreed, "The thing about the old days, they the old days" in its judgment against restoring the right to carry a handgun in public without a permit in the name of self-defense.[26] Therefore, journalist Jacob Weisberg's prediction that "people are going to be watching *The Wire* in 50 years, the way they're reading Dickens 150 years later" feels ever more likely.[27] *The Wire* continues to challenge enduring cultural perceptions of American law enforcement, deindustrialization, drug trafficking, racial archetypes and stereotypes, the international war on drugs, critical race theory, inner-city education policy, political discourse, and modern journalism, as has been outlined through this book. The precise change that *The Wire* will ignite and inspire throughout American society and the rest of the world remains to be seen. After all, 20 years later, it is still very much "all in the game."

THE EPISODES

An Opinionated Compendium

You will rarely see "Top 10 Episodes of *The Wire*" articles published because it is difficult to delineate episodes from one another. This episode list serves as a guide for readers to locate key plot points regarding drug investigations by the Major Crimes Unit and character arcs overlooked in this book thus far.

EPISODE 1.2: "THE DETAIL"

Daniels is given a useless office space, and Burrell assigns him hopeless officers to fill the rest of the detail, including Roland "Prez" Pryzbylewski. Prez foolhardily pistol-whips young dealer Kevin Johnston, leading the young man to permanently lose vision in one eye.

EPISODE 1.4: "OLD CASES"

Bodie escapes from the juvenile detention center and challenges D'Angelo on his return. To command respect, D'Angelo confesses to killing Avon's ex-girlfriend Deirdre Kresson. Later, it transpires that he witnessed Wee-Bey carrying it out. Coincidentally, McNulty and Bunk investigate the very same crime scene and find a previously unnoticed shell casing. Here they link the closed case to Barksdale solely by communicating through the word "fuck" in many different intonations and inflections.

EPISODE 1.9: "GAME DAY"

Freamon trains Sydnor and Prez in detective work and has them research city records to identify Barksdale's and Bell's business fronts and confirm the drug kingpins have donated to politicians, including Senator Clay Davis. Meanwhile, Omar robs a stash house, simply standing outside with his shotgun, and the bag is dropped to him. He then uses the obtained drugs to exchange Barksdale's pager code from Prop Joe. As Omar lures Barksdale out into the open to kill him, Wee-Bey realizes what is happening and saves his boss.

EPISODE 1.12: "CLEANING UP"

Bell orders Wallace's death given his proclivity to inform on the Barksdale crew, which Poot and Bodie reluctantly carry out. As the Barksdales stop using phones entirely, D'Angelo's stripper girlfriend Shardene maps out the dimensions of Barksdale's office at Orlando's strip club, enabling the detectives to install a camera in the neighboring building. After hearing Avon order D'Angelo to pick up a drug shipment, they fit D'Angelo's car with a tracker and then arrest him.

EPISODE 2.6: "ALL PROLOGUE"

Omar's testimony outsmarts Levy's line of questioning to ensure that Bird is found guilty for Gant's murder. Ziggy and Nick begin smuggling chemicals, and as part of their deal, the Greek settles Ziggy's debt with Cheese through Prop Joe. Russell and Bunk learn how to operate the port computers and discover that the container of dead women was purposefully moved. Greggs cases strip clubs, learning that Madam Ilona Petrovich controls several trafficked women. D'Angelo's mother, Brianna, fails to convince her son to inform on prison guard Tilghman. Believing that D'Angelo is planning to snitch, Bell has D'Angelo murdered in the prison library, where his body is staged as a suicide.

EPISODE 2.10: "STORM WARNINGS"

As the detail focuses on the Greeks over union finances, an annoyed Valchek calls the FBI, which agrees to split work with the detail if it returns to focusing on Frank Sobotka. Valchek tries to take Prez off the detail while mocking Daniels, prompting Prez to punch his powerful father-in-law square in the face. Glekas shorts Ziggy his payment for stealing cars from the docks and beats Ziggy when he protests. An enraged Ziggy then shoots Glekas dead and is suitably arrested.

EPISODE 2.11: "BAD DREAMS"

The detail arrests several Greeks and stevedores. Bell convinces Omar that hired enforcer Brother Mouzone helped kill his dead lover, Brandon Wright. When Omar breaks into Mouzone's motel room and shoots him, Mouzone convinces the stickup artist of his innocence. Frank Sobotka agrees to cooperate with the detail as long as no stevedores are implicated. Agent Koutris informs the Greek of this deal, so the mob boss lures Frank to a meeting, promising to produce witnesses that will get Ziggy freed from jail only to execute the union treasurer.

EPISODE 3.6: "HOMECOMING"

As dealers are still skeptical that Colvin's Hamsterdams are a trap, Colvin sanctions his officers to slam dealers against police vans, pepper spray them, and then abandon them, handcuffed in the woods. As the drug dealers and users begin to comply, a much more peaceful and idyllic district emerges where homeowners of all ages are happy to congregate outside their properties and in the street without fear of getting caught in turf war crossfire. Bunk meets with Omar and expresses disgust at the lost sense of community they once shared in high school together. Omar then helps uncover the gun that killed Officer Dozerman. Cutty retires with Barksdale's consent.

EPISODE 3.8: "MORAL MIDGETRY"

Unsettled by the Hamsterdams, the Deacon convinces Colvin to take ownership of his experiment and work with charities to provide aid for the area. Cutty is shown an abandoned boxing gym and vows to repair it for the local corner kids. With the Barksdale crew's position weakening, Bell bribes a social services agent for Omar's grandmother's address and has men stake it out. He also continues to bribe Davis to ensure that he gets a federal grant to renovate his properties. Barksdale accuses Bell of going soft, and they end up in a tussle after Bell spitefully reveals that he had D'Angelo murdered all along, insisting that he did it to protect both of them.

EPISODE 3.11: "MIDDLE GROUND" (EMMY NOMINATED)

Cutty secures funding from Barksdale for gym repairs and fresh equipment and holds a tournament between his corner boys and another out-of-town gym. Having been informed of the drug free zones, Mayor Royce decides to sit on the revelation with his advisers and consultants to find a legal loophole that will leave them operational and keep crime rates low. Levy informs Bell that Davis is known for pocketing bribes. Incensed that Barksdale will not sanction a Davis execution, Bell relinquishes Barksdale's safe house address directly to Colvin. Meanwhile, Mouzone threatens to cut off Barksdale from his New York drug contacts unless he gives up Bell. Barksdale gives the hit man details of Bell's meeting with property developer Andy Krawczyk. Mouzone and Omar confront Bell in his West Side property and murder him.

EPISODE 4.3: "HOME ROOMS"

The Deacon convinces the now retired Colvin to work for a Johns Hopkins sociology project at Tilghman Middle School, looking to identify repeat offenders. Prez struggles to maintain order in his classroom. The situation grows out of control to the point where the episode concludes with one pupil, Laetitia, slashing another, Chiquan, with a box cutter.

EPISODE 4.10 "MISGIVINGS"

Carver arrests Namond for dealing drugs. Scared of being booked into a youth detention facility while his mother is away for the weekend, Namond is taken in by his teacher, Colvin, instead. Namond impresses Colvin's wife with his manners. However, when the assistant superintendent observes Colvin's special class, she is of a mind to shut the entire program down due to its lack of results in socializing the kids, especially having witnessed a classroom role-playing exercise escalate into a fight when the all-important state tests are looming. Marlo has Kevin killed on learning that he involved

Randy in Lex's murder and spreads word that Randy talked to the police. When Michael implies that his father molested him, Partlow brutally beats Michael's father to death.

EPISODE 4.11: "A NEW DAY"

The school board shuts down Colvin's class. Having successfully completed their project on the qualities of an effective corner boy, Albert refuses to take part in a follow-up trust exercise, disrupting the whole class in the process. After calming down, Albert confesses to Colvin that his mother died that morning of a drug overdose. Randy is rescued by Prez after being attacked outside the school gates for being a snitch, and Carver assigns police patrols to guard the boy's house. Carcetti pledges to focus on community-based policing only to learn that the school system is $54 million over budget. Freamon learns from Prez where Randy lured Lex. At the site, Freamon realizes that Marlo's murder victims are being hidden in boarded-up vacants.

EPISODE 5.8: "CLARIFICATIONS"

McNulty is unsettled by the FBI's profile of his faked serial killer replicating his own personality traits, leading him to confess the truth to Greggs. Bunk runs a DNA check on Michael's father's body that matches Partlow. Sydnor realizes that the page numbers of a street atlas match the numbers that Marlo's dealers are messaging one other and that the corresponding cell phone photographs of clock hands are coordinates for meeting locations. Haynes encourages Fletcher to keep reporting on Bubbles's life. Kernard notices Omar and shoots the stickup artist dead in a store.

EPISODE 5.9: "LATE EDITIONS"

The heads of Marlo's crew are arrested, as is Partlow for the murder of Michael's father. Herc relays to Levy that Marlo was arrested on evidence obtained from an illegal wiretap. Greggs reports McNulty's serial killer scheme to Daniels after a homeless man is genuinely murdered, and the body features all the hallmarks of McNulty's faked serial killer.

EPISODE 5.10: "-30-" (EMMY NOMINATED)

Carcetti keeps McNulty's confession under wraps to keep his governor campaign alive. Another man is murdered, but McNulty catches the perpetrator—another homeless man—whom they frame for all the previous killings. Levy gets Marlo freed due to his illegal wiretap on the condition that the young kingpin retire from the drug trade altogether. Daniels becomes commissioner but refuses to doctor statistics and so resigns after promoting Carver to lieutenant of the Major Crimes Unit. Slim Charles kills Cheese for his previous role in Prop Joe's murder and starts heading negotiations with Vondas and the Greek as the new de facto head of Baltimore's illicit drug trade.

NOTES

INTRODUCTION

1. Steve Johnson, "*The Wire* Review," *Chicago Tribune*, May 31, 2002, 4.

2. Adam Buckman, "*The Wire* Review," *New York Post*, May 31, 2002, 122.

3. Eric Deggans, "Why *The Wire* Is the Greatest TV Series of the 21st Century," *BBC Culture*, October 19, 2021, https://www.bbc.com/culture/article/20211015-why-the -wire-is-the-greatest-tv-series-of-the-21st-century (accessed March 8, 2024).

4. Jonathan Abrams, *All the Pieces Matter: The Inside Story of "The Wire"* (Harpenden: No Exit Press, 2018), 244.

5. David Simon, "Fuck the Casual Viewer" (interview conducted by Charlie Brooker at the annual Edinburgh Television Festival, Edinburgh, August 28, 2009), https:// www.theguardian.com/media/video/2009/aug/29/david-simon-edinburgh-interview-full (accessed March 8, 2024).

6. Simon, "Fuck the Casual Viewer."

7. Simon, "Fuck the Casual Viewer."

8. Dennis Walder, Stephen Regan, Pam Morris, and Richard Allen, "The Novel and Society," in *The Realist Novel*, ed. Dennis Walder (London: Routledge, 1995), 103.

9. Marsha Kinder, "Re-Wiring Baltimore: The Emotive Power of Systematic, Seriality, and the City," *Film Quarterly* 62, no. 2 (2008): 50–57.

10. Kweisi Mfume, "Virtual Whitewashing in Programming," *CNN*, July 28, 1999, http://edition.cnn.com/SHOWBIZ/TV/9907/28/lack.tv.color/index.html.

11. Julia Hallam and Margaret Marshment, *Realism and Popular Cinema* (Manchester: Manchester University Press, 2000),184.

12. Abrams, *All the Pieces Matter*, 19.

13. Raymond Williams, *What I Came to Say* (London: Hutchinson Books, 1990), 232.

14. J. Patrick Coolican, "Obama Goes Gloves Off, Head-On," *Las Vegas Sun*, January 14, 2008, https://lasvegassun.com/news/2008/jan/14/obama-gloves-off (accessed March 8, 2024).

15. Tom Jackman, "After Crime Plummeted in 2020, Baltimore Will Stop Drug, Sex Prosecutions," *Washington Post*, March 26, 2021, https://www.washingtonpost.com/ dc-md-va/2021/03/26/baltimore-reducing-prosecutions (accessed March 8, 2024).

16. Phil Hoad, "When Good TV Goes Bad: How *The Wire* Lost Its Spark," *The Guardian*, August 14, 2017, https://www.theguardian.com/tv-and-radio/2017/aug/14/ when-good-tv-goes-bad-how-the-wire-lost-its-spark (accessed March 8, 2024).

17. Cas Mudde, *Populist Radical Right Parties in Europe* (Cambridge: Cambridge University Press, 2007), 23.

18. Jonathan Abrams, *"The Wire* at 20: This Show Will Live Forever," *New York Times*, June 2, 2022, https://www.nytimes.com/2022/05/31/arts/television/david-simon-ed -burns-the-wire-anniversary.html (accessed March 8, 2024).

19. Abrams, *"The Wire* at 20."

20. Abrams, *All the Pieces Matter*, 256.

CHAPTER 1

1. David Simon, "Episode 698—David Simon," *WTF with Marc Maron*, podcast audio. April 14, 2016, https://www.youtube.com/watch?v=w_eHu_R4AcI (accessed March 8, 2024).

2. Brett Martin, *Difficult Men. Behind the Scenes of a Creative Revolution: From "The Sopranos" and "The Wire" to "Mad Men" and "Breaking Bad"* (London: Faber & Faber, 2013), 113.

3. Margaret Talbot, "Stealing Life: The Crusader behind 'The Wire,'" *The New Yorker*, October 14, 2007, https://www.newyorker.com/magazine/2007/10/22/stealing-life (accessed March 8, 2024).

4. David Simon, *Homicide: A Year on the Killing Streets* (Boston: Houghton Mifflin, 1991; Edinburgh: Canongate, 2009), 14.

5. Simon, *Homicide*, 16–73.

6. Simon, *Homicide*, 131, 241.

7. David Simon and Ed Burns, *The Corner* (New York: Broadway Books, 1997; Edinburgh: Canongate, 2010), 51.

8. David Simon, "Introduction," in *"The Wire": Truth Be Told*, ed. Rafael Alvarez (Edinburgh: Canongate, 2009), 13.

9. Method Man, "Episode 1 with David Simon," *The Wire at 20 Official Podcast*, podcast audio, June 2, 2022, https://www.youtube.com/watch?v=xljB94DkS88&t=1s (accessed March 8, 2024).

10. Martin, *Difficult Men*, 122.

11. "Interview with Ed Burns," *HBO*, January 24, 2010, http://web.archive.org/web /20170606141306/http://www.hbo.com/the-wire/inside/interviews/interview/ed-burns .html (accessed March 8, 2024).

12. Simon, "Introduction," 14.

13. Simon, "Introduction," 14.

14. Martin, *Difficult Men*, 130.

15. Simon, "Introduction," 15.

16. Simon, "Introduction," 16.

17. Dorian Lynskey, *"The Wire,* 10 Years On: 'We Tore the Cover Off a City and Showed the American Dream Was Dead,'" *The Guardian*, March 6, 2018, https://www .theguardian.com/tv-and-radio/2018/mar/06/the-wire-10-years-on-we-tore-the-cover-off-a -city-and-showed-the-american-dream-was-dead (accessed March 8, 2024).

18. Simon, "Introduction," 6.

19. David Simon, interviewed by Simon Mayo, *BBC Radio 5 Live*, September 16, 2008.

20. Simon, "Introduction," 5.

21. Talbot, "Stealing Life."

22. Man, "Episode 1 with David Simon."

23. Talbot, "Stealing Life."

24. David Simon, "Letter to HBO," in Alvarez, *The Wire*, 32–36.

CHAPTER 2

1. David Simon, "Introduction," in *"The Wire": Truth Be Told*, ed. Rafael Alvarez (Edinburgh: Canongate, 2009), 19.

2. Method Man, "Episode 3 with Wendell Pierce and Andre Royo," *The Wire at 20 Official Podcast*, podcast audio, June 16, 2022, https://www.youtube.com/watch?v =mSU1D_OH1VI (accessed March 8, 2024).

3. Man, "Episode 3 with Wendell Pierce and Andre Royo."

4. Alvarez, *The Wire*, 110.

5. Jonathan Abrams, *All the Pieces Matter: The Inside Story of "The Wire"* (Harpenden: No Exit Press, 2018), 21.

6. Man, "Episode 3 with Wendell Pierce and Andre Royo."

7. Abrams, *All the Pieces Matter*, 23.

8. Method Man, "Episode 7 with Idris Elba and Jermaine Crawford," *The Wire at 20 Official Podcast*, podcast audio, July 14, 2022, https://www.youtube.com/watch?v =Zx0U2xMQ50s (accessed March 8, 2024).

9. Idris Elba, interviewed by Steve Rose, "You Can Make Sparkling Wine in Portsmouth or Champagne in Champagne. My Ambition Was to Make Champagne," *The Guardian*, March 3, 2023, https://www.theguardian.com/film/2023/mar/03/idris-elba-you -can-make-sparkling-wine-in-portsmouth-or-champagne-in-champagne-my-ambition-was -to-make-champagne.

10. bell hooks, *Black Looks: Race and Representation* (London: Routledge, 2014), 96.

11. Man, "Episode 3 with Wendell Pierce and Andre Royo."

12. David Simon, "Life as a Snitch: Anonymous to the End, 'Possum' tells Secrets," *The Baltimore Sun*, March 16, 1992, https://www.baltimoresun.com/1992/03/16/life-as-a -snitch-anonymous-to-the-end-possum-tells-secrets (accessed March 8, 2024).

13. readjack.wordpress.com/2009/10/15/imdb-wire-character-poll-and-the-win ner-is.

14. Method Man, "Episode 6 Remembering Michael Kenneth Williams," *The Wire at 20 Official Podcast*, podcast audio, July 7, 2022, https://www.youtube.com/watch?v =zJmuaB8M4Ok (accessed March 8, 2024).

15. Tim Walker, "Donnie Andrews: The Road to Redemption," *The Independent*, June 21, 2009, https://www.independent.co.uk/news/people/profiles/donnie-andrews-the -road-to-redemption-1711563.html (accessed March 8, 2024).

16. Jessica Anderson and Justin Fenton, "Donnie Andrews, Inspiration for Omar Character on 'The Wire,' Dies," *The Baltimore Sun*, December 4, 2012, https://www.bal timoresun.com/news/crime/bs-xpm-2012-12-14-bal-donnie-andrews-inspiration-for-omar -character-on-the-wire-dies-20121214-story.html (accessed March 8, 2024).

17. hooks, *Black Looks*, 112.

18. Patricia Hill Collins, *Black Sexual Politics: African Americans, Gender, and the New Racism* (New York: Routledge, 2004), 171–76.

19. Michael K. Williams and Jon Sternfeld, *Scenes from My Life: A Memoir* (London: Pan Macmillan, 2022), 148.

20. Man, "Episode 6 Remembering Michael Kenneth Williams."

21. Lorraine Gamman, "Watching the Detectives: The Enigma of the Female Gaze," in *The Female Gaze: Women as Viewers of Popular Culture*, ed. Lorainne Gamman and Margaret Marshment (London: Women's Press, 1988), 11.

22. Sonja Sohn, "Sonja Sohn: Changing Baltimore Long after *The Wire*," NPR, *Fresh Air*, podcast audio, March 15, 2012, https://www.npr.org/2012/03/15/148294942/sonja-sohn-changing-baltimore-long-after-the-wire (accessed March 8, 2024).

CHAPTER 3

1. Dorian Lynskey, "*The Wire*, 10 Years On: 'We Tore the Cover Off a City and Showed the American Dream Was Dead,'" *The Guardian*, March 6, 2018, https://www.theguardian.com/tv-and-radio/2018/mar/06/the-wire-10-years-on-we-tore-the-cover-off-a-city-and-showed-the-american-dream-was-dead (accessed March 8, 2024).

2. Alasdair McMillan, "Heroism, Institutions, and the Police Procedural," in *"The Wire": Urban Decay and America Television*, ed. Tiffany Potter and C. W. Marshall (New York: Continuum, 2009), 63.

3. Linda Williams, *On the Wire* (Durham, NC: Duke University Press, 2014), 4.

4. Jonathan Nichols-Pethick, *TV Cops: The Contemporary American Television Police Drama* (London: Routledge, 2012), 153.

5. Sue Turnbull, *The TV Crime Drama* (Edinburgh: Edinburgh University Press, 2014), 93.

6. Sherryl Vint, "*The Wire*" (Detroit: Wayne State University Press, 2013), 12.

7. Kyle Barrett, "'A Man Must Have a Code': Good Po-Lice and Representations of Masculinity in HBO's *The Wire*," in *Watching the Cops: Essays on Police and Policing in 21st Century Film and Television*, ed. Marcus K. Harmes, Barabara Harmes, and Meredith A. Harmes (Jefferson, NC: McFarland, 2023), 91.

8. Jonathan Abrams, *All the Pieces Matter: The Inside Story of "The Wire"* (Harpenden: No Exit Press, 2018), 173.

9. Mareike Jenner, "*The Wire*," in *The Television Genre Book*, 3rd ed., ed. Glen Creeber (London: BFI, 2015), 31.

10. Jason Mittell, "*The Wire* in the Context of American Television" in *"The Wire": Race, Class and Genre*, edited by Liam Kennedy and Stephen Shapiro, (Ann Arbor: University of Michigan Press, 2012), 29.

11. Leslie Raddatz, "Jack Webb Revisited," *TV Guide*, February 2, 1963, 16.

12. Jason Mittell, "Policing Genres—*Dragnet*'s Texts and Generic Contexts," in *Genre and Television: From Cop Shows to Cartoons in American Culture*, ed. Jason Mittell (New York: Routledge, 2004), 133–38.

13. Robert E. Fitzgibbons, "*Naked City*: The Relativist Turn in TV Noir," in *The Philosophy of TV Noir*, ed. Steven Sanders and Aeon J. Skoble (Lexington: University Press of Kentucky, 2014), 50–54.

14. Paul Cobley, "'Who Loves Ya, Baby?' Kojak, Action and the Great Society," in *Action TV: Tough-Guys, Smooth Operators and Foxy Chicks*, ed. Anna Gough-Yates and Bill Osgerby (London: Routledge, 2001), 65.

15. Roger Sabin, *"Kojak,"* in Sabin et al., *Cop Shows*, 73.

16. Sabin, *"Kojak,"* 75.

17. Paul Owen, "Episode 6: Where's Jimmy," in *"The Wire" Re-Up*, ed. Steve Busfield and Paul Owen (London: Guardian Books, 2009), 172.

18. Ben Bethell, *"Starsky and Hutch,"* in Sabin et al., *Cop Shows*, 87.

19. Robin Wood, *Hollywood from Vietnam to Reagan . . . and Beyond* (New York: Columbia University Press, 1986), 228.

20. Wood, *Hollywood from Vietnam to Reagan*, 228–29.

21. Todd Gitlin, *Inside Primetime* (Berkeley: University of California Press, 1994), 285.

22. Nichols-Pethick, *TV Cops*, 81–104.

23. David Simon, "The Target," director's commentary, in *The Wire: Season 1* (HBO, 2005), DVD.

24. James L. Longworth, *TV Creators: Conversations with America's Top Producers of Television Drama* (Syracuse, NY: Syracuse University Press, 2000), 93.

25. Nichols-Pethick, *TV Cops*, 119–26.

26. Jonathan Bignell, "The Police Series," in *Close-Up 03*, ed. Jonathan Gibbs and Douglas Pye (London: Wallflower, 2009), 50.

27. Brian G. Rose, *"The Wire,"* in *The Essential HBO Reader*, ed. Gary R. Edgerton and Jeffrey P. Jones (Lexington: University Press of Kentucky, 2008), 88.

CHAPTER 4

1. Sean O'Connell, "The Wire Cast Pay Tribute to Michael K. Williams as the HBO Show Turns 20 Years Old," *Cinemablend*, June 22, 2022, https://www.cinemablend.com/interviews/watch-the-wire-cast-pay-tribute-to-michael-k-williams-as-the-hbo-show-turns-20-years-old (accessed March 8, 2024).

2. Dorian Lynskey, *"The Wire*, 10 Years On: 'We Tore the Cover Off a City and Showed the American Dream Was Dead,'" *The Guardian*, March 6, 2018, https://www.theguardian.com/tv-and-radio/2018/mar/06/the-wire-10-years-on-we-tore-the-cover-off-a-city-and-showed-the-american-dream-was-dead (accessed March 8, 2024).

3. David Simon, "Down to the Wire," 2008, https://davidsimon.com/down-to-the-wire (accessed March 8, 2024).

4. Rober Alter, *Imagined Cities: Urban Experience and the Language of the Novel* (New Haven, CT: Yale University Press, 2005), 52.

5. Sherry H. Olson, *Baltimore: The Building of an American City* (Washington, DC: Beard Books, 2004), 262.

6. Stephen Lucasi, "Networks of Affiliation: Familialism and Anticorporatism in Black and White," in *"The Wire": Urban Decay and America Television*, ed. Tiffany Potter and C. W. Marshall (New York: Continuum, 2009), 143.

7. Marc Levine, "Downtown Redevelopment as an Urban Growth Strategy: A Critical Appraisal of the Baltimore Renaissance," *Journal of Urban Affairs* 9 (June 1987): 103–23.

8. Julia Hallam and Margaret Marshment, *Realism and Popular Cinema* (Manchester: Manchester University Press, 2000), 184.

9. Stanley Corkin, *Connecting "The Wire": Race, Space, and Postindustrial Baltimore* (Austin: University of Texas Press, 2017), 48.

10. Sherryl Vint, *"The Wire"* (Detroit: Wayne State University Press, 2013), 35.

11. Vint, *"The Wire,"* 36.

12. Vint, *"The Wire,"* 92.

13. Vint, *"The Wire,"* 39.

14. Frederick Douglass, *Narrative of the Life of Frederick Douglass: An American Slave* (Boston: Anti-Slavery Office, 1845), 41, 89.

15. bell hooks, *We Real Cool: Black Men and Masculinity* (New York: Routledge, 2004), 42.

16. hooks, *We Real Cool*, 104.

17. hooks, *We Real Cool*, 84–104.

18. hooks, *We Real Cool*, xiii.

19. Rafael Alvarez, *"The Wire": Truth Be Told* (Edinburgh: Canongate, 2009), 115.

20. hooks, *We Real Cool*, 17–18, 142.

21. Alvarez, *"The Wire,"* 134–35.

22. Method Man, "Episode 3 with Wendell Pierce and Andre Royo," *The Wire at 20 Official Podcast*, podcast audio, June 16, 2022, https://www.youtube.com/watch?v=mSU1D_OH1VI (accessed March 8, 2024).

23. Margaret Talbot, "Stealing Life: The Crusader behind 'The Wire,'" *The New Yorker*, October 14, 2007, https://www.newyorker.com/magazine/2007/10/22/stealing-life (accessed March 8, 2024).

CHAPTER 5

1. Dorian Lynskey, "*The Wire*, 10 Years On: 'We Tore the Cover Off a City and Showed the American Dream Was Dead,'" *The Guardian*, March 6, 2018, https://www.theguardian.com/tv-and-radio/2018/mar/06/the-wire-10-years-on-we-tore-the-cover-off-a-city-and-showed-the-american-dream-was-dead (accessed March 8, 2024).

2. Jonathan Abrams, *All the Pieces Matter: The Inside Story of "The Wire"* (Harpenden: No Exit Press, 2018), 173.

3. Rafael Alvarez, *"The Wire": Truth Be Told* (Edinburgh: Canongate, 2009), 273.

4. David Simon and Ed Burns, *The Corner* (New York: Broadway Books, 1997; Edinburgh: Canongate, 2010), 70.

5. Gregg Barak, Paul Leighton, and Jeanne Flavin, eds., *Class, Race, Gender and Crime: The Social Realities of Justice in America*, 2nd ed. (Lanham, MD: Rowman & Littlefield, 2007).

6. Vernon Guidry Jr., "Baltimore Is among Best in Using Drug Kingpin Law," *The Baltimore Sun*, February 16, 1983, A1.

7. Simon and Burns, *The Corner*, 74.

8. Ryan S. King and Marc Mauer, "Distorted Priorities: Drug Offenders in State Prisons," *Prison Policy Initiative*, 2002, http://www.sentencingproject.org/doc/publications/dp_distortedpriorities.pdf (accessed March 8, 2024).

9. Elliott Currie, *Reckoning: Drugs, the Cities and the American Future* (New York: Farrar, Straus and Giroux, 1993), 104–13.

10. Currie, *Reckoning*, 113–16.

11. Edward Preble, "Social and Cultural Factors Related to Narcotic Use among Puerto Ricans in New York City," *International Journal of the Addictions* 1, no. 1 (1966): 40.

12. Currie, *Reckoning*, 116–19.

13. George Pelecanos, "Middle Ground," director's commentary, in *The Wire: Season 3* (HBO, 2007), DVD.

14. Currie, *Reckoning*, 119–21.

15. Currie, *Reckoning*, 122.

16. Ron Cassie, "Back to the Future: Kurt Schmoke Was Vilified for Wanting to End the Drug War. Today, His Ideas Are Becoming Reality," *Baltimore Magazine*, April 2018, https://www.baltimoremagazine.com/section/health/thirty-years-ago-kurt-schmoke -openly-advocating-for-decriminalization-of-marijuana (accessed March 8, 2024).

17. Susan E. Kirkpatrick, James P. Lester, and Mark R. Peterson, "The Policy Termination Process: A Conceptual Framework and Application to Revenue Sharing," *Policy Studies Review* 16, no. 1 (Spring 1999): 211–16.

18. David Simon, "Time after Time," director's commentary, *The Wire: Season 3* (HBO, 2007), DVD.

19. Dante Alighieri, *The Divine Comedy*, trans. Rev. H. F. Cary (London: Cassell & Company, 1892), cantos VI–XXV, https://www.gutenberg.org/files/8800/8800-h/8800-h .htm (accessed March 8, 2024).

20. Joe Chappelle, "Middle Ground," director's commentary, *The Wire: Season 3* (HBO, 2007), DVD.

21. David Simon, "Mission Accomplished," director's commentary, *The Wire: Season 3* (HBO, 2007), DVD.

22. Pelecanos, "Middle Ground."

23. Simon, "Mission Accomplished."

24. Simon, "Mission Accomplished."

25. Simon, "Mission Accomplished."

CHAPTER 6

1. Method Man, "Episode 3 with Wendell Pierce and Andre Royo," *The Wire at 20 Official Podcast*, podcast audio, June 16, 2022.

2. Jonathan Abrams, *All the Pieces Matter: The Inside Story of "The Wire"* (Harpenden: No Exit Press, 2018), 244.

3. Method Man, "Episode 5 with Dominic West, Clarke Peters, Jim True-Frost," *The Wire at 20 Official Podcast*, podcast audio, June 30, 2022.

4. David Forrest, *Social Realism: Art, Nationhood and Politics* (Cambridge: Cambridge Scholars Publishing, 2013), 16.

5. Rafael Alvarez, *"The Wire": Truth Be Told* (Edinburgh: Canongate, 2009), 287.

6. Margaret Talbot, "Stealing Life: The Crusader behind 'The Wire,'" *The New Yorker*, October 14, 2007, https://www.newyorker.com/magazine/2007/10/22/stealing-life (accessed March 8, 2024).

7. Method Man, "Episode 7 with Idris Elba and Jermaine Crawford," *The Wire at 20 Official Podcast*, podcast audio, July 14, 2022.

8. Abrams, *All the Pieces Matter*, 216.

9. Stephen King, "Stephen King on the Brilliant New Season of *The Wire*," *Entertainment Weekly*, February 1, 2007, https://ew.com/article/2007/02/01/stephen-king-brilliant-new-season-wire (accessed March 8, 2024).

10. Mark Athitakis, "Q&A with Novelist and Wire Writer Richard Price," *Washington City Paper*, February 1, 2008, https://washingtoncitypaper.com/article/236151/qa-with-novelist-and-wire-writer-richard-price (accessed March 8, 2024).

11. "Interview with Ed Burns," *HBO*, April 27, 2010, http://web.archive.org/web/20170603052358/http://www.hbo.com/the-wire/inside/interviews/interview/ed-burns.html (accessed March 8, 2024).

12. Mekeisha Madden Toby, "The Wire's Hard Truths about How Our Schools Fail Us All," *Cracking the Wire during Black Lives Matter*, ed. Ronda Racha Penrice (New York: Fayetteville Mafia Press, 2022), 72.

13. John D. Kasarda, "Urban Industrial Transition and the Underclass," *Annals of the American Academy of Political and Social Science* 501 (1989): 33.

14. Peter L. Szanton, *Baltimore 2000: A Choice of Futures: A Report to the Morris Goldseker Foundation* (Baltimore, MD: The Foundation, 1980).

15. Marion Orr, *Black Social Capital: The Politics of School Reform in Baltimore, 1986–98* (Lawrence: University Press of Kansas, 1999), 193.

16. Margaret Zamudio, Christopher Russell, Francisco Rios, and Jacquelyn L. Bridgeman, *Critical Race Theory Matters: Education and Ideology* (New York: Routledge, 2011), 107.

17. Tara J. Yosso, "Toward a Critical Race Curriculum," *Equity & Excellence in Education* 35, no. 2 (2002): 98.

18. Linda Perlstein, *Tested: One American School Struggles to Make the Grade* (New York: Griffin, 2008).

19. Claudine Raynaud, "Coming of Age in the African American Novel," in *The Cambridge Companion to the African American Novel*, ed. Maryemma Graham (Cambridge: Cambridge University Press, 2006), 106–21.

20. Raynaud, "Coming of Age in the African American Novel," 111.

21. Raynaud, "Coming of Age in the African American Novel," 110.

22. James Poniewozik, "*The Wire* Gives TV Drama a Good Schooling," *Time*, September 8, 2006, https://entertainment.time.com/2006/09/08/the_wire_gives_tv_drama_a_good (accessed March 8, 2024).

CHAPTER 7

1. Margaret Talbot, "Stealing Life: The Crusader behind *The Wire*," *The New Yorker*, October 14, 2007, https://www.newyorker.com/magazine/2007/10/22/stealing-life (accessed March 8, 2024).

2. Simon, interviewed by Amon Warmann, "*The Wire* 20th Anniversary: 'The King Stay the King': In Conversation with Creator David Simon," *BFI*, June 29, 2022, https://www.youtube.com/watch?v=iNGQc6hDNvE (accessed March 8, 2024).

3. Jonathan Abrams, *All the Pieces Matter: The Inside Story of "The Wire"* (Harpenden: No Exit Press, 2018), 300–302.

4. Mark Athitakis, "What Happened to Our Show? For Four Seasons *The Wire* Reinvented the Crime Drama. Now the Viewer's the Victim," *Washington City Paper*,

February 1, 2008, https://washingtoncitypaper.com/article/236177/what-happened-to-our
-show (accessed March 8, 2024).

5. Ta-Nehisi Coates, "The Problem with Season Five of *The Wire*," *The Atlantic*, January 26, 2008, https://www.theatlantic.com/entertainment/archive/2008/01/the-prob lem-with-season-five-of-the-wire/5542 (accessed March 8, 2024).

6. Darren Franich, "The Bitter Resonance of *The Wire*'s Fake News Plotline, a Decade Later," *Entertainment Weekly*, March 9, 2018, https://ew.com/tv/2018/03/09/the -wire-finale-10-year-anniversary-essay (accessed March 8, 2024).

7. Phil Hoad, "When Good TV Goes Bad: How *The Wire* Lost Its Spark," *The Guardian*, August 14, 2017, https://www.theguardian.com/tv-and-radio/2017/aug/14/ when-good-tv-goes-bad-how-the-wire-lost-its-spark (accessed March 8, 2024).

8. David Zurawik, "'*The Wire*' Finale Is a Cop-Out for a Once-Great Show," *The Baltimore Sun*, March 9, 2008, https://www.baltimoresun.com/entertainment/bal-thewire finale-story.html (accessed March 8, 2024).

9. Rafael Alvarez, *"The Wire": Truth Be Told* (Edinburgh: Canongate, 2009), 409.

10. Harold A. Williams, *The Baltimore Sun: 1837–1987* (Baltimore, MD: Johns Hopkins University Press, 1987), 307.

11. Williams, *The Baltimore Sun*, 301.

12. Cas Mudde, *Populist Radical Right Parties in Europe* (Cambridge: Cambridge University Press, 2007), 23.

13. Koen Abts and Stefan Rummens, "Populism versus Democracy," *Political Studies* 55 (2007): 420.

14. Joe Chapelle, "More with Less," director's commentary, in *The Wire: Season 5* (HBO, 2008), DVD.

15. Alvarez, *"The Wire*," 402–3.

16. Jonathan Abrams, *"The Wire* at 20: 'This Show Will Live Forever,'" *New York Times*, May 31, 2022, https://www.nytimes.com/2022/05/31/arts/television/david-simon -ed-burns-the-wire-anniversary.html (accessed March 8, 2024).

17. Benjamin Moffitt and Simon Tormey, "Rethinking Populism: Politics, Mediati- sation and Political Style," *Political Studies* 62 no. 2 (2014): 391–92.

18. Kate Sanford, "Took," director's commentary, in *The Wire: Season 5* (HBO, 2008), DVD.

19. Steve Chibnall, *Law-and-Order News: An Analysis of Crime Reporting in the British Press* (London: Routledge, 1977), 23–44.

20. Chibnall, *Law-and-Order News*, 32–33.

21. David Simon, "-30-," director's commentary, in *The Wire: Season 5* (HBO, 2008), DVD.

CONCLUSION

1. Jonathan Abrams, *All the Pieces Matter: The Inside Story of "The Wire"* (Harpen- den: No Exit Press, 2018), 11.

2. Alan Sepinwall, "*The Wire* Reunion," *PaleyFest 2014*, Paley Center for Media, New York, October 16, 2014, https://www.youtube.com/watch?v=SGuy6ITOJsI (accessed March 8, 2024).

3. Abrams, *All the Pieces Matter*, 11.

4. Drake Bennett, "This Will Be on the Midterm. You Feel Me? Why So Many Col- leges Are Teaching The Wire," *Slate*, March 24, 2010, https://slate.com/culture/2010/03/

why-are-professors-at-harvard-duke-and-middlebury-teaching-courses-on-david-simon-s
-the-wire.html (accessed March 8, 2024).

5. David John Nutt, "Season 1 Episode 05: The Pager," *The Wire: Stripped*, podcast audio, March 12, 2018, https://podcasts.apple.com/gb/podcast/s1-ep05-the-pager/
id1321861159?i=1000400119734 (accessed March 8, 2024).

6. Sherryl Vint, *The Wire* (Detroit: Wayne State University Press, 2013), 104.

7. Carolyn Younce, "Ella Thompson Fund Special with Carolyn Younce," *The
Wire: Stripped*, podcast audio, June 30, 2021, https://podcasts.apple.com/gb/podcast
/ella-thompson-fund-special-with-carolyn-younce/id1321861159?i=1000527413446
(accessed March 8, 2024).

8. Sepinwall, "*The Wire* Reunion."

9. Annalies Winny, "'Gentrification without Displacement': Wire Actor's Property
Plan Causes Storm," *The Guardian*, March 28, 2018, https://www.theguardian.com/cit
ies/2018/mar/28/weldell-pierce-gentrification-without-displacement-wire-actors-property
-plan-causes-storm (accessed March 8, 2024).

10. Andre Royo, April 27, 2015, https://twitter.com/andreroyo/status
/592821336025726978 (accessed March 8, 2024).

11. David Simon, "Baltimore," *The Audacity of Despair: Collected Prose, Links
and Occasional Venting from David Simon*, April 27, 2015, https://davidsimon.com/balti
more (accessed March 8, 2024).

12. https://www.baltimoresun.com/entertainment/tv/z-on-tv-blog/bs-ae-zontv-wire
-reunion-20150716-story.html#page=2 (accessed March 8, 2024).

13. Mark Kennedy, "*The Wire* Star Makes Documentary *Baltimore Rising*," *Maryland Daily Record*, November 14, 2017, https://thedailyrecord.com/2017/11/21/the-wire
-star-makes-documentary-baltimore-rising (accessed March 2024).

14. Justin Fenton, *We Own This City: A True Story of Crime, Cops and Corruption
in an American City* (London: Faber & Faber, 2021), 269.

15. Veronica Chambers, *Call and Response: The Story of Black Lives Matter* (New
York: HarperCollins, 2021), 26.

16. Jennifer Cobbina, *Hands Up, Don't Shoot: Why the Protests in Ferguson and
Baltimore Matter and How They Changed America* (New York: New York University
Press, 2019), 87.

17. Inkoo Kang and Daniel Fienberg, "Critics' Conversation: Is TV Afraid to
Tackle Police Brutality or Just Unable to Do It Well?" *Hollywood Reporter*, June 4,
2020, https://www.hollywoodreporter.com/tv/tv-news/critics-conversation-has-tv-been
-afraid-tackle-police-brutality-just-unable-do-it-well-1297134 (accessed March 8,
2024).

18. Wendell Pierce, June 7, 2020, https://twitter.com/WendellPierce/status
/1269582087855710209?lang=en (accessed March 8, 2024).

19. Ronda Racha Penrice, "Conclusion: Why *The Wire* Still Matters," in *Cracking
The Wire during Black Lives Matter*, ed. Ronda Racha Penrice (New York: Fayetteville
Mafia Press, 2022), 121.

20. Gary Gately, "Baltimore Is More Murderous Than Chicago. Can Anyone Save
the City from Itself?" *The Guardian*, November 2, 2017, https://www.theguardian.com/us
-news/2017/nov/02/baltimore-murder-rate-homicides-ceasefire (accessed March 8, 2024).

21. Tom Jackman, "After Crime Plummeted in 2020, Baltimore Will Stop Drug,
Sex Prosecutions," *Washington Post*, March 26, 2021, https://www.washingtonpost.com/
dc-md-va/2021/03/26/baltimore-reducing-prosecutions (accessed March 8, 2024).

22. Ashlee Banks, "Mayor Brandon Scott Is the Unapologetically Black 'Son of Baltimore,'" *Revolt*, February 25, 2022, https://www.revolt.tv/article/2022-02-25/154040/baltimore-mayor-brandon-scott-black-history-month-interview (accessed March 8, 2024).

23. Julian Sancton, "David Simon, Jon Bernthal and the Makers of HBO's *We Own This City* on Dirty Cops, the Drug War and the Legacy of *The Wire*," *Hollywood Reporter*, April 21, 2022, https://www.hollywoodreporter.com/tv/tv-features/we-own-this-city-simon-pelecanos-bernthal-green-1235132991/#! (accessed March 8, 2024).

24. Sancton, "David Simon, Jon Bernthal and the Makers of HBO's *We Own This City* on Dirty Cops, the Drug War and the Legacy of *The Wire*."

25. Alexey Navalny, March 22, 2022, https://twitter.com/navalny/status/1506247694804783113?lang=en-GB (accessed March 8, 2024).

26. *State of Hawai'i v. Christopher L. Wilson*, CAAP-22-0000561, case no. 2CPC-17-0000964, Supreme Court of the State of Hawai'i, February 7, 2024, https://www.courts.state.hi.us/wp-content/uploads/2024/02/SCAP-22-0000561.pdf&sa=U&ved=2ahUKEwj0pNeDgr2EAxUqFBAIHXiNA9cQFnoECAIQAg&usg=AOvVaw366R02qKPLgDhZ97nTk6bp (accessed March 8, 2024).

27. *The Wire Odyssey* (2007).

BIBLIOGRAPHY

Abrams, Jonathan. *All the Pieces Matter: The Inside Story of "The Wire"*. Harpenden: No Exit Press, 2018.

———. "The Wire at 20: This Show Will Live Forever." *New York Times*. June 2, 2022. https://www.nytimes.com/2022/05/31/arts/television/david-simon-ed-burns-the-wire-anniversary.html (accessed March 8, 2024).

Abts, Koen, and Stefan Rummens. "Populism versus Democracy." *Political Studies* 55, no. 2 (2007).

Albertazzi, Daniele, and Duncan McDonnell. *Twenty-First Century Populism: The Spectre of Western European Democracy*. London: Palgrave Macmillan, 2007.

Albrecht, Chris, "HBO: No Verdict on *The Wire*." *TV Week*. January 13, 2005. https://www.tvweek.com/in-depth/2005/01/hbo-no-verdict-on-the-wire (accessed March 8, 2024).

Alff, David M. "Yesterday's Tomorrow Today: Baltimore and the Promise of Reform." In *"The Wire": Urban Decay and America Television*, edited by Tiffany Potter and C. W. Marshall. New York: Continuum, 2009.

Alighieri, Dante. *The Divine Comedy*. Translated by Rev. H. F. Cary. London: Cassell & Company, 1892). https://www.gutenberg.org/files/8800/8800-h/8800-h.htm (accessed March 8, 2024).

Alter, Rober. *Imagined Cities: Urban Experience and the Language of the Novel*. New Haven, CT: Yale University Press, 2005.

Alvarez, Rafael. *"The Wire": Truth Be Told*. Edinburgh: Canongate, 2009.

Anderson, Jessica, and Justin Fenton. "Donnie Andrews, Inspiration for Omar Character on 'The Wire,' Dies." *The Baltimore Sun*. December 14, 2012. https://www.baltimoresun.com/news/crime/bs-xpm-2012-12-14-bal-donnie-andrews-inspiration-for-omar-character-on-the-wire-dies-20121214-story.html (accessed March 8, 2024).

Aslanidis, Paris. "Coalition-Making under Conditions of Ideological Mismatch: The Populist Solution." *International Political Science Review* 42, no. 5 (2021).

Associated Press. "Baltimore Mayor Supports Legalization of Illicit Drugs." *New York Times*. September 30, 1988. https://www.nytimes.com/1988/09/30/us/baltimore-mayor-supports-legalization-of-illicit-drugs.html (accessed March 8, 2024).

Athitakis, Mark, "Q&A with Novelist and Wire Writer Richard Price." *Washington City Paper*. February 1, 2008. https://washingtoncitypaper.com/article/236151/qa-with-novelist-and-wire-writer-richard-price (accessed March 8, 2024).

———. "What Happened to Our Show? For Four Seasons *The Wire* Reinvented the Crime Drama. Now the Viewer's the Victim." *Washington City Paper*. February 1, 2008. https://washingtoncitypaper.com/article/236177/what-happened-to-our-show (accessed March 8, 2024).

Baltimore Afro-American. "Drug Agents Claim Victories in Ongoing War against Drugs." January 10, 1987.

Baltimore Police Department. "Crime Statistics." https://www.baltimorepolice.org/crime -stats (accessed March 8, 2024).

Banks, Ashlee. "Mayor Brandon Scott Is the Unapologetically Black 'Son of Baltimore.'" *Revolt*. February 25, 2022. https://www.revolt.tv/article/2022-02-25/154040/balti more-mayor-brandon-scott-black-history-month-interview (accessed March 8, 2024).

Barak, Gregg, Paul Leighton, and Jeanne Flavin, eds. *Class, Race, Gender and Crime: The Social Realities of Justice in America*. 2nd ed. Lanham, MD: Rowman & Littlefield, 2007.

Barr, Robert R. "Populists, Outsiders and Anti-Establishment Politics." *Party Politics* 15, no. 1 (January 2009).

Barrett, Kyle. "'A Man Must Have a Code': Good Po-Lice and Representations of Mascu-linity in HBO's *The Wire*." In *Watching the Cops: Essays on Police and Policing in 21st Century Film and Television*, edited by Marcus K. Harmes, Barbara Harmes, and Meredith A. Harmes. Jefferson, NC: McFarland, 2023.

Bennett, Drake. "This Will Be on the Midterm. You Feel Me? Why So Many colleges Are Teaching *The Wire*." *Slate*. March 14, 2010. https://slate.com/culture/2010/03/why -are-professors-at-harvard-duke-and-middlebury-teaching-courses-on-david-simon-s -the-wire.html (accessed March 8, 2024).

Bethell, Ben. "*Starsky and Hutch*." In *Cop Shows: A Critical History of Police Dramas on Television*, edited by Roger Sabin, Ronald Wilson, Linda Speidel, and Ben Bethell. Jefferson, NC: McFarland, 2015.

Bianco, Robert. "10 Reasons We Still Love TV." *USA Today*. May 16, 2004. https://web .archive.org/web/20060813180544/http://www.usatoday.com/life/television/news /2004-05-26-tv-mvps_x.htm (accessed March 8, 2024).

Bignell, Jonathan. "The Police Series." In *Close-Up 03*, edited by Jonathan Gibbs and Douglas Pye. London: Wallflower, 2009.

Biskind, Peter. *Pandora's Box: The Greed, Lust, and Lies That Broke Television*. London: Penguin, 2022.

Bluestone, Barry, and Bennet Harrison. *The Deindustrialization of America: Plant Clos-ings, Community Abandonment and the Dismantling of Basic Industry*. New York: Knopf, 1996.

Bonikowski, Bart, and Noam Gidron. "The Populist Style in American Politics: Presiden-tial Campaign Discourse, 1952–1996." *Social Forces* 94, no. 4 (2016).

Bourgeois, Philippe. "In Search of Horatio Alger: Culture and Ideology in the Crack Econ-omy." *Contemporary Drug Problems* (Winter 1989).

Brooks, Tim, and Earl Marsh. *The Complete Directory to Prime-Time Network and Cable Shows, 1946–Present*. 7th ed. New York: Ballantine Books, 1999.

Brown, Lawrence. "Baltimore Has Been Flattening the Curve on Murders." *Baltimore Banner*. December 11, 2023. https://www.thebaltimorebanner.com/opinion/com munity-voices/baltimore-murders-violence-intervention-housing-monse-63SOCYQ 4MBD3FNIYQFD7AY4PRE (accessed March 8, 2024).

Brown, Sheila. *Crime and Law in Media Culture*. Maidenhead: Open University Press, 2003.

Buckman, Adam. "*The Wire* Review." *New York Post*. May 31, 2002.

Burns, Ed. "Interview with Ed Burns." *HBO*. January 24, 2010. http://web.archive.org/web/20170606141306/http://www.hbo.com/the-wire/inside/interviews/interview/ed-burns.html (accessed March 8, 2024).

Busfield, Steve, and Paul Owen, eds. The Wire *Re-Up*. London: Guardian Books, 2009.

Bzdak, David, Joanna Crosby, and Seth Vannatta, eds. The Wire *and Philosophy: This America, Man*. Chicago: Open Court, 2013.

Campbell, Christopher. "A Post-Mortem Time for Racial Imperialism." *Television Quarterly* 2 (Winter 2000).

Canovan, Margret. "Taking Politics to the People: Populism as the Ideology of Democracy." In *Democracies and the Populist Challenge*, edited by Yves Mény and Yves Surel. Basingstoke: Palgrave Macmillan, 2001.

Carnoy, Martin. *Faded Dreams: The Politics and Economics of Race in America*. Cambridge: Cambridge University Press, 1994.

Cassie, Ron. "Back to the Future: Kurt Schmoke Was Vilified for Wanting to End the Drug War. Today, His Ideas Are Becoming Reality." *Baltimore Magazine*. April 2018. https://www.baltimoremagazine.com/section/health/thirty-years-ago-kurt-schmoke-openly-advocating-for-decriminalization-of-marijuana (accessed March 8, 2024).

Chambers, Veronica. *Call and Response: The Story of Black Lives Matter*. New York: HarperCollins, 2021.

Chibnall, Steve. *Law-and-Order News: An Analysis of Crime Reporting in the British Press*. London: Routledge, 1977.

City of Baltimore. *The History of Baltimore*. 2020. https://www.baltimorecity.gov/sites/default/files/5_History.pdf (accessed March 8, 2024).

Coates, Ta-Nehisi. "The Problem with Season Five of *The Wire*." *The Atlantic*. January 26, 2008. https://www.theatlantic.com/entertainment/archive/2008/01/the-problem-with-season-five-of-the-wire/5542 (accessed March 8, 2024).

Cobbina, Jennifer. *Hands Up, Don't Shoot: Why the Protests in Ferguson and Baltimore Matter and How They Changed America*. New York: New York University Press, 2019.

Cobley, Paul. "'Who Loves Ya, Baby?' Kojak, Action and the Great Society." In *Action TV: Tough-Guys, Smooth Operators and Foxy Chicks*, edited by Anna Gough-Yates and Bill Osgerby. London: Routledge, 2001.

Collins, Patricia Hill, *Black Sexual Politics: African Americans, Gender, and the New Racism*. New York: Routledge, 2004.

Coolican, J. Patrick. "Obama Goes Gloves Off, Head-On." *Las Vegas Sun*. January 14, 2008. https://lasvegassun.com/news/2008/jan/14/obama-gloves-off (accessed March 8, 2024).

Corkin, Stanley. *Connecting* The Wire*: Race, Space, and Postindustrial Baltimore*. Austin: University of Texas Press, 2017.

Creeber, Glen, and Matt Hills, eds. "Editorial TV III: Into, or towards, a New Television Age?" *New Review of Film and Television Studies* 5, no. 1 (2007).

———. *Serial Television: Big Drama on the Small Screen*. London: BFI, 2004.

Crenson, Matthew A., *Baltimore: A Political History*. Baltimore, MD: Johns Hopkins University Press, 2019.

Curato, Nicole. "Flirting with Authoritarian Fantasies? Rodrigo Duterte and the New Terms of Philippine Populism." *Journal of Contemporary Asia* 47, no. 1 (2017).

Currie, Elliott. *Reckoning: Drugs, the Cities and the American Future.* New York: Farrar, Straus and Giroux, 1993.

Deggans, Eric. "Why The Wire Is the Greatest TV Series of the 21st Century." *BBC Culture.* October 19, 2021. https://www.bbc.com/culture/article/20211015-why-the-wire-is-the-greatest-tv-series-of-the-21st-century (accessed March 8, 2024).

Delgado Bernal, Dolores. "Critical Race Theory, Latino Critical Theory, and Critical Raced-Gendered Epistemologies: Recognizing Students of Color as Holders and Creators of Knowledge." *Qualitative Inquiry* 8, no. 1 (2002).

Delgado, Richard, and Jean Stefancic. *Critical Race Theory: An Introduction.* 3rd ed. New York: New York University Press, 2017.

DeVance Taliaferro, Jocelyn, and Tia Sherèe Gaynor, eds. *Teaching the Wire: Frameworks, Theories and Strategies for the Classroom.* Jefferson, NC: McFarland, 2016.

Deylami, Shirin, and Jonathan Havercroft, eds. *The Politics of HBO's* The Wire*: Everything Is Connected.* London: Routledge, 2015.

DiBennardo, Rebecca A. "Ideal Victims and Monstrous Offenders: How the News Media Represent Sexual Predators." *Socius: Sociological Research for a Dynamic World* 4 (2018).

Douglass, Frederick. *Narrative of the Life of Frederick Douglass: An American Slave.* Boston: Anti-Slavery Office, 1845.

Edgerton, Gary R., and Jeffrey P. Jones, eds. *The Essential HBO Reader.* Lexington: University Press of Kentucky, 2008.

Elba, Idris, interviewed by Steve Rose. "You Can Make Sparkling Wine in Portsmouth or Champagne in Champagne. My Ambition Was to Make Champagne." *The Guardian.* March 3, 2023. https://www.theguardian.com/film/2023/mar/03/idris-elba-you-can-make-sparkling-wine-in-portsmouth-or-champagne-in-champagne-my-ambition-was-to-make-champagne (accessed March 8, 2024).

Elliott, Stuart. "Controversy May Sell, but Only a Few Marketers Took a Chance with *NYPD Blue*." *New York Times*, September 23, 1993.

Ellner, Steve. "The Contrasting Variants of the Populism of Hugo Chávez and Alberto Fujimori." *Journal of Latin American Studies* 35, no. 1 (2003).

Federal Bureau of Investigation. "Crime in the United States: Uniform Crime Report." 2000. http://www.fbi.gov/ucr/cius_00/contents.pdf (accessed March 8, 2024).

Fenton, Justin. *We Own This City: A True Story of Crime, Cops and Corruption in an American City.* London: Faber & Faber, 2021.

Fitzgerald, Scott. *The Last Tycoon.* New York: Charles Scribner's Sons, 1947; London: Penguin, 2002.

Fitzgibbons, Robert E. "*Naked City*: The Relativist Turn in TV Noir." In *The Philosophy of TV Noir*, edited by Steven Sanders and Aeon J. Skoble. Lexington: University Press of Kentucky, 2014.

Fitzpatrick, Joseph P. "Addiction Prevention and Correction among Puerto Ricans: The Cultural and Social Context." In *Drugs in Hispanic Communities*, edited by Ronald Glick and Joan Moore. New Brunswick, NJ: Rutgers University Press, 1990.

Fleming, Neil D. "The Case against Learning Styles: 'There Is No Evidence . . .'" 2012. https://vark-learn.com/wp-content/uploads/2014/08/The-Case-Against-Learning-Styles.pdf (accessed March 8, 2024).

Fleming, Neil D., and David Baume. "Learning Styles Again: VARKing Up the Right Tree!" *Educational Developments* 7, no. 4 (November 2006).

Fleming, Neil D., and Colleen Mills. "Not Another Inventory, Rather a Catalyst for Reflection." *To Improve the Academy* 11 (1992).

Forrest, David. *Social Realism: Art, Nationhood and Politics*. Cambridge: Cambridge Scholars Publishing, 2013.

Franich, Darren. "The Bitter Resonance of *The Wire*'s Fake News Plotline, a Decade Later." *Entertainment Weekly*. March 9, 2018. https://ew.com/tv/2018/03/09/the-wire -finale-10-year-anniversary-essay (accessed March 8, 2024).

Gamman, Lorraine. "Watching the Detectives: The Enigma of the Female Gaze." In *The Female Gaze: Women as Viewers of Popular Culture*, edited by Lorainne Gamman and Margaret Marshment. London: Women's Press, 1988.

Gately, Gary. "Baltimore Is More Murderous Than Chicago. Can Anyone Save the City from Itself?" *The Guardian*. November 2, 2017. https://www.theguardian.com/us-news /2017/nov/02/baltimore-murder-rate-homicides-ceasefire (accessed March 8, 2024).

Gibson, Campbell. "Populations of the 100 Largest Cities and Other Urban Places in the United States: 1790 to 1990." U.S. Census Bureau. June 1998. www.census .gov/population/www/documentation/twps0027/twps0027.html (accessed March 8, 2024).

Gitlin, Todd. *Inside Primetime*. Berkeley: University of California Press, 1994.

Goodnough, Abby. "In Cities Where It Once Reigned, Heroin Is Disappearing." *New York Times*. May 18, 2019, https://www.nytimes.com/2019/05/18/health/heroin-fentanyl -deaths-baltimore.html#:~:text=The%20rise%20of%20the%20more,far%20greater %20risk%20of%20overdose (accessed March 8, 2024).

Graham, Maryemma. "Introduction." In *The Cambridge Companion to the African American Novel*, edited by Maryemma Graham. Cambridge: Cambridge University Press, 2006.

Graziosi, Graig. "Baltimore Ends War on Drugs with Plot Line Straight from *The Wire*." *The Independent*. April 8, 2021. https://www.independent.co.uk/news/world/ameri cas/baltimore-drugs-the-wire-b1828185.html (accessed March 8, 2024).

Greer, Chris. "News, Media, Victims and Crime." In *Victims, Crime and Society*, 2nd ed., edited by Pamela Davies, Peter Francis, and Chris Greer. London: Sage, 2017.

Griffith, Kristen. "New Maryland School Ratings Are Out. Baltimore City and County Performed among the Worst." *Baltimore Banner*. September 3, 2023. https://www .thebaltimorebanner.com/education/k-12-schools/maryland-school-report-card-2022 -V63KWIZHCVHYZDYSN6Z4ZEVEHI/#:~:text=Each%20Baltimore%2Darea %20district%2C%20with,from%2053%25%20to%2075%25 (accessed March 8, 2024).

Guidry, Vernon, Jr. "Baltimore Is among Best in Using Drug Kingpin Law." *The Baltimore Sun*. February 16, 1983.

Hallam, Julia, and Margaret Marshment. *Realism and Popular Cinema*. Manchester: Manchester University Press, 2000.

Hamid, Ansley. "Political Economy of Crack Related Violence." *Contemporary Drug Problems* 17, no. 1 (Spring 1990).

Hawkins, Kirk A. *Venezuela's Chavismo and Populism in Comparative Perspective*. Cambridge: Cambridge University Press, 2010.

Hillyard, Paddy, Christina Pantazis, Dave Gordon, Steve Tombs, and Daniek Dorling. *Beyond Criminology: Taking Harm Seriously*. London: Pluto Press, 2004.

Hillyard, Paddy, and Steve Tombs. "From 'Crime' to Social Harm?" *Crime, Law and Social Change* 48 (2007).

Hoad, Phil. "When Good TV Goes Bad: How The Wire Lost Its Spark." *The Guardian*. August 14, 2017. https://www.theguardian.com/tv-and-radio/2017/aug/14/when -good-tv-goes-bad-how-the-wire-lost-its-spark (accessed March 8, 2024).

hooks, bell. *Black Looks: Race and Representation*. 2nd ed. London: Routledge, 2014.

———. *We Real Cool: Black Men and Masculinity*. London: Routledge, 2004.

Human Rights Watch. "Racially Disproportionate Drug Arrests." 2000. http://www.hrw .org/reports/2000/usa/Rcedrg00-05.htm (accessed March 8, 2024).

Intlekofer, Kristen. "The Real Mean Streets of *The Wire*." *Johns Hopkins University Gazette*. September 2012. https://hub.jhu.edu/gazette/2012/september/the-real-mean -streets-of-the-wire (accessed March 8, 2024).

Jackman, Tom. "After Crime Plummeted in 2020, Baltimore Will Stop Drug, Sex Prosecutions." *Washington Post*. March 26, 2021. https://www.washingtonpost.com/dc-md -va/2021/03/26/baltimore-reducing-prosecutions (accessed March 8, 2024).

Jansen, Robert S. "Populist Mobilization: A New Theoretical Approach to Populism." *Sociological Theory* 29, no. 2 (2011).

Jenner, Mareike. "*The Wire*." In *The Television Genre Book*, 3rd ed., edited by Glen Creeber. London: BFI, 2015.

Jensen, Mikkel. *David Simon's American City*. Manchester: Manchester University Press, 2024.

Jewkes, Yvonne. *Crime and the Media*. 3rd ed. London: Sage, 2015.

Johnson, Steve. "*The Wire* Review." *Chicago Tribune*. May 31, 2002.

Kang, Inkoo, and Daniel Fienberg. "Critics' Conversation: Is TV Afraid to Tackle Police Brutality or Just Unable to Do It Well?" *Hollywood Reporter*. June 4, 2020. https://www.hollywoodreporter.com/tv/tv-news/critics-conversation-has-tv-been -afraid-tackle-police-brutality-just-unable-do-it-well-1297134 (accessed March 8, 2024).

Kasarda, John D. "Urban Industrial Transition and the Underclass." *Annals of the American Academy of Political and Social Science* 501 (January 1989).

Keeble, Arin, and Ivan Stacy, eds. The Wire *and America's Dark Corners: Critical Essays*. Jefferson, NC: McFarland, 2015.

Kennedy, Liam, and Stephen Shapiro, eds. The Wire*: Race, Class, and Genre*. Ann Arbor: University of Michigan Press, 2012.

Kennedy, Mark. "*The Wire* Star Makes Documentary *Baltimore Rising*." *Maryland Daily Record*. November 14, 2017. https://thedailyrecord.com/2017/11/21/the-wire-star -makes-documentary-baltimore-rising (accessed March 8, 2024).

Kessler, Glenn, Salvador Rizzo, and Meg Kelly. "Trump's False or Misleading Claims Total 30573 over Four Years." *Washington Post*. January 14, 2021. https://www .washingtonpost.com/politics/2021/01/24/trumps-false-or-misleading-claims-total -30573-over-four-years (accessed March 8, 2024).

Kinder, Marsha. "Re-Wiring Baltimore: The Emotive Power of Systematic, Seriality, and the City." *Film Quarterly* 62, no. 2 (2008).

King, Ryan S., and Marc Mauer. "Distorted Priorities: Drug Offenders in State Prisons." *Prison Policy Initiative*. 2002. http://www.sentencingproject.org/doc/publications/ dp_distortedpriorities.pdf (accessed March 8, 2024).

King, Stephen. "Stephen King on the Brilliant New Season of *The Wire*." *Entertainment Weekly*. February 1, 2007. https://ew.com/article/2007/02/01/stephen-king-brilliant -new-season-wire (accessed March 8, 2024).

Kirkpatrick, Susan E., James P. Lester, and Mark R. Peterson. "The Policy Termination Process: A Conceptual Framework and Application to Revenue Sharing." *Policy Studies Review* 16, no. 1 (Spring 1999).

Kohl, Herbert R. *"I Won't Learn from You": And Other Thoughts on Creative Maladjustment*. New York: New Press, 1995.

Kolker, Robert Philip. *A Cinema of Loneliness*. 4th ed. Oxford: Oxford University Press, 2011.

Kompare, Derek. "Publishing Flow: DVD Box Sets and the Reconception of Television." *Television New Media* 7 (2006).

Lamont, Michèle, Bo Yun Park, and Elena Ayala-Hurtado. "Trump's Electoral Speeches and His Appeal to the American White Working Class." *British Journal of Sociology* 68, no. 1 (2017).

Leverette, Marc, Brian L. Ott, and Cara Louise Buckley, eds. *It's Not TV: Watching HBO in the Post-Television Era*. London: Routledge, 2008.

Levine, Marc. "Downtown Redevelopment as an Urban Growth Strategy: A Critical Appraisal of the Baltimore Renaissance." *Journal of Urban Affairs* 9 (June 1987).

LoLordo, Ann. "City Narcotics Squad Seeks 'Containment.'" *The Baltimore Sun*. September 18, 1983.

Longworth, James L. *TV Creators: Conversations with America's Top Producers of Television Drama*. Syracuse, NY: Syracuse University Press, 2000.

Lucasi, Stephen. "Networks of Affiliation: Familialism and Anticorporatism in Black and White." In The Wire*: Urban Decay and America Television*, edited by Tiffany Potter and C. W. Marshall. New York: Continuum, 2009.

Lynskey, Dorian. *"The Wire*, 10 Years On: 'We Tore the Cover Off a City and Showed the American Dream Was Dead." *The Guardian*. March 6, 2018. https://www.theguardian.com/tv-and-radio/2018/mar/06/the-wire-10-years-on-we-tore-the-cover-off-a-city-and-showed-the-american-dream-was-dead (accessed March 8, 2024).

Macro Trends. "Baltimore MD Murder/Homicide Rate 2000–2018." https://www.macrotrends.net/cities/us/md/baltimore/murder-homicide-rate-statistics (accessed March 8, 2024).

Man, Method. "Episode 1 with David Simon." *The Wire at 20 Official Podcast*. Podcast audio. June 2, 2022. https://www.youtube.com/watch?v=xljB94DkS88&t=1s (accessed March 8, 2024).

———. "Episode 3 with Wendell Pierce and Andre Royo." *The Wire at 20 Official Podcast*. Podcast audio. June 16, 2022. https://www.youtube.com/watch?v=mSU1D_OH1VI (accessed March 8, 2024).

———. "Episode 4 with Delicia 'Snoop' Pearson." *The Wire at 20 Official Podcast*. Podcast audio. June 23, 2022. https://www.youtube.com/watch?v=PdBqFbW9OIk&t=1162s (accessed March 8, 2024).

———. "Episode 5 with Dominic West, Clarke Peters, Jim True-Frost." *The Wire at 20 Official Podcast*. Podcast audio. June 30, 2022. https://www.youtube.com/watch?v=2hDM1b8ObVE (accessed March 8, 2024).

———. "Episode 6 Remembering Michael Kenneth Williams." *The Wire at 20 Official Podcast*. Podcast audio. July 7, 2022. https://www.youtube.com/watch?v=zJmuaB8M4Ok (accessed March 8, 2024).

———. "Episode 7 with Idris Elba and Jermaine Crawford." *The Wire at 20 Official Podcast*. Podcast audio. July 14, 2022. https://www.youtube.com/watch?v=Zx0U2xMQ50s (accessed March 8, 2024).

Mares, David R. *Drug Wars and Coffee Houses: The Political Economy of the International Drug Trade*. Washington, DC: CQ Press, 2005.

Maron, Marc. "Episode 698—David Simon." *WTF with Marc Maron*. Podcast audio. April 14, 2016. https://www.youtube.com/watch?v=w_eHu_R4AcI (accessed March 8, 2024).

Marsh, Jeanne, and Steven Shevell. "Males' and Females' Perceived Reasons for Their Use of Heroin." *Social Service Review* 57, no. 1 (March 1983).

Martin, Brett. *Difficult Men. From* The Sopranos *and* The Wire *to* Mad Men *and* Breaking Bad*: Behind the Scenes of a Creative Revolution*. London: Faber & Faber, 2013.

Maryland Historical Trust. 2004. https://mht.maryland.gov/nr/NRDetail.aspx?NRID =1464&COUNTY=Baltimore%20City&FROM=NRCountyList.aspx (accessed March 8, 2024).

Mbete, Sithembile Nombali. "The Economic Freedom Fighters: South Africa's Turn towards Populism?" *Journal of African Elections* 14, no. 1 (2015).

McCabe, Brent, and Van Smith. "Down to the Wire: Top 10 Reasons Not to Cancel *The Wire*." *Baltimore City Paper*. April 16, 2005. https://web.archive.org/web /20050416234720/http://cpgo.citypaper.com/film/story.asp?id=9538 (accessed March 8, 2024).

McCabe, Janet, and Kim Akass, eds. *Quality TV: Contemporary American Television and Beyond*. London: I. B. Tauris, 2007.

McConnell, Frank. "Smart, Hip and Real: Bochco's 'NYPD Blue.'" *Commonweal*. October 8, 1993.

McMillan, Alasdair. "Heroism, Institutions, and the Police Procedural." In The Wire*: Urban Decay and America Television*, edited by Tiffany Potter and C. W. Marshall. New York: Continuum, 2009.

Mfume, Kweisi. "Virtual Whitewashing in Programming." *CNN*. July 28, 1999. http://edition .cnn.com/SHOWBIZ/TV/9907/28/lack.tv.color/index.html (accessed March 8, 2024).

Milch, David, and Bill Clark. *True Blue: The Real Stories behind NYPD Blue*. New York: Willliam Morrow, 1995.

Mittell, Jason. "Policing Genres—*Dragnet*'s Texts and Generic Contexts." In *Genre and Television: From Cop Shows to Cartoons in American Culture*, edited by Jason Mittell. New York: Routledge, 2004.

Moffitt, Benjamin. "Populism in Australia and New Zealand." In *The Oxford Handbook of Populism*, edited by Cristóbal Rovira Kaltwasser, Paul Taggart, Paulina Ochoa Espejo, and Pierre Ostiguy. Oxford: Oxford University Press, 2017.

———. *Populism (Key Concepts in Political Theory)*. Cambridge: Polity, 2020.

Moffitt, Benjamin, and Simon Tormey. "Rethinking Populism: Politics, Mediatisation and Political Style." *Political Studies* 62 no. 2 (2014).

Moore, Wes. "Governor Moore Announces Strong First Quarter Growth for Port of Baltimore Key Commodities." June 6, 2023. https://governor.maryland.gov/news/press /pages/Governor-Moore-Announces-Strong-First-Quarter-Growth-for-Port-of-Balti more-Key-Commodities.aspx#:~:text=The%20Port%20of%20Baltimore%20gener ates,overall%20linked%20to%20port%20activities (accessed March 8, 2024).

Mudde, Cas. *Populist Radical Right Parties in Europe*. Cambridge: Cambridge University Press, 2007.

Mudde, Cas, and Cristobal Rovira Kaltwasser. "Voices of the Peoples: Populism in Europe and Latin America Compared." *Kellogg Working Paper* 37, no. 8 (2023).

Müller, Jan-Werner. *What Is Populism?* Philadelphia: University of Pennsylvania Press, 2016.

Navalny, Alexey. 2022. https://twitter.com/navalny/status/1506247694804783113?lang =en-GB (accessed March 8, 2024).

Nelson, Robin. *State of Play: Contemporary "High-End" TV Drama.* Manchester: Manchester University Press, 2007.

———. *TV Drama in Transition: Forms, Values and Cultural Change.* London: Palgrave Macmillan, 1997.

Nichols-Pethick, Jonathan. *TV Cops: The Contemporary American Television Police Drama.* London: Routledge, 2012.

Nutt, David John. "Season 1 Episode 05: The Pager." The Wire: *Stripped.* Podcast audio. March 12, 2018. https://podcasts.apple.com/gb/podcast/s1-ep05-the-pager/ id1321861159?i=1000400119734 (accessed March 8, 2024).

O'Connell, Sean. "The Wire Cast Pay Tribute to Michael K. Williams as the HBO Show Turns 20 Years Old." *Cinemablend.* June 22, 2022. https://www.cinemablend.com/ interviews/watch-the-wire-cast-pay-tribute-to-michael-k-williams-as-the-hbo-show -turns-20-years-old (accessed March 8, 2024).

Oborne, Peter. *Lies, Falsehoods and Misrepresentations from Boris Johnson to Rishi Sunak.* https://boris-johnson-lies.com (accessed March 8, 2024).

Olson, Sherry H. *Baltimore: The Building of an American City.* Washington, DC: Beard Books, 2004.

Orr, Marion. *Black Social Capital: The Politics of School Reform in Baltimore, 1986–98.* Lawrence: University Press of Kansas, 1999.

Ostiguy, Pierre. "The Socio-Cultural, Relational Approach to Populism." *Partecipazione e Conflitto* 13, no. 1 (2020).

Owen, Paul. "Episode 6: Where's Jimmy?" In The Wire *Re-Up*, edited by Steve Busfield and Paul Owen. London: Guardian Books, 2009.

Parker, Howard, Russell Newcombe, and Keith Bakx. *Living with Heroin: The Impact of a Drug Epidemic on an English Community.* Maidenhead: Open University Press, 1988.

Patashnik, Ben. "An Interview with Donnie Andrews, the Real-Life Omar Little." *Vice.* June 29, 2009. https://www.vice.com/sv/article/nnmkmw/an-interview-with-donnie -andrews-the-real-life-omar-little (accessed March 8, 2024).

Pearson, Geoffrey. *The New Heroin Users.* Oxford: Basil Blackwell, 1987.

Perlstein, Linda. *Tested: One American School Struggles to Make the Grade.* New York: Griffin, 2008.

Pierce, Wendell. December 28, 2014. https://twitter.com/WendellPierce/status /549345133989076992 (accessed March 8, 2024).

———. June 7, 2020. https://twitter.com/WendellPierce/status/1269582087855710209 ?lang=en (accessed March 8, 2024).

Poniewozik, James. "*The Wire* Gives TV Drama a Good Schooling." *Time.* September 8, 2006. https://entertainment.time.com/2006/09/08/the_wire_gives_tv_drama_a_good (accessed March 8, 2024).

Potter, Tiffany, and Marshall, C.W. eds. The Wire: *Urban Decay and American Television* (New York: Continuum, 2009).

Preble, Edward. "Social and Cultural Factors Related to Narcotic Use among Puerto Ricans in New York City." *International Journal of the Addictions* 1, no. 1 (1966).

Preble, Edward, and John J. Casey. "Taking Care of Business—The Heroin User's Life on
    the Street." *International Journal of the Addictions* 4, no. 1 (1969).
Racha Penrice, Ronda. "Conclusion: Why *The Wire* Still Matters." In *Cracking the Wire
    during Black Lives Matter*. New York: Fayetteville Mafia Press, 2022.
Raddatz, Leslie. "Jack Webb Revisited." *TV Guide*. February 2, 1963.
Rapping, Elayne. *The Movie of the Week: Private Stories, Public Events*. Minneapolis:
    University of Minnesota Press 1992.
Raynaud, Claudine. "Coming of Age in the African American Novel." In *The Cambridge
    Companion to the African American Novel*, edited by Maryemma Graham. Cam-
    bridge: Cambridge University Press, 2006.
Reiner, Robert. "Media-Made Criminality: The Representation of Crime in the Mass
    Media." In *The Oxford Handbook of Criminology*, 4th ed., edited by Mike Maguire,
    Rodney Morgan, and Robert Reiner. Oxford: Oxford University Press, 2007.
Remnick, Noah. "Michael K. Williams Is More Than Omar from *The Wire*." *New York
    Times*. June 3, 2017. https://www.nytimes.com/2017/06/30/nyregion/michael-k-wil
    liams-is-more-than-omar-from-the-wire.html (accessed March 8, 2024).
Rickard, Diana. *The New True Crime: How the Rise of Serialized Storytelling Is Trans-
    forming Innocence*. New York: New York University Press, 2023.
Roberts, Kenneth. "Populism, Political Mobilizations, and Crises of Political Representa-
    tion." In *The Promise and Perils of Populism: Global Perspectives*, edited by Carlos
    de la Torre. Lexington: University Press of Kentucky.
Rooduijn, Matthijs. "The Nucleus of Populism: In Search of the Lowest Common Denom-
    inator." *Government and Opposition* 49, no. 4 (2014).
Rose, Brian G. "'*The Wire*.'" In *The Essential HBO Reader*, edited by Gary R. Edgerton
    and Jeffrey P. Jones. Lexington: University Press of Kentucky, 2008.
Rovira Kaltwasser, Cristobal. "The Ambivalence of Populism: Threat and Corrective for
    Democracy." *Democratization* 19, no. 2 (2012).
Royo, Andre. April 17, 2015. https://twitter.com/andreroyo/status/592821336025726978
    (accessed March 8, 2024).
Sabin, Roger. "*Dragnet*." In *Cop Shows: A Critical History of Police Dramas on Televi-
    sion*, edited by Roger Sabin, Ronald Wilson, Linda Speidel, and Ben Bethell. Jeffer-
    son, NC: McFarland, 2015.
———. "*Kojak*." In *Cop Shows: A Critical History of Police Dramas on Television*,
    edited by Roger Sabin, Ronald Wilson, Linda Speidel, Ben Bethell. Jefferson, NC:
    McFarland, 2015.
Sancton, Julian. "David Simon, Jon Bernthal and the Makers of HBO's *We Own This City*
    on Dirty Cops, the Drug War and the Legacy of *The Wire*." *Hollywood Reporter*.
    April 21, 2022. https://www.hollywoodreporter.com/tv/tv-features/we-own-this-city
    -simon-pelecanos-bernthal-green-1235132991/#! (accessed March 8, 2024).
Sayles, Justin. "The Bloody Bubble: From *Tiger King* to *The Vanishing at the Cecil Hotel*
    to *The Vow*, True-Crime Documentaries Are More Popular Than Ever. But as Film-
    makers Wrestle with the Ethical Concerns That Come with the Genre, Some Are
    Asking whether It Needs to Adapt to Stay." *The Ringer*. July 9, 2021. afloat. https://
    www.theringer.com/tv/2021/7/9/22567381/true-crime-documentaries-boom-bubble
    -netflix-hbo (accessed March 8, 2024).
Sepinwall, Alan. "*The Wire* Reunion." *PaleyFest 2014*. Paley Center for Media. October 16,
    2014. https://www.youtube.com/watch?v=SGuy6ITOJsI (accessed March 8, 2024).

Silverman, Elizabeth. "Compstat's Innovation." In *Police Innovation: Contrasting Perspectives*, edited by David Weisburd and Anthony A. Braga. Cambridge: Cambridge University Press, 2006.

Simon, David. "Baltimore." In *The Audacity of Despair: Collected Prose, Links and Occasional Venting from David Simon*. April 27, 2015. https://davidsimon.com/baltimore (accessed March 8, 2024).

———. "Behind Bars, Melvin Williams Still a Ghetto Legend: 'Avenue' Hustler Called Heroin Czar." *The Baltimore Sun*. January 11, 1987.

———. "David Simon Interview Special: Part II." The Wire*: Stripped*. Podcast audio. May 23, 2022. https://podcasts.apple.com/gb/podcast/david-simon-interview-special -part-ii/id1321861159?i=1000563221356 (accessed March 8, 2024).

———. "Fuck the Casual Viewer." Interview conducted by Charlie Brooker at the annual Edinburgh Television Festival, Edinburgh, August 28, 2009. https://www.theguard ian.com/media/video/2009/aug/29/david-simon-edinburgh-interview-full (accessed March 8, 2024).

———. "Heroin Trade Enlists Ever-Younger Kids for Reign by Bloodletting." *The Baltimore Sun*. January 13, 1987.

———. *Homicide: A Year on the Killing Streets*. Boston: Houghton Mifflin, 1991; Edinburgh: Canongate, 2009.

———. Interviewed by Amon Warmann. "The Wire 20th Anniversary: 'All the Pieces Matter' Panel Discussion with Cast & Creatives." *BFI*. June 28, 2022. https://www .youtube.com/watch?v=CQAQYnu4k50 (accessed March 8, 2024).

———. Interviewed by Simon Mayo. *BBC Radio 5 Live*. September 16, 2008.

———. "Life as a Snitch: Anonymous to the End, 'Possum' Tells Secrets." *The Baltimore Sun*. March 16, 1992. https://www.baltimoresun.com/1992/03/16/life-as-a -snitch-anonymous-to-the-end-possum-tells-secrets (accessed March 8, 2024).

———. "Loyal Underlings Insulated Williams: Ring Members Called Him 'Dad' Police Say." *The Baltimore Sun*. January 12, 1987.

———. "The Metal Men: With Quick Drug Money as Their Goal." *The Baltimore Sun*. September 3, 1995. https://www.baltimoresun.com/1995/09/03/the-metal-men-with -quick-drug-money-as-their-goal-theyre-stealing-and-selling-every-bit-of-alumi num-iron-brass-and-copper-they-can-cart-out-of-city-buildings (accessed March 8, 2024).

———. "Woman's Death Leads to Beeper Codes, Little Melvin: Caught in the Act." *The Baltimore Sun*. January 15, 1987.

Simon, David, and Ed Burns. *The Corner*. New York: Broadway Books, 1997; Edinburgh: Canongate, 2010.

Smart, Reginald, and Edward Adlaf. "Substance Use and Problems among Toronto Street Youth." *British Journal of Addiction* 86 (1991).

Smith, Adam. *The Wealth of Nations*. London: W. Strahan and T. Cadell, 1776.

Smith, Austin. "Tough Cookie—Can't Help but Love 'Wired' Kids." *New York Post*. September 9, 2006. https://nypost.com/2006/09/09/tough-cookie-cant-help-but-love -wired-kids (accessed March 8, 2024).

Smith, David. "Interview: The Wire's Sonja Sohn on Her Baltimore Documentary: 'We Are Seeing Multilayered Corruption.'" *The Guardian*. December 9, 2021. https:// www.theguardian.com/tv-and-radio/2021/dec/09/the-wire-sonja-sohn-baltimore -documentary-slow-hustle-hbo (accessed March 8, 2024).

Soderberg, Brandon. "Baltimore City 2021 Crime Data: A Closer Look." *The Real News Network*. January 28, 2022. https://therealnews.com/baltimore-city-2021-crime-data -a-closer-look (accessed March 8, 2024).

Sohn, Sonja. "Sonja Sohn: Changing Baltimore Long after 'The Wire.'" *NPR: Fresh Air*. Podcast audio. March 15, 2012. https://www.npr.org/2012/03/15/148294942/sonja -sohn-changing-baltimore-long-after-the-wire (accessed March 8, 2024).

Solórzano, Daniel. "Critical Race Theory, Race and Gender Microaggressions and the Experience of Chicana and Chicano Scholars." *Qualitative Studies in Education* 1, no. 1 (1998).

Somashekhar, Sandhya, Wesley Lowery, Keith L. Alexander, Kimberley Kindy, and Julie Tate. "Black and Unarmed." *Washington Post*. August 8, 2015. https://www.washing tonpost.com/sf/national/2015/08/08/black-and-unarmed (accessed March 8, 2024).

Stanley, Ben. "The Thin Ideology of Populism." *Journal of Political Ideologies* 13, no. 1 (2008).

Stolworthy, Jacob. "Nathan Barksdale, the Inspiration behind Characters from *The Wire*, Dies in Prison." *The Independent*. February 17, 2016. https://www.independent.co .uk/arts-entertainment/tv/news/the-wire-inspiration-nathan-barksdale-dies-in-prison -a6879331.html (accessed March 8, 2024).

Supreme Court of the State of Hawai'i. *State of Hawai'i v. Christopher L. Wilson*, CAAP- 22-0000561. Case no. 2CPC-17-0000964. February 7, 2024. https://www.google .com/url?client=internal-element-cse&cx=015176889377364375695:awlaikvly0a &q=https://www.courts.state.hi.us/wp-content/uploads/2024/02/SCAP-22-0000561 .pdf&sa=U&ved=2ahUKEwj0pNeDgr2EAxUqFBAIHXiNA9cQFnoECAIQAg &usg=AOvVaw366R02qKPLgDhZ97nTk6bp (accessed March 8, 2024).

Szanton, Peter L. *Baltimore 2000: A Choice of Futures: A Report to the Morris Goldseker Foundation*. Baltimore, MD: The Foundation, 1980.

Talbot, Margaret. "Stealing Life: The Crusader behind 'The Wire.'" *The New Yorker*. October 14, 2007. https://www.newyorker.com/magazine/2007/10/22/stealing-life (accessed March 8, 2024).

Taylor, Carl. *Dangerous Society*. East Lansing: Michigan State University Press, 1989.

Thompson, Robert J. *Television's Second Golden Age: From* Hill Street Blues *to* ER. Syr- acuse, NY: Syracuse University Press, 1997.

Toby, Mekeisha Madden. "*The Wire*'s Hard Truths about How Our Schools Fail Us All." In *Cracking the Wire during Black Lives Matter*, edited by Ronda Racha Penrice. New York: Fayetteville Mafia Press, 2022.

Truslow Adams, James. *The Epic of America*. New York: Blue Ribbon Books, 1931.

Tumulty, Brian, and Ellyn Ferguson. "Budget Battle Begins." *The Coloradoan*. May 11, 1997.

Turnbull, Sue. *The TV Crime Drama*. Edinburgh: Edinburgh University Press, 2014.

Twomey, Ryan. *Examining* The Wire: *Authenticity and Curated Realism*. New York: Pal- grave Pivot, 2020.

Urbinati, Nadia. "Populism and the Principle of Majority." In *The Oxford Handbook of Populism*, edited by Cristóbal Rovira Kaltwasser, Paul Taggart, Paulina Ochoa Espejo, and Pierre Ostiguy. Oxford: Oxford University Press, 2017.

Valliant, George E. "What Can Long-Term Follow-Up Teach Us about Relapse and Preven- tion of Relapse in Addiction?" *British Journal of Addiction* 83, no. 10 (October 1988).

van Ghent, Dorothy. *The English Novel: Form and Function*. New York: Harper & Row, 1953.

Vint, Sherryl. The Wire. Detroit: Wayne State University Press, 2013.

Waisbord, Silvio, and Adriana Amado. "Populist Communication by Digital Means: Presidential Twitter in Latin America." *Information Communication & Society* 20, no. 9 (2017).

Walder, Dennis, Stephen Regan, Pam Morris, and Richard Allen. "The Novel and Society." In *The Realist Novel*, edited by Dennis Walder. London: Routledge, 1995.

Walker, Tim. "Donnie Andrews: The Road to Redemption." *The Independent*. June 21, 2009. https://www.independent.co.uk/news/people/profiles/donnie-andrews-the-road -to-redemption-1711563.html (accessed March 8, 2024).

Webster, Daniel W., Carla G. Tilchin, and Mitchell L. Doucette. *Estimating the Effects of Safe Streets Baltimore on Gun Violence 2007–2022*. Johns Hopkins Bloomberg School of Public Health, Center for Gun Violence Solutions. March 2023. https:// publichealth.jhu.edu/sites/default/files/2023-10/estimating-the-effects-of-safe-streets -baltimore-on-gun-violence-july-2023.pdf (accessed March 8, 2024).

Weyland, Kurt. "Clarifying a Contested Concept: Populism in the Study of Latin American Politics." *Comparative Politics* 34, no. 1 (2001).

———. "Populism: A Political-Strategy Approach." In *The Oxford Handbook of Populism*, edited by Cristóbal Rovira Kaltwasser, Paul Taggart, Paulina Ochoa Espejo, and Pierre Ostiguy. Oxford: Oxford University Press, 2017.

Williams, Harold A. *The Baltimore Sun: 1837–1987*. Baltimore, MD: Johns Hopkins University Press, 1987.

Williams, Linda. *On the Wire*. Durham, NC: Duke University Press, 2014.

Williams, Michael K., and Jon Sternfeld. *Scenes from My Life: A Memoir*. London: Pan Macmillan, 2022.

Williams, Raymond. *What I Came to Say*. London: Hutchinson Books, 1990.

Wilson, David. *Cities and Race: America's New Black Ghetto*. New York: Routledge, 2006.

Wilson, Ronald. "*Naked City*." In *Cop Shows: A Critical History of Police Dramas on Television*, edited by Roger Sabin, Ronald Wilson, Linda Speidel, and Ben Bethell. Jefferson, NC: McFarland, 2015.

Winny, Annalies. "'Gentrification without Displacement': Wire Actor's Property Plan Causes Storm." *The Guardian*. March 28, 2018. https://www.theguardian.com/cities /2018/mar/28/weldell-pierce-gentrification-without-displacement-wire-actors-prop erty-plan-causes-storm (accessed March 8, 2024).

Wood, Robin. *Hollywood from Vietnam to Reagan . . . and Beyond*. New York: Columbia University Press, 1986.

Yang, Carter M. "Part I: Baltimore Is the U.S. Heroin Capital." *ABC News*. March 14, 2001. https://abcnews.go.com/US/story?id=92699&page=1#:~:text=Government %20agencies%20estimate%20that%20as,taking%20control%20of%20my%20life .%22 (accessed March 8, 2024).

Yosso, Tara J. "Toward a Critical Race Curriculum." *Equity & Excellence in Education* 35, no. 2 (2002).

Younce, Carolyn. "Ella Thompson Fund Special with Carolyn Younce." The Wire: Stripped. Podcast audio. June 30, 2021. https://podcasts.apple.com/gb/podcast/ella -thompson-fund-special-with-carolyn-younce/id1321861159?i=1000527413446 (accessed March 8, 2024).

Zamudio, Margaret, Christopher Russell, Francisco Rios, and Jacquelyn L. Bridgeman. *Critical Race Theory Matters: Education and Ideology*. New York: Routledge, 2011.

Zilney, Lisa Anne. *Drugs: Policy, Social Costs, Crime, and Justice*. Englewood Cliffs, NJ: Prentice Hall, 2010.

Zurawik, David. "'*The Wire*' Finale Is a Cop-Out for a Once-Great Show." *The Baltimore Sun*. March 9, 2008. https://www.baltimoresun.com/entertainment/bal-thewirefinale -story.html (accessed March 8, 2024).

INDEX

African American culture,
  literature, 136–143
  masculinity, 88–94
  rap music, 92–94
  stereotypes, 31–35
  unions, 86–87
Albrecht, Chris, 11, 14–15, 18–19, 21, 71, 119–120, 145–146
Alvarez, Rafael, 72
American dream, x, xviii, 12, 139–140
American Revolution, 75
Andrews, Donnie, xvii, 29–30

Baltimore and Ohio Railroad, 76, 86
Baltimore City,
  show's impact on the city, 73, 170–172
  as a character, xiv–xv
  crime rates, xxi, 5, 97–98, 177–178
  housing projects, 25, 30 45, 52, 60–61, 64, 66 –67, 98, 172
  mayors, xv, xxi, 72–73, 96, 106, 109, 112, 115–117, 123, 135–136, 146, 152–155, 160, 178–179, 186
  immigration, xxiv, 81–83
  riots, 24, 172–174
  state attorneys, 19, 34, 38, 53, 68, 157–158, 160, 175 177–179
Baltimore County Public Schools (BCPS), 122–123

Baltimore Police Department (BPD), 2, 6, 12, 19, 21, 35, 37, 38, 40, 42, 44–46, 68–69, 112, 154, 166, 172, 174, 178–180
  Barksdale Detail, 20, 38, 39, 43, 45, 46, 51, 53, 54, 55, 56, 57, 58, 61, 66–7, 73
  Major Crimes Unit, 9, 98, 108, 146, 157, 183, 188
  Gun Trace Task Force, 179–180
  harbor patrol, 74–80
  homicide department, xv, 3, 4, 7, 19, 21, 25, 27, 34, 38, 41–42, 50, 54, 57, 58–59, 97– 98, 109–110, 162–165, 178
  narcotics department, 19, 38, 41, 106
  Southeastern District, 73, 74, 78, 85
  Western District, xiv, 4, 6, 8–9, 23– 24, 29, 32, 38, 55, 73, 92, 101, 106, 116, 125, 139, 142, 159, 161, 172, 186
Baltimore Rising (2017), 174, 176
Baltimore Sun, ix, xiv, xxi, xxiv, 2– 6, 8, 9, 13, 72, 95, 109, 145–149, 164, 166–167, 180
Barskdale, Brianna, 90–91 138
Barksdale crew, 32, 38, 43, 44–47, 52, 53, 64–68, 72, 85, 88, 98, 99, 103, 104, 121, 138, 140, 184, 185

Barksdale, Avon, xiv, xviii, xix, xxiv,
    21, 22, 23–26, 32, 37, 38, 40–42,
    45, 46, 51, 60–61, 64, 68, 88–94, 98,
    100–101. 103–104, 115, 119, 183,
    184, 185, 186,
Barksdale, D'Angelo, xix, 18, 38,
    45–47, 52, 60–61 64–68, 88–94, 167,
    183, 184, 186
Barksdale, Nathan "Bodie," 24–26, 30
Bates, Ivan, J., 178
Battle of Baltimore 1814, 75–77, 79
Bell, Roland, 25
Bell, Stringer, xvi, xvii, 21–23, 26, 38,
    43, 45, 47, 60–61, 64, 67, 88, 91, 93,
    98, 100–101, 115, 184, 185, 186
Bellerophon, xviii
bell hooks, 26–31, 88–94
Bethlehem Steel, 72, 77–78
binge watching, xii–xiv
Black Lives Matter (BLM), xxiii–xxiv,
    122, 174– 177
Boardley, Warren, 19, 30
Bochco, Steven, 57, 62
Bolsonaro, Jair, xxii, 147,
Bond, Rupert, 157
Boyd, Fran, 7, 30
Brice, Namond, xxiv, 121–122, 127–
    143, 186
Briesewitz, Uta, xviii
Broadus, Bodie, 45–57, 52, 64–66, 88,
    104, 108, 140, 183, 184
broken windows theory, 109
Brooklyn Nine–Nine (2013–2021), 31
Brown v. Board of Education 1954, 122
Brown, Michael, 175
Bubbles, 26–28, 38, 47–48, 55, 68, 93,
    102, 110–111, 116, 120, 167, 187
buddy genre, 54–57
Burns, Ed, ix, xiii, xiv, xxii–xxiii, 6–9,
    11–14, 18–20, 23, 29–31, 71–72, 92,
    94, 95, 121, 146, 170, 172, 180
Burrell, Ervin, 35, 38, 43, 106, 108,
    112, 114–116, 152, 154, 183

Cagney and Lacey (1981–1988),
    33–34

Carcetti, Tommy, xv, xxi, 95–96, 106,
    109, 111–112, 116–117, 119, 135–
    136, 139, 146, 152–158, 164–166,
    187–188
Carver, Ellis, 33–35, 38, 42, 61, 67,
    99–102, 107–108. 140, 154, 169,
    186, 187, 188
Chappelle, Joe, 150
Charles, Slim, 100–101, 104, 106 166,
    181, 188
Chesapeake Bay, 75–76, 80, 86
Civil Rights, xxiii, 21, 49, 122–125,
    127, 129, 148
closing montage, xv, 167
Colesberry, Bob, 10–11, 14, 18, 67, 95
Collins, Patricia Hill, 31–32
Columbo (1968–2003), 49
Coleman, Chad, 24, 174
Colvin, Howard "Bunny," 105–116,
    122, 128–133, 135, 137, 140–143,
    174, 185–187
Corner, The (2000), xv, 1, 10–11, 15,
    30, 170
*Corner, The: A Year in the Life of an
    Inner-City Neighborhood* (1997),
    6–9, 30, 170
CompStat, 114–115
COVID-19 criminal justice policies
    2021, xxi, 178
COVID-19, xxi–xiii, 178
Crawford, Jermaine, 121,
crime reporting, 162–167
critical criminology, 106–107
critical race theory, xxiv, 122, 123–136,
    143, 181
CSI: Crime Scene Investigation (2000–
    2015), 15, 17
"Cutty" Wise, Dennis, 24, 93, 98, 100,
    103–104, 140, 141 185, 186

Daniels, Cedric, xv, 35, 38, 43, 50–51,
    53, 55, 57–58, 61, 98, 146, 164 183,
    185, 187, 188
Dante's *Inferno*, 110–112
Davis, Senator Clay, 98, 101, 128, 146,
    157–162, 184, 185, 186

Dickens, Charles, xiv, xix, xx, 74, 154, 165 181
Donnelly, Marcia, 121, 124, 127, 137–139
Douglass, Frederick, 86, 124–125, 173
"Dukie" Weems, Duquan, xxiv, 122, 136,137, 139–140, 166
Duterte, Rodrigo, xxii
Duvall, Tootsie, 121
DVD, xi–xiii

Elba, Idris, xvi–xvii 21–23, 38, 169
Emancipation Proclamation, 86
Emmy Awards, ix, xvi, 11, 46, 47, 186, 188
Erdoğan, Recep Tayyip, xxii, 147

Farmer, Lamont "Chin," 22–23, 25
FBI, xxi, 74, 83, 84, 175, 184, 187
Fells Point, 75, 79, 86–87
Fenton, Justin, 179–180
film noir, 40, 45
flexi narrative, xii, xxii 57–58
Floyd, George, xxiii, 174, 176
Fogel, Alexa, xvi, 17–20, 27, 29, 121
Fontanta, Tom, 9, 10, 13
Fort McHenry, 76, 79
Francis Scott Key Bridge, 79
Freamon, Lester, xv, 38–39, 43–44, 50, 127, 146, 157, 163–165, 167, 169, 184, 187

Game of Thrones (2011–2019), xvii, xxii
Generation Kill (2008), 145
Gillen, Aidan, xv, xvii, 95–96
Gilliam, Seth, 33, 38, 169 174,
Gilliard Jr., Larry, xix, 38,174
Glekas, George, 84, 185
Glover, Anwan, 100, 174
Gray, Freddie, xxiv, 12, 172–175, 177–179
Greek mythology, xviii–xix, 75, 131
Greek, the, 74, 81, 83–85, 184, 185, 188

Greggs, Shakima "Kima," 32–35, 38, 39, 42, 48, 50, 108, 171, 184, 187
Gutierrez, Alma, 152, 163

Hades, xix
Hamsterdam free zones, xxi, xxiv, 106–117, 178, 185
Harris, Wood, xiv, 37, 23–26
Harrison, Michael, 178
Haynes, Gus, 10, 146, 149, 150–152, 166, 187
HBO, ix, xi–xii, xv, xxiii–xxiv, 9–12, 15, 18–19 27, 29, 37–38, 40, 60, 72, 93, 95, 119, 120, 170, 180
Heracles, xix
Hector, Jamie, 26,98, 174
"Herc" Hauk, Thomas, 33, 38, 42, 61, 67–68, 99, 107, 109, 127, 139
Highway Patrol (1955–1959), 40
Hill Street Blues (1981–1987), 57–58
Homicide: A Year on the Killing Streets (1991), xiii, 3–5, 6–7
Homicide: Life on the Street (1993–1999), xiii, 5, 9–10, 14, 58–62, 67–68,

Ironside (1967–1975), 49

Jason and the Argonauts, xix
Jenkins, Wayne, 179
JFK, 148
Johnson, Boris, xxii, 147
Johnson, Clark, 10, 18, 58, 146, 150
Johnson, Lyndon B., 148
Jordan, Michael B., xvi, 45

King, Maurice "Peanut," 97
Klebanow, Thomas, 149–150. 152
Kojak (1973–1978), 4, 49–54, 68

Lee, Michael, xxiv, 122, 130, 134, 136, 139, 141, 187
Lehane, Dennis, xiii, 38, 121
Levinson, Barry, 5, 9–10, 59
Levy, Maurice, 43, 90, 146, 186, 187, 188

Little, Omar, xvii, xix, 25, 28–32, 35, 45, 53, 55, 61, 66, 67, 98, 115, 146, 173, 184, 185–187
Locust Point, 72–73, 75, 81–82, 86
Lovejoy, Deirdre, 34, 38, 174
Luther King Jr., Martin, 24, 51, 170

Marshall, Thurgood, 124–125
Martin, Trayvon, 175
Max, ix
McNulty, James "Jimmy," xiv–xvi, xviii–xix, xxi, 17–20, 21, 22, 34, 38, 40–42, 46–57, 61, 67–68, 74–81, 83, 85, 108, 146, 147, 157, 162–167, 183, 187, 188
Milch, David, 62
Milei, Javier, 147
Mills, David, 1, 5, 10
Moreland, Bunk, xxiii, 18, 20–21, 38, 50, 54–57, 60, 68, 127, 162–163, 165, 171, 183, 184, 185, 187
Mosby, Marilyn, xxi, 175, 178
Mouzone, Brother, 115, 185, 186
Myers, Isaac, 86–87

Naked City (1958–1963), 45–48, 67, 68
Napoleonic Wars, (1806–1815) 75
National Association for the Advancement of Colored People (NAACP), xvi
Navalny, Alexei, 181
Nelson Kohl building, 171
Netflix, xi, xvi
Nixon, Richard, 96
novel for television, xiii–xiv
NPYD Blue (1993–2005), 5, 10, 15, 17, 62–67, 68

O'Malley, Marty, 72–73, 96, 136, 154
Obama, Barack, xx, 28, 153
Orbán, Viktor, 147
Oz (1997–2003), 9, 17

Parks, Rosa, 124–129
Patapsco River, 74, 76

Pearlman, Rhonda, 34, 38, 51, 53, 55, 68, 162
Pelecanos, George, xiii, 13, 38, 73, 95, 103, 111, 146, 180
Peters, Clarke, xv, xvii, 38, 71–72, 169
Phelan, Judge Daniel, xviii, 38, 41, 46–47, 49, 165
Pierce, Wendell, xxiii, 20–21, 38, 120, 171–174, 176
policy termination theory, 106–117
political science, 96, 106–117,
"Poot" Carr, Malik, 45, 47, 64–67 184
popular criminology, xxiv, 147, 162–167
populism, 145–168
    ideology, 149–153
    performance, 157–162
    politicians, xvii, 12, 147 153–168
    strategy, 153–157
Port of Baltimore, 74–80
    deindustrialization 74–75, 78–80
    grain elevator (pier), 76–77, 80–85, 87
    industrialisation, 76–77
    gentrification of the inner harbor, 78
    longshoremen, 85–88, 93–94
    race relations, 85–88, 93,94
    shipbuilding, 75
    War of Independence, 75
Possum, 27–28
"Prez" Pryzbylewski, Roland, 38, 43–44, 67, 122–136, 139, 140, 141, 143, 183, 184, 185, 186, 187
Price, Richard, 95, 121, 146
Proposition Joe, 88, 184
Pulitzer Prize, xv, xxi, 5, 12, 148, 166

quality TV, x–xii, xv–xvi

Rawls, William, xv, 38, 42, 46, 50, 53, 57, 106, 108–109, 112, 114–116, 152, 154, 166
Reilly, John C., 18
ReWired for Change, 171, 174
Royce, Clarence, 112–116 ,160–161, 186

Royo, Andre, 26–28, 31, 38, 120, 173–174
Russell, Beadie, 73, 184

Schmoke, Kurt, 106, 115, 123, 154
Scott, Brandon, 178
serial killers, xxi, 146–147, 157, 162–167, 187
Simon, David, ix, xii–xv, xvii–xx, xxiv, 1–16, 17, 20, 22–23, 26, 28–31, 38, 46, 58, 60–61, 69, 71–73, 94, 95–96, 110, 112, 114, 116–117, 119–120, 143, 145–149, 153, 157, 166–167, 170, 172–174, 177, 179–180
Slow Hustle, The (2021), 180
"Snoop" Pearson, Felicia, 121–122, 141, 174
Sobotka, Frank, xiv, xix, 73–74, 80–88, 91 93, 185
Sobotka, Nick, 74, 81–85, 91, 154, 184
Sobotka, Ziggy, xix, 81–84, 92, 184 185
social realism, xvii–xviii, 80–81, 120
Sohn, Sonja, 32–35, 38, 120, 171–176, 180
Sopranos, The (1999–2007), 29, 120
Stanfield, Marlo, 26, 98, 102, 121, 139, 141, 146, 162–164, 166, 186, 187–188
Starsky and Hutch (1975–1979), 54
Station North, 171
Stinkum, 67, 53
Strauss, Carolyn, 11, 14–15 119–120, 145
streaming services, ix, xi, xii–xiv, xxii–xxiii
Suiter, Sean, 180
Sydnor, Leander, 43–44, 61, 108, 157–158, 165, 184, 187

Templeton, Scott, xv, xxi, 146, 152, 164–166
Thompson, Ella, 170
Trump, Donald, xxii, 12, 147, 153, 157, 160
Tubman, Harriet, 124–129

Underground Railroad, 124
US Supreme Court, 49, 122, 124, 125, 181

Valchek, Stan, 73, 91, 166, 184, 185
VARK education theory, 131

Wagstaff, Randy, xxiv, 121, 125, 127, 130–131, 136–140, 187
Wallace, Justin, 45, 47, 64–66, 184
Wallace, Latonya Kim, 4
war on drugs, the, 96–98
    decriminalising drug use, 106–117, 177–179
    criminological studies of, 105–106
    impact on Baltimore, 96, 97, 98, 117–179
    racial inequity, 97–98, 177–178
We Own This City (2022), 179–180
Webb, Jack, 39–40
"Wee–Bey" Brice, Roland, 53, 66, 68, 88, 91, 121, 138, 140, 166, 183, 184
Weeks, Johnny, 46–47, 102, 111
West, Dominic, xiv, xvi, xvii, 17–20, 120–121, 174
West Wing, The (1999–2006), xi
Whiting, James, 149–153
Williams, "Little" Melvin, xvii, 2, 7–8, 19, 22–26, 30, 92, 97, 103
Williams, Michael K., xvi–xvii, 28–31, 71–72, 121, 174
Williams, Raymond, xvii, 81
Williams, Robin, 5
Winstone, Ray, 18
Wired Up!, 173–174, 176
Wisdom, Robert, 105, 174
World War I, 77
World War II, xxiii, 2, 47
Wright, Brandon, 25, 29, 32, 55, 61, 66 185,

X, Malcolm, 125

Zorzi, Bill, 95–96, 119, 146, 149, 180

ABOUT THE AUTHOR

Dr. Ben Lamb is the world's leading expert on British television crime drama, having published the definitive academic work, *You're Nicked: Investigating British Television Police Series*, for Manchester University Press. He is a senior lecturer in media studies and is currently the English studies and creative writing course leader at Teesside University, United Kingdom. As a cultural theorist specializing in television studies, his published research examines modes of realism within different television production systems, genre theory, ideology, gender politics, and representations of crime and social class. He is the producer of the films *Rewinding the Welfare State: A Social History of the North East on Film* and *In the Veins: Coalmining Communities*, supported by the Yorkshire and North East Film Archive. He is a passionate supporter of the Middlesbrough Football Club and is grateful to his wife, son, and two dogs for being patient with him when it came to writing this book.